THE INTELLIGENT
Conversationalist

Also by Imogen Lloyd Webber

The Single Girl's Survival Guide:
Secrets for Today's Savvy, Sexy, and Independent Women

The Twitter Diaries:
A Tale of 2 Cities, 1 Friendship, 140 Characters
(with Georgie Thompson)

THE INTELLIGENT
Conversationalist

31 Cheat Sheets

That Will Show You
How to Talk to Anyone
About Anything, Anytime

IMOGEN LLOYD WEBBER

ST. MARTIN'S GRIFFIN
NEW YORK

THE INTELLIGENT CONVERSATIONALIST. Copyright © 2016 by Imogen Lloyd Webber. All rights reserved. Printed in the United States of America. For information, address St. Martin's Press, 175 Fifth Avenue, New York, N.Y. 10010.

www.stmartins.com

Designed by Maura Rosenthal

Library of Congress Cataloging-in-Publication Data

Names: Lloyd Webber, Imogen, author.
Title: Intelligent conversationalist, the : 31 cheat seats that will show you how
   to talk to anyone about anything, anytime / Imogen Lloyd Webber.
Description: First Edition. | New York: St. Martin's Griffin, 2016.
Identifiers: LCCN 2016000034| ISBN 9781250040473 (paperback) |
   ISBN 9781466835849 (e-book)
Subjects: LCSH: Conversation. | BISAC: SELF-HELP / Personal Growth /
   Success.
Classification: LCC BJ2121 .L55 2016 | DDC 395.5/9—dc23
LC record available at http://lccn.loc.gov/2016000034

Our books may be purchased in bulk for promotional, educational, or business use. Please contact the Macmillan Corporate and Premium Sales Department at 1-800-221-7945, extension 5442, or by e-mail at MacmillanSpecialMarkets@ macmillan.com.

First Edition: June 2016

For the first man I remember

CONTENTS

SUBJECT EIGHT—CULTURE

ACKNOWLEDGMENTS

This is my third (published—there are a few that will fortunately never see the light of day) book. It has been the toughest—and most rewarding—professional challenge of my life. I am so sorry to everyone I've let down with my juggling act over the past couple of years. I promise I'm now back in the land of the living.

First of all, a massive thank-you to my long-suffering agent, Sam Hiyate, without whom there would be no *The Intelligent Conversationalist*, St. Martin's, or Michael Flamini. Michael—thank you so much to you, Vicki Lame, and the entire team at St. Martin's for all your support.

Thank you to everyone who has ever invited me on air, but in particular, Neil Cavuto, Don Imus, Greg Gutfeld, Steve Friedman, and Dylan Ratigan—I learned so much from you.

On a personal note I'm indebted to Paul Wontorek, Beth Stevens, Anthony Mendoza, and the whole team at Broadway.com, Eleanor Wilkinson, Darryl Samaraweera, Daniel Bee, Sierra Boggess, Thomas Jones, Bella Webber Design, Michael "shut up" Riedel, Peter Brown, and all my friends and family. Thank you for putting up with me.

All the mistakes contained in *The Intelligent Conversationalist* are my own. My sincere apologies if I've been a muppet (see p. 24) anywhere (although as per p. 32 I should probably just say: "Being right is highly overrated. Even a stopped clock is right twice a day").

THE INTELLIGENT
Conversationalist

INTRODUCTION

It has happened to us all. Including me. And most of my coworkers. On live television.

We are embroiled in a quasi-intellectual debate or perhaps watching (even appearing on) the television news. And it occurs to us that we have a situation on our hands. We are lacking the killer fact that would enable us to win the aforementioned argument. Or the news anchor says something that makes us realize we are unable to quite account for why something has happened or where somewhere is—but we know we really should know. We somehow forgot or quite possibly missed the moment when it was explained to us.

We are also all sometimes wrong. There are the certain beliefs we hold for years that nobody has bothered or felt fitting to correct us about. We are the victims of a Chinese whisper that has stuck.

These are the times that we needed to have a "Cheat Sheet," a concise set of notes of accurate, useful knowledge. Because whether we admit it or not, all of us, at all times, prefer to be never knowingly short of an opinion. On no occasion is it a good look to be one of those people who repeatedly says, "You know," which is an immediate tip-off that they either have little idea what they're talking about or are lazy linguists. The only type of linguist you want to be is a cunning one. An intelligent conversationalist, if you will.

It is not that we are stupid or that we couldn't look anything up on the Internet. But there is just too much information out there for anyone with a pulse as opposed to a CPU to disseminate. Especially now that we are expected to think of everything in social media soundbites and are so time poor. Well, according to our artfully constructed social networking profiles, we are extremely busy and important, aren't we?

This book will ensure you will be able to talk to anyone about anything at any time; that you will never be short of an opinion, shut out of a conversation, or written off as an empty head. It came about after I spoke to over a hundred people—male and female, aged eighteen to eighty. Even the most educated, successful, and televised among them admitted—often in whispers, usually inebriated—that they too had gaps in their knowledge. The pages in this volume contain invaluable information for our overextended, supremely busy 140-character world. Presented with tongue firmly embedded in cheek, this is a series of Cheat Sheets on a variety of topics essential to modern-day survival for the man and woman about town.

As the only female, often on air with four mouthy men, I have to be better prepared than any of them. One mistake from the blond girl, and the best-case scenario is that your Twitter followers don't let you forget it. Worst case normally involves YouTube and work drying up. So I know my stuff—watch my Fox News *Red Eye* appearances and you'd be surprised how many statistics I've slipped in over the years while hamming it up in the "leg chair." To write this book, I've employed my research and presentational skills learned at Cambridge University and honed since 2009 on hundreds of "hits" for American cable news outlets. Fox News host Neil Cavuto, whom I've done coming on a hundred segments with, once said one of the nicest things to me anyone ever has after we'd finished a debate on obesity: "You have a way of making everything very clear." That has always been my raison d'être every time I turn up on TV and what I try to do here.

Of course, this slim tome cannot cover everything, nor will you be able to remember it all. So within it I reveal the tricks of the trade that those who permanently appear to be in the know use to switch the discussion onto safe territory, so that they always swim, not sink, in conversation. Perception is reality, after all. The first time Sean Hannity invited me onto his Fox News show one-on-one, he changed the topic as he introduced me to the nation. All my careful hours of research were suddenly worthless as I faced down a barrage of questions. Putting the tears on hold until after I left the News Corp. building, I fought back using every technique I could muster from my Cambridge debating-my-professor days to my experiences appearing on other programs. The confrontational segment won me a contributorship at MSNBC. Wish I'd known that as I sobbed my way down Sixth Avenue.

The Intelligent Conversationalist is made up of a series of Cheat Sheets, and in homage to their origins—they were invented by students who used them without their instructor's knowledge to cheat on a test—each chapter is a school subject split into various Cheat Sheets. Laid out in textbook style, the material contained within is what we wish we had been taught, an aid to appearing top dog today. At all times the maxim of Albert Einstein, himself no slouch in the brains department, will be kept in mind: "If you can't explain it to a six-year-old, you don't understand it yourself." There will be some subjects that you are already teacher's pet in that you can skim through. And then there are others where you don't quite make the grade and linger longer.

This book is for dipping in and out of. For you to discover or be reminded of a factual gem in a way that will hopefully amuse you and can be utilized to impress your lovers, colleagues, and parental figures. To an extent, most life encounters are akin to exams. And as with exams, you will revise the most relevant Cheat Sheet(s) prior to a rendezvous. Dinner with a banker? It would be wise to peruse the section on math and economics, so you can differentiate your euro bailout from your Marshall Plan. Job interview with a Brit? Discover what the UK version of a muppet is and why you want to avoid appearing like one. Christmas lunch *en famille*? It's all pagan, don't you know, or you will after you've read up on religion.

The Intelligent Conversationalist contains background briefings, explains why the topic matters today, and features talking points along with red flags in case you end up in a debate over it. For the Internet Age is not merely about possessing mere knowledge—we can all find out pretty much anything with a click of a mouse—it is about how we use that knowledge, how we present our opinions. Within these pages you may just alight on one or two items that help you win the girl, job, or quiz night.

We begin with the basis of a good conversation in North America, the UK, and many other places around the globe: English. Without correct use of it, both written and spoken, you will not be taken seriously. I became convinced I should write this book when the then prime minister of Great Britain's wife misspelt the word "definitely" on Twitter. In my guise as author of *The Single Girl's Survival Guide,* I came across men and women who have fallen in love or broken up with their partners over spelling and grammar. Desperate, perhaps, but *desperately* seems another word to confuse, along with the use of apostrophes. Split infinitives can be as divisive as their title suggests. Oh, you may jest, but thanks to social networking the world is a stage for all of us. Every time we make an inadvertent spelling or grammatical mistake on a Twitter or Facebook "status update," a good percentage of those reading our broadcast to the world have knocked our IQ down a percentage point or two. And heaven forbid you do it on your Tinder profile, it could cause unnecessary multiple swipes left. When should we put it into *affect,* or is it *effect*? *Lose* or *loose*? You may think you know. I'm sure the prime minister of the time's wife did when she wrote *definately*. However, she really didn't, and several hundred thousand people became even more convinced her husband was doing a lousy job of educating the people of Britain. This did nothing to help his ultimately unsuccessful electoral cause. Additionally, the adage is true: England and America *are* separated by a common language. Therefore, to help you understand those from across the pond and how they may interpret you, we look at the differences in words such as *quite,* the American use of which can cause mortal offense to an Englishman. This book is for the real as well as the virtual world, so this section will also include a few words to drop into conversation to impress, along with some smart one-liners to deflect anyone who verbally attacks you and methods to buy time while you remember a fact or work out how to change the topic to something you know about without anyone noticing. Equally helpful if you're one-on-one with Hannity live or yelling at him on your television set sitting next to someone on your sofa who agrees with him. The one thing you want to avoid is blanking, which I've only ever done twice on air. But enough of your author's Rick Perry moments . . .

Moving on, we turn to math and economics, the subject that many were tempted to cut at school, which possibly goes a long way in explaining the dire straits of the past few years. Before you switch off entirely, I'm talking *relevant* math and economics. If you are going to date a Wall Street type, which variety of financier fits your schedule. How none of us really have any money. A look at tax, exchange rates, a quick review of economists in history, and an even quicker guide to the credit crunch and Eurogeddon. There will also be a few case studies so we can derive some real-life tips about what and what not to do from notorious business "brains."

We follow this with the subject of religion, it being the root cause of most of the world's trouble and strife. We have a reference grid of religions containing some bullet points on the main religions that have far too often translated into real bullets, along with answers to such important questions as: Can you drink? Can you have sex? Is there a life-after-death plan? We also list the major religious holidays so you avoid offering a Muslim water during daylight hours in Ramadan and ripostes for religion being used as justification for bad behavior.

Subject four is history, for as Churchill put it: "The farther back you can look, the farther forward you are likely to see." History is crucial for explaining why we are in the state we are in, but it is such a large topic, it is only natural we all feel all at sea. Our first Cheat Sheet of the section covers basic American history, which is targeted at, say, anyone from outside the United States wanting to sound smart at a Thanksgiving party or anyone who grew up in the US but did not pay attention to the lecture on the Puritans or to the one on holidays established by President Lincoln. We also look at American "imperialism," the British royals (what I'm probably most notorious for here on US TV), the world wars, and the Middle East. (I know I have missed out large swaths of the globe—if I get to do a follow-up to *The Intelligent Conversationalist,* Africa, China, India, and Pakistan will all feature prominently.) All of this is condensed into bite-size, need-to-know chunks. Yes, I needed a small lie-down/extremely large alcoholic beverage after finishing this section.

Our fifth subject encompasses politics and the variety of questions that topic brings up. Cable news pundits spend a lot of time bellowing at us about what is in the American Constitution—but what is actually in it? How can it get amended, again? SCOTUS—who, what, where, why? Congress: Why can't they get anything done? What is up with all those naughty political corruption and sex scandals? Finally, jargon in American politics will be deconstructed, and we supply some solid election talking points such as "a week is a long time in politics," "all politics is local," "you don't win campaigns by playing defense." They've been sufficient to get me through enough election cycles on air, anyway.

We are now pretty good at why, but what about where? Subject six is geography. This is something we should all be world experts in, really. We're all part of a globalized society, so chances are you're trying to chat a foreigner up for sex or cash. Hopefully not both. But too often our education—or what we remember of it—leaves much to be desired. Even President Bush II was somewhat befuddled about the difference between Wales and Great Britain. (It wasn't the special relationship's finest hour.) We'll see that Brunei isn't anywhere near Saudi Arabia and why Austria has no kangaroos. And yes, there are maps to help you out. Finally, the topic of geography of course includes climate, so we have enough information here to give short shrift to anyone still denying climate change.

Our penultimate subject gets down to that fundamental of subjects, biology. Now, let's all get real. In the real world, will you ever need to know about amoebae, plankton, or osmosis rates of houseplants in New Guinea? Of course not, so we cover sex and gender and the agendas they bring in. Contraception. Abortion. Feminism. LBGTQ. And circumcision, which I contemplated covering under religion, until I realized that when I thought of the male member, it rarely had anything to do with worship. Sorrynotsorry, boys. For despite our being well into the twenty-first century, these matters still seem to be front and center of too many debates. Since we're talking about life, we also cover death—including the death penalty.

We conclude with a cultural roundup so you appear a fully balanced human being. And so you don't embarrass yourself if you've got Van Gogh's ear for music and are trying to seduce someone arty. It would be best if you admit you don't know everything about the person you're wooing's specific genre, but you should be able to match their interest in other ones. Don't worry, you're in good company: Everyone is telling tall tales in this area. A recent study showed that 62 percent of adults lie about reading the classics in order to appear more intelligent. We cover everything from notable authors, artists, and composers to theater, before finishing up with some winning awards-season conversation.

If all this sounds a bit too much like hard work, never fear. For those downright time-poor (or lazy—that's perfectly acceptable too), there's a helpful summary, a general plan of attack if you will, at the beginning of each subject that will get you through cocktail conversation, at the very least. At the end of every Cheat Sheet, I lay out a social survival strategy that should see you through a dinner. The first part of the approach provides you an "argument"—aka a line of thought for you to make your case and to spark a discussion. The argument is followed by a clever "crisp fact" (as one of my college professors always insisted on) to support your position. But perhaps most important, I supply a pivot to get you out of a sticky situation. At the end of the day, if you don't like a conversation, the intelligent thing to do is change it.

Once you've perused these Cheat Sheets, you will be able to go out into the world fully confident in your ability to commentate on everything but sports (what am I, Superwoman?). Well, at least you should at least have enough wisdom to blag (British slang for *bluff*) your way through a tweet without humiliating yourself.

SUBJECT ONE—ENGLISH LANGUAGE

ENGLISH LANGUAGE SUMMARY

The key theme to keep in mind is that unless your spelling and grammar are accurate and your vocabulary is appropriate, you will find it impossible to win any debate. That is to say, if you use *arguement,* you've lost the argument, end of. Speaking of winning, the word *xenon* (a chemical element) may save you at Scrabble one day. And a pivot to stop an unseemly disagreement? Try "What's been your funniest ever autocorrect?" We all love it when we can blame technology, not ourselves.

We begin with the basis of communication in North America, the UK, and many places around the world—the English language. Incorrect usage will automatically negate any opinion you opine and indeed possibly lose you the job—or sexual partner—of your dreams. I ran into problems with the big tribute I wrote about Margaret Thatcher when she died. I made a typo, using *concurrent* instead of *consecutive* about her three terms in office. I probably didn't lose any sex over the error, but from the comments underneath the piece, possibly jobs and certainly reputation.

This series of Cheat Sheets aims to prevent such minor catastrophes, focusing on the most common and embarrassing errors. Convinced that you never make mistakes such as mine? Take the following pop quiz.

ENGLISH POP QUIZ

1. *Definitely* or *definately*?
2. Do you *lose* or *loose* your virginity?
3. Fever *affects* or *effects* your temperature?
4. Is it "*It's* a shame" or "*Its* a shame"?
5. Should it be "to boldly go where no man has gone before" or "to go where no man has gone before"?
6. What does a Brit hear when you say they are "quite pretty"?
7. What do you say to get someone to shut up and listen?

Correct answers: 1. Definitely. 2. Lose. 3. Affect. 4. It's. 5. Star Trek *is wrong: The* boldly *is an offense (to some) against grammar. 6. You think they're fugly. 7. "Surely it's no coincidence that the word* listen *is an anagram of the word* silent*."*

Perhaps it's worth having a quick skim read of this subject, just in case? Bad puns are pretty much the only excuse for bad spelling, and they're unlikely to further your career or love life unless you're the *New York Post*'s headline writer.

Our first Cheat Sheet examines spelling. Nobody is asking you to be spelling bee champion, and yes, English is an impossibly inconsistent language—urban legend has it that 923 words break the "*i* before *e*" rule and only 44 follow it—but to make basic spelling errors in the age of spell-check is unforgivable unless you are one of the 10 to 15 percent of Americans who are dyslexic. We will thus take a look at the most common words that people seem to ignore spell-check on and also homophones, words that are pronounced alike but different in meaning.

Our second Cheat Sheet is an index of common grammatical terms and errors. We're not going to get bogged down on the minutiae here. We'll give you just enough to make sure you don't irritate a pedant you need on side by splitting an infinitive or using an apostrophe in an ill-informed way. We also quickly "remind" you of the difference between verbs, adverbs, and such like.

Cheat Sheet 3 will focus on how, as George Bernard Shaw is widely attributed to have remarked, the United States and Great Britain are "separated by a common language." A portion of the blame can land at the feet of Noah Webster, he of the dictionary fame. Webster was all about asserting America's cultural independence through tweaking the language and believing words should be spelled as they sound. However, we won't be focusing so much on spelling or grammar. Let's be honest: The *get/gotten* and quotation-mark debates or the use of the phrase "I could care less" when it should be "I couldn't care less" will not destroy Anglo-American relations. Instead we will look at a number of words, especially those involving the police, sex, and alcohol, that have very different meanings to British and American ears. We highlight them to avoid unintended and unfortunate consequences.

The fourth and final Cheat Sheet under the banner of the English language will encompass a list of impressive words and one-liners to drop into any sort of communication and provide some methods to get you out of any oratory holes you may have dug for yourself. Of course, the most important thing to keep in mind is this: Never, ever use *like* or *you know* unless Shakespeare would have felt the need to.

English literature, in the form of Cheat Sheets on authors and theater, is covered under culture, for here we are still covering the basics. The subject after this one must therefore be math. Sorry. Money makes the world go round and all that.

WISE WORDS

If the English language made any sense, a catastrophe would be an apostrophe with fur.

—Doug Larson

CHEAT SHEET 1—SPELLING

SPELLING DISPUTE	INTERPRETATIONS
Affect/Effect	An affect is an influence. An effect is a result. So an affect causes an effect. "Twitter affects people's egos in a negative way." "Twitter's effects can also be positive." There are exceptions, it's English; blame the baffling Brits. If in any doubt, Google your phrase BEFORE you press send.
Allude/Elude	Allude is to hint. Elude is to escape.
A Lot/Allot	It is NEVER alot. A lot means to a large extent. Allot means to allocate something.
Altar/Alter	You'll find an altar in a church. You can't alter that.
Anyone/Any one	Anyone is referring to any person, often multiple people: "Anyone can buy my book." Any one refers to a single person: "Any one of my friends can buy my book."
Ascent/Assent	You have to assent, agree, to climb a mountain, an ascent.
Argument	Use arguement and you've lost the argument, end of.
Aural/Oral	Aural relates to what you hear, oral to the mouth.
Bachelor	You're liable to remain a batchelor if you spell this wrong in a communiqué to your beloved.

SPELLING DISPUTE	INTERPRETATIONS
Bare/Bear	Bare skin involves fur removal. A bear is furry.
Bridal/Bridle	A bridle is for horses. The bride may look like a horse, but the bridal party won't be happy if they hear you say that.
Canopy/Canapé	You eat canapés under a canopy at a wedding.
Censer/Censor/ Sensor	A censer is a container for incense. A censor is something Americans don't take too kindly to, as it's against free speech. Triggering a sensor sets alarm bells off.
Columbus	Spell it Colombus and it's clear you're not really American, are you?
Coolly	It is not cool to omit the second L on this one.
Connecticut	The thinking man's Mississippi, as everyone knows to spell-check that. It is not spelled how it is said— Conneticut. It has an extra C.
Chauvinism	Use chauvanism and you've lost the argument, which was probably pretty brutal if you're on the topic anyway.
Chord/Cord	You use chords in music, cords in sex games.
Definite/Definitely	Definitive, finite, decision. You are an ignorant idiot if you use definately.
Desert/Dessert	Desert—full of sand. Dessert—full of sugar. If a restaurant gets this wrong, you need to desert it before it gives you food poisoning.
Desperate	You write desparate and it's grounds for your spouse to separate from you.
Discreet/Discrete	Discreet—what you try to be when you're having an affair. Discrete means distinct.
Elicit/Illicit	"She was trying to elicit a response from him when she had an illicit affair."
Gorilla/Guerrilla	Gorillas are animals. Humans involved with guerrilla warfare may be acting like animals, but they still receive a different spelling.
Grateful	Your spell-check is right, it is not greatful. Be grateful for that.

SPELLING DISPUTE	INTERPRETATIONS
Hangar/Hanger	Hangars are for airplanes. Hangers are for evening dresses.
Heroin/Heroine	Tragic heroines may end up junkies on heroin.
Eminent/Immanent/ Imminent	Eminent refers to those who are respected. Immanent is rarer and means inherent. Imminent means threatening.
Independent	Don't go independent of the spell-check here. Trust it. It really isn't independant.
Lightning	Lightning doesn't strike twice. Spell-check is right, it isn't lightening.
Loose, Lose, Loser	You're a loser if you get this wrong. You lose your virginity. As a Desperate Housewife, to spice up your sex life, you may play around with loose handcuffs.
Misspell	It is not mispell. It is miss+spell=misspell.
Principal/Principle	The school principal will teach you principles to live by.
Retch/Wretch	Retching, vomiting, makes you feel wretched.
Site/Sight	A site is a location you visit. Sight refers to your sense of vision.
Stationary/ Stationery	Stationary is what you are most of the time in an NYC cab—stopped. You go to buy envelopes in the stationery section at Staples.
Their/There	Their is possessive. It is about ownership: "their penthouse." There refers to a place: "the penthouse over there." "They're" is covered in the grammar (apostrophe) section.
Too/To/Two	There's too much on your to-do list. Task number two is especially tricky.
Tragedy	Tradgedy. That extra D is tragic, especially if you're also using it in the word "privilege."
Wether/Weather/ Whether	Whether you need an umbrella depends on the weather. A wether is a castrated sheep—vaguely bringing up bestiality in conversation still isn't the done thing, so best avoid.
Whined/Wind/Wined	Wind can make you whine if it ruins your hair. You will also whine if the wine is corked.

WISE WORDS

A synonym is a word you use when you can't spell the other one.

—Baltasar Gracián

SOCIAL SURVIVAL STRATEGY

Argument: "Use arguement and you've lost the argument, end of."
You will obviously be utilizing this Cheat Sheet for when you are deploying the written word. Keep in mind that anyone who makes a spelling or grammatical error instantly renders the point they are making pointless. This is how Piers Morgan wins so many of his Twitter fights—he may be in the wrong, but his good grasp of the English language allows him to embarrass his opponents into if not submission, mild humiliation. Triple-check before you post or press send—you can never be too careful.

Crisp Fact: "You use chords in music, cords in sex games."
If you're floundering, counter with a fact about the spelling of a word or the word itself. It'll take the sting out of the situation.

Pivot: "What's been your funniest ever autocorrect?"
Made a mistake? Try blaming autocorrect. People almost always have an amusing anecdote about theirs or an acquaintance's.

CHEAT SHEET 2—GRAMMAR

GRAMMATICAL DISPUTE	INTERPRETATIONS
Adjective	A word that is used to describe a noun (a person or thing). For instance, hideous: "Why didn't we realize in the 1980s that leg warmers were hideous?"
Adverb	Used to give more information about an adjective, verb, or other adverb, such as really. E.g., "That's really not a good look." Does not suffer from underuse in twenty-first century America.

Apostrophes	Apostrophes are used to make a contraction and show possession. Which translates to:
	1. Replacing a letter (or two). For example:
	  • Do not=don't.
	  • Cannot=can't.
	  • It is=it's.
	  • There is=there's. Not to be confused with they're.

GRAMMATICAL DISPUTE	INTERPRETATIONS
Apostrophes (*cont.*)	• They are=they're. Not to be confused with their. See Cheat Sheet 1, Spelling. • We will=we'll. • Will not=won't. • You are=you're. 2. Showing ownership. Even if there's already an S at the end of a word. • John Oliver's show. • The boss's office. Could also be "boss'," as there's already an S there. • Ben and Jerry's ice cream (need an S only on the second). NB: Do NOT add an apostrophe if ownership is already shown. Basically, if you're not abbreviating anything. • That's yours. • The snake's escaped from its cage. • Markets boomed under Clinton.
Lay and Lie	I could bore you with talk of transitive verbs, direct subjects, and intransitive verbs. Instead I'll just say: "You lied to lay or get laid by Kate Upton." Don't suppose you'll be making that grammatical mistake again. Or get laid by Kate Upton, for that matter.
Noun	A word that refers to a person, place, animal, thing, or idea, for example: president, dildo, Washington, DC, sheep, or bestiality.
Pronoun	A word that is used often to avoid repeating a noun: *I, he, she, it, we, hers, us, yours,* or *they.* For instance, "Derek was so bored he skipped to the next Cheat Sheet."

GRAMMATICAL DISPUTE	INTERPRETATIONS
Split Infinitive	The world is divided into those who tolerate split infinitives and those who loathe them, to the extent they may come between you and a book deal, or even worse, sex. It's when an adverb is added between to and a verb. For instance, "He appears to really hate him." The grammatically correct version is "He appears to hate him."
That or Which	You are forgiven for being confused by this—take one look at the *Chicago Manual of Style* and you'll know what I'm talking about. Basically, the vast majority won't pick you up on this if you follow these rules: Which refers to animals or things, never to people. That can refer to people, animals, and things. So that or which? Well, what's attached to *that* is essential to the meaning of the sentence and what's attached to *which* is not—it's just some extra information. "Dogs that yap are the worst." "A dog, which sometimes drools, is man's best friend."
Who or Whom	An English language expert will launch into a tremendously boring lecture about nominative/objective pronouns and throw the word *clause* around a lot. We just have a cunning trick: When you're trying to figure out whether to use *who* or *whom*, decide whether the answer to the question is *he* or *him*. If it's him, use whom, and if it's he, it's who. "Whom do you love?" " I love him." "Who trod on the cat?" "He trod on the cat."

GRAMMATICAL DISPUTE	INTERPRETATIONS
Verb	A word that describes what a person or thing does, or what happens— for example, run, sing, grow, occur, seem.

WISE WORDS

I will not go down to posterity talking bad grammar.

—Benjamin Disraeli

SOCIAL SURVIVAL STRATEGY

Argument: "The world is divided into those who tolerate, those who loathe, and those who don't understand what a split infinitive is."

Split infinitives are one of the few areas that are up for debate in grammar, so are relatively safe to deliberate if for some reason you've ended up on this topic. Some people have no problem with them; until the 1800s, nobody raised an eyebrow over their use. For others, they are positively painful. Of course, many have no idea what they even are.

Crisp Fact: "*Which* refers to animals or things, never to people."

This is a good one to have in your back pocket—so you never go there and can pick someone up on incorrect use if you feel the need.

Pivot: "Have you ever ditched someone for using bad grammar?"

This will provide an interesting insight into all partaking in the conversation. Grammar Nazis may not be even able to bring themselves to court, let alone bed, someone who can't place an apostrophe in the appropriate place in a text message.

CHEAT SHEET 3—SEPARATED BY A COMMON LANGUAGE— ENGLISH AND AMERICAN

Don't scoff at the Brits. It is somewhat telling that probably the greatest communicator in history, Winston Churchill, had an American mother and an English father. The perfect language is a combination of the two. This section is specifically for Americans who would like to close the deal while engaged in a business meeting, cocktail chat, or pre-hookup explorations with a Brit. Or maybe all three.

EXPRESSION	BRITS HEAR	AMERICAN DOS, DON'TS, AND GENERAL INFO
Bang	Have sex with.	Don't use when referring to a hairstyle with a Brit. The British call American bangs a fringe.
Banger	A sausage, as in a frankfurter. Or an old car.	You can use ironically with the word *mash*. Nothing to do with head-bangers, who are people who wave their greasy hair about at rock concerts.
Bill	Police or invoice.	Try not to call for the first if you can possibly avoid it, but definitely call for the second in a restaurant. If you

EXPRESSION	BRITS HEAR	AMERICAN DOS, DON'TS, AND GENERAL INFO
Bill (cont.)		ask for the check, the waitress will be wondering why she should be paying you.
Bird	One's girlfriend or any young female.	Use with extreme caution if you're unsure of the sense of humor of any females in the vicinity.
Bin	To throw away, discard.	What straight male Brits do to a bit of fluff.
Bit of fluff	Sexually attractive female lacking in brains.	Not exactly a term of endearment.
Blag	Bluff.	If you want to improve your blagging, don't skip any of these Cheat Sheets.
Bollocking	A severe reprimand.	If working for a Brit, avoid being on the receiving end of.
Bollocks	1. Testicles; 2. Rubbish, nonsense, drivel.	Don't worry about this. It's impossible to say without a genuine Brit accent.
Bonk	To have sex.	Your call. If an attractive Brit suggests it, why not?
Bugger	Anal sex; joking term for addressing someone. Buggered—something's broken, couldn't be bothered. Bugger up—to make a mess of something. Bugger off—go away, leave me alone. Bugger all—absolutely nothing at all.	When in doubt, ask for clarification. The abundance of multiple meanings is unfair.
Can't be arsed	Can't be bothered.	Note for once, nothing to do with sex.

EXPRESSION	BRITS HEAR	AMERICAN DOS, DON'TS, AND GENERAL INFO
Cheers	Thank you. Also used in toasts.	Use sparingly. Brits tend not to mind if an American utilizes it. However, some Americans object.
Cider	Alcoholic drink derived from apples.	In a pub, don't ask for it "hot with a cinnamon stick" unless you'd like a group of burly Manchester United fans to laugh you out of the building.
Crumpet	Attractive female.	Not something worth risking saying within earshot of any female.
Dogging	Anonymous, public sex between strangers, usually taking place in cars or outdoors and in the presence of voyeurs.	In the age of camera phones, it might be best not to engage in this.
Drivel	To talk stupidly and carelessly.	Something you won't be doing once you've read *The Intelligent Conversationalist*.
Fanny	Vagina.	In general, stay away from this word, even when discussing one's Aunt Fanny in a concerned way.
Fancy	1. Feel like; 2. Find attractive. Fancy dress—costume party attire.	Not to be confused with posh, which is what Brits call Americans' use of fancy. ("Port Out, Starboard Home" was the side of the boat Brits wanted to be on when they traveled to check out the Empire in the East.)
Fit	Attractive person.	You want to be this.
Fry-up	Also known as the full English. A large breakfast that may include any/all of the following: bacon, eggs, black pudding, sausages, and baked beans.	Proper black pudding is made from pork blood—you have been warned.

EXPRESSION	BRITS HEAR	AMERICAN DOS, DON'TS, AND GENERAL INFO
Gooseberry	Third person, outsider.	What you were at one time in high school or college, but would never admit to now.
Graft	Hard work.	Employ a Brit who says he or she will do this.
Grill	What you do to bacon when you're being healthy.	Americans would say broil.
Gutted	Disappointed.	Good word. Okay for Americans to use.
Knob	1. Penis or dim-witted person. 2. Door handle.	If this is said of you in your presence and nowhere near a door, be worried.
IRA	Terrorist group. If you are in the company of a Brit over age thirty, he or she will have a story about missing a bomb by minutes and some choice words about Ted Kennedy and Peter King.	Probably best not bring it up, even if you're referring to individual retirement accounts.
Jock	A Scotsman or a small dog.	Not something American jocks want to be, unless they've Scottish roots.
Mid-Atlantic	Halfway between the US and the UK; Madonna's accent when married to Guy Ritchie.	Clarify your use unless you want to confuse a Brit.
Muppet	Foolish and incompetent person.	Has nothing to do with Jim Henson, Sesame Street, or films showcasing Miss Piggy.
Natter	Talk pleasantly.	Brits not being sarcastic here, for once.
Nick	1. Prison; 2. Police station; 3. To steal.	Avoid.

EXPRESSION	BRITS HEAR	AMERICAN DOS, DON'TS, AND GENERAL INFO
Pants	Underpants or something that's not very good.	Unless you want a Brit to laugh at you, don't refer to your trousers as pants.
Paralytic	Extremely drunk.	This has nothing to do with neuromuscular functioning. It is the normal state of a Brit who's been at a pub for several hours.
Peckish	Slightly hungry.	Use this either when you'd like a little snack or when you're paralytic and need a fry-up to deal with the alcohol from the cider you drank before the Manchester United fans threw you out the pub's front door.
Piss	Urinate. To take the piss—tease. On the piss—out drinking. Pissed—drunk. Pissed off—annoyed.	If in doubt, ask for clarification.
Plank	A right idiot.	Give a Brit a bollocking if he or she calls you this when it's undeserved.
Pull	To persuade someone to be one's date or sex partner. On the pull—to seek a date or sex partner.	Americans arguably better at this than Brits.
Quite	A little bit. Often used sarcastically. "Quite good" means "not very good."	Never use in the company of a Brit. People have been fired over misunderstanding this phrase.
Roast(ing)	Either roasting meat or a gangbang involving one girl and many men, normally football (aka soccer) players.	Tell a Brit you went to a great "roasting" and he or she will use you as the punch line of all his or her jokes for the rest of time.

EXPRESSION	BRITS HEAR	AMERICAN DOS, DON'TS, AND GENERAL INFO
Roger	Roger—to have sexual intercourse. Roger that—I heard you.	Very important for you to listen carefully here. Ask them to repeat if not quite sure.
Row	Argument.	Not pronounced in the way you would pronounce the verb that has to do with how one propels a canoe or where your seat is in a theater.
Sacked	Fired from a job.	No laughing matter.
Section	To detain under the Mental Health Act.	Scary ground here.
Skint	Penniless/broke.	Good word; Americans allowed to utilize.
Slag	A promiscuous woman. Also occasionally heard with reference to such men.	Practice safe sex if with one or if you are one.
Sod	Unpleasant person, exclamation of frustration originally short for sodomite. Or if preceded by "poor"—an unfortu-nate person. Sod it—exclamation of contempt or frustration	If you mean turf and you're with a Brit, say turf.
Strop, Stropping, Stroppy	A bad mood, a fit of fury more fitting for a toddler but indulged in by an adult.	Good insult; consider adopting.
Tit	Fool.	If someone tells you that you're "making a total tit of yourself," it's time to change course, especially if you're hoping to hook up with them.

EXPRESSION	BRITS HEAR	AMERICAN DOS, DON'TS, AND GENERAL INFO
Tosser	Also a wanker, which as you know is someone who masturbates. And is an idiot.	Nothing to do with salad.
Twat	The female genitals (from the 1600s). A contemptible person, an idiot.	Brits couldn't just leave it at vagina. I apologize for my countrymen.

WISE WORDS

I didn't know he was dead; I thought he was British.

—Woody Allen

SOCIAL SURVIVAL STRATEGY

Argument: "There are some words, such as *bollocks*, that just shouldn't be said in anything other than a British accent."
Americans usually sound like Dick Van Dyke gone wrong when they try to speak the Queen's English (although Jake Gyllenhaal's enunciation was perfection on Broadway in 2015). Leave the Brits to their colloquialisms; you've plenty of "awesome" slang of your own that can be rendered properly only in an American accent.

Crisp Fact: American cider will disappoint British people.
Most Brits love their alcohol, so either embrace us for it or judge from afar. (The former is far more fun.)

Pivot: "Madonna's tweed-wearing British phase seems so long ago. Seen her Instagram lately?"

Nicely inclusive, as everyone can summon up an opinion on Madonna, even if it's just "what has she done to her face?"

CHEAT SHEET 4—DEBATE

This final English language Cheat Sheet gives you some strategies to come out champion of any conversation. We first focus on an A to Z of impressive words to throw into your chat now and again. We then follow these up with a few one-liner get-outs and steer-aways to ensure you can dig yourself out of any holes you may find yourself in.

DISARMING WORD	TRANSLATION
Avarice	Excessive greed. Use when describing bankers, politicians, realtors, and the IRS. Except to their face. Or in writing.
Borborygmus	Your tummy is rumbling. Could be used as some sort of icebreaker when trying to convince someone to have dinner with you.
Connive	To plot, scheme. This book is somewhat conniving.
Disestablish-mentarianism	Opposes having an established religion within a state. Antidisestablishmentarianism is thus basically radical GOP—dismissive of evolution and for school prayer.
Erudite	Learned. What you will be when you've read all the Cheat Sheets.

DISARMING WORD	TRANSLATION
Fractious	Irritable, troublesome. Normally used in connection with a child, thus suitably insulting when deployed on an adult.
Gluttony	Aka what goes on at the Super Bowl, Thanksgiving, and Christmas.
Hauteur	Haughtiness—take care that you don't take arrogance too far after completing this book. Not to be confused with couture, though the two words have much in common.
Inveterate	Stubbornly established by habit. "He's an inveterate taker of dinner off the mirror." (If you missed my *Single Girl's Survival Guide,* those who "do dinner off the mirror" eschew food for hoovering cocaine.)
Jabberwock	Nonsense, gibberish; not to be confused with a character in *Star Wars.*
Kismet	Fate; destiny. Not to be confused with Katniss, an aquatic plant and the heroine in *The Hunger Games.*
Lackadaisical	Lacking spirit, liveliness; languid. NB: You'd be lax—not to mention incorrect—to spell it laxidasical.
Malapropism	Aka Dogberryism. Misusing or switching words that are similar. Often amusing—to everyone else. Example, Dan Quayle, vice-president: "Republicans understand the importance of bondage between a mother and child."
Nadir	Lowest point of something. Regularly—and accurately—describes relations with nations in the Middle East.
Obtuse	Irritatingly insensitive or difficult to understand. In other words, anyone who disagrees with you.
Panacea	Cure-all; a remedy for all disease or ills. Not ever going to happen to the US health-care system.
Qoph	The 19th letter of the Hebrew alphabet and a Scrabble-winning word.
Repudiate	Refuse to accept; reject. Sarah Palin infamously riffed on this word and came up with "refudiate." Safest for you not to, clearly.
Sycophant	Person who flatters someone for self-gain. Troubles politicians and celebrities more than us mere mortals.

DISARMING WORD	TRANSLATION
Truculent	Quick to fight; aggressively defiant. Often used in relation to teenagers and thus all the more damning if employed against an adult.
Umbrage	Dolores Umbridge was the awful woman in pink in the Harry Potter books. J. K. Rowling undoubtedly playing with *umbrage*, which means taking resentment.
Vex	Upmarket way of saying to confuse or annoy.
Wanton	Deliberate and unprovoked; promiscuous person (usually female); play or frolic. Essential element to have in one's existence, whichever meaning is being referred to.
Xenon	Colorless, odorless gas; Scrabble savior.
Yack	To talk incessantly and tiresomely. What everyone apart from you does occasionally.
Zenith	The highest point.

The next sets of phrases are there to get you out of a tight spot, for sometimes we all find ourselves a little out of our depth. Every single television personality has a tell, a filler word or phrase they employ while they try to figure out what to say on air without looking like a muppet. One of the most successful cable news hosts I've ever worked with uses *exactly*. My get-out-of-jail card is to say "on some levels, yes." It buys enough time for me to figure out, under the X-ray that is the TV camera, how I'm going to steer the conversation to an area I want to talk about. And this is worth repeating: Never use the words *like* or *you know*. You are not an ignorant fool; you are an intelligent member of society.

To buy time while you figure out how to respond:
- Repeat the question.
- Use pauses and remark "good question" or "interesting point."
- Direct the question to someone else.

Be vague if you're unsure:

- "Recently"—could mean at any point in the past few years.
- "In my opinion."

Counterpunches:

- "You're being defensive."
- "Surely it's no coincidence that the word *listen* is an anagram of the word *silent*."
- "I don't have an attitude problem. You have a perception problem."
- "Frankness is usually a euphemism for rudeness."

To win a debate with a conservative:

- "A conservative is a politician who wants to keep what the liberals fought for a generation ago."

To win a debate with a liberal:

- "Show me a young Conservative and I'll show you someone with no heart. Show me an old Liberal and I'll show you someone with no brains." —Winston Churchill
- "The principal feature of American liberalism is sanctimoniousness." —P. J. O'Rourke

When you've won a debate:

- "Sarcasm is just one more service we offer."
- "The shortest complete sentence in the English language is 'Go.' Shall we go to the bar?"

When you're sinking:

- "Don't take life too seriously, you won't get out alive."
- "Being right is highly overrated. Even a stopped clock is right twice a day."

To end the debate and come out with some of your reputation intact:

- "Talk is cheap because supply exceeds demand."
- "After all is said and done, more is said than done."

On the very rare occasions you initially appear to have lost:

- "You can't learn anything while you're talking."
- "Waste no more time arguing about what a good man should be. Be one." —Marcus Aurelius

---

WISE WORDS

I love argument, I love debate. I don't expect anyone just to sit there and agree with me, that's not their job.

—Margaret Thatcher

SOCIAL SURVIVAL STRATEGY

Argument: "After all is said and done, more is said than done."
The above phrase will shut everyone up, but avail yourself of it sparingly. You don't want a reputation as a killjoy, you want to be known for your sparkling chitchat.

Crisp Fact: The word *xenon* may save you at Scrabble one day.
Always important to commit a few good Scrabble words to memory; not using your phone to cheat will always be admired, if not appreciated.

Pivot: "I think we should all just follow Marcus Aurelius: 'Waste no more time arguing about what a good man should be. Be one.'"
Take the high road—this is cocktail conversation, not a GOP primary.

SUBJECT TWO—MATH AND ECONOMICS

MATH AND ECONOMICS SUMMARY

The key theme to think about when discussing anything related to this subject is that you agree with John Kenneth Galbraith's infamous appraisal: "The only function of economic forecasting is to make astrology look respectable." This shuts up people who think they know something, as they really don't. It then allows you to throw in a brilliant but appropriately obscure crisp fact to show your sophistication. Try "the monuments on euro notes are fictional so no country's national pride is offended." This will allow you the perfect segue to your pivot out of a financial discussion, which is not somewhere you ever want to linger in polite company. Ask "What's your favorite European city?" Even if the people you're speaking to have never crossed the pond, there's normally somewhere they wouldn't mind stopping by—and if they don't, why are you talking to them? Food! Wine! Real monuments that are over three hundred years old everywhere! Sex! (You should always travel hopefully.)

Welcome to math and economics. Before your eyelids droop and you flip to the political sex scandal Cheat Sheet, let us recall that this subject is a necessary evil. Indeed, it is quite possibly the backbone to any useful knowledge gained from this tome.

As Groucho Marx put it, "Money frees you from doing things

you dislike. Since I dislike doing nearly everything, money is handy."

So don't get too grouchy here. I've tried to keep this subject as entertaining as possible for all you Oscar the Grouch Muppets out there. If you're going to blame anyone, blame the Scottish for inventing banking. Well, branch banking anyway.

Our first Cheat Sheet on this subject concerns the history of money, and the fact that if one considers the concept of cash too carefully, we're basically in an "emperor's new clothes" situation. This is followed up with a grid of the major economists throughout civilization and their thoughts—thoughts that have dubious links to reality, as we will see in the seventh Cheat Sheet, which covers the economic crisis of 2008, including Eurogeddon.

In an attempt to end the section on a hopeful note and actually get some concrete tips on money matters, in our eighth Cheat Sheet we look at three case studies, of the good, the bad, and the aha! Namely Warren Buffett, Bernie Madoff, and Oprah Winfrey.

The good news is that it turns out we shouldn't be watching CNBC in the morning if we want to get ahead—we should be glued to reruns of Tom Cruise types bouncing on *The Oprah Winfrey Show*'s sofa.

CHEAT SHEET 5—HISTORY OF MONEY

BACKGROUND BRIEFING

"Money makes the world go round." "It's a rich man's world." Clichés are clichés for a reason. "Money" is defined as anything that is generally accepted as payment for goods and services and repayment of debts.

Initially, it all made perfect sense. The use of barter dates back tens of thousands of years. Many cultures around the world eventually developed the use of commodity money, such as gold coins. This eventually evolved into a system of representative money known as fiat money. Fiat money has nothing to do with the car. Instead, in itself, it is without intrinsic use or value—i.e., it's just a bit of paper. It gets its value by being declared by a government to be legal tender.

NOTEWORTHY NUGGET

The Chinese, trailblazers that they are, came up with paper money during the Song Dynasty (although the notes were used alongside commodity money).

Starting in the seventeenth century, European traders got bored of lugging gold around. So commodity money—gold coins—was eventually replaced by representative money—paper notes—linked to the gold standard. This still makes perfect sense. The supply of gold can only grow slowly, so the gold standard would restrain governments' spending and keep inflation in check. By the beginning of the twentieth century almost all countries had adopted the gold standard.

And then the world decided to shoot itself in the foot. Life is a cabaret, old chum.

There was World War I, followed by the Wall Street crash and Great Depression. To help bring the United States out of the Depression (and most economists agree that it did), President Franklin D. Roosevelt cut most of the dollar's ties with gold, allowing the American government to pump money into the economy and lower interest rates. But the United States did continue to allow foreign governments to exchange dollars for gold.

However, the world continued self-sabotaging itself, this time in the form of World War II. The winner takes it all and all that jazz (sorry, I've been senior editor at Broadway.com too long; I'll leave it with the musical theater references). And in this case, the real winner was America. Europe lay in ruins and the United States became the preeminent global economic power.

So in 1944, off the world (well, at least "experts" representing all forty-four Allied nations, who battled the Axis powers of Hitler and co.) trotted to America, specifically to Bretton Woods in New Hampshire, to begin to resolve the mess. At Bretton Woods, most countries adopted fiat currencies that were fixed to the US dollar, which still maintained at least a link to gold.

Currencies basically swam along until 1971, when the Nixon administration suspended the convertibility of the US dollar to gold, at which point many countries depegged their currencies from the US dollar and most of the world's currencies weren't backed by anything except governments' fiat of legal tender.

WHY IT MATTERS TODAY

Now pause for a moment. Take a deep breath. Try not to panic too much. Yes, you are correct in thinking that our financial system has evolved to something akin to the emperor's new clothes. Everyone is telling everyone else we've got money (clothes on), but we don't really. Thanks to what went on in 1971—and I'm not talking about the recreational drug use, which actually didn't play a part in America's decision; it was because foreigners flush with dollars were depleting US gold reserves—our money is not linked to gold or anything real anymore. It's just a bit of paper that some bloke somewhere says is worth something.

The only thing that's stopping out-and-out chaos is inflation—print too much money and the economy will go haywire. So that's all right then.

KEY TERMS: INFLATION AND DEFLATION

Inflation

- Inflation is the persistent, substantial rise in the general level of prices. If prices don't rise, it's deflation.
- In the United States, this is measured by the Consumer Price Index, which is based on a shopping "basket" of goods and services on which we typically spend our money.
- To combat inflation, the Federal Reserve, aka the Fed, will increase short-term interest rates so it costs more for businesses and consumers to borrow money.

Deflation

- The Fed fears this more than inflation—it's when the general level of prices goes down.
- Best analogy, think of a car. Say thanks to deflation in 2017 a new car costs $30,000; in 2018 it's $10,000, and by 2019 it's

> $5,000. What sane consumer would buy a car in 2017? As a result, spending dries up on cars and the industry collapses. This would be mirrored across the board. You are in the deflation "death spiral."

And then again, maybe not. There's also a young pretender to the whole monetary system called the bitcoin. Stuff of nightmares? Quite possibly.

KEY TERM: BITCOIN

- Bitcoin has massive potential and challenges the banking system as we know it. A bitcoin is a form of digital currency, sometimes called a cryptocurrency or a virtual currency, that was started in 2009 by an unknown person called Satoshi Nakamoto. Bitcoins basically exist only online and you hold them in an online "wallet."

- You can trade bitcoins for goods or services with vendors who'll accept them for payment, but it is not legal tender anywhere. It is not backed by any government.

- The payment system is supposed to be designed so only a certain number of bitcoins can exist, preventing inflation.

- The "real" monetary value of bitcoins fluctuates, like equities.

- Governments are freaking out. People can anonymously trade, sometimes even naughty things, and avoid taxes!

- You'll keep hearing about it as everyone tries to figure out what to do and how to regulate the system.

- It could really work; just think of the currency thing for normal people. If my mum in London wants to buy me a birthday present in New York, the banks will screw her on the exchange rate. If she could use bitcoin, that wouldn't be an issue.

- At time of going to press, the world's largest bitcoin wallet is owned by the US government (of course it is). The largest bitcoin holder is Nakamoto, who holds many wallets.
- Interesting sidenote: Just 8 percent of the world's currency exists as physical cash; the remainder is electronic.

TALKING POINTS

- If you're going to date a bankster type, you won't see them much (might be a good thing), what with globalization and all, but you'll possibly get more face time with someone who is primarily in equities—stocks and shares—rather than Forex. Forex, or FX, is what businessmen—not a breed best known for their spelling ability, but who do like to confuse us with jargon in the hope we will believe that they are masters of the universe—call the foreign exchange rate between two currencies. Forex is unique because it trades twenty-four hours a day except weekends. The New York Stock Exchange trades weekdays from 9:30 AM to 4:00 PM EST and has public holidays off.

- Taxation has been used by states throughout history to carry out many functions, from war to welfare. Historically, the nobility were supported by taxes on the poor. This has now flipped, and modern social security systems are intended to support the poor, the disabled, or the retired by taxes on those who are still working. Some might say that certain conservative types have embraced this "grudgingly."

  * The first known system of taxation was in ancient Egypt, and our ancestors have flirted with all sorts ever since. Some obsolete forms of taxation include taxes being clamped on beards in tsarist Russia (we should probably have one on mustaches now—for men and women—to encourage the end of this fashion faux pas). The window tax lasted in the UK from 1696 to 1851, so if you were showing off, you'd

build a house with lots of windows, and if you were broke, you'd fill them in.

* It may be a statement of the obvious, but a nation's tax system tends to be a reflection of its communal values or the values of those in power. Hence the Germans are still forking out for a solidarity surcharge, which was introduced back in 1991 to help pay for reunification. Can you see (insert the name of whichever selfish country or political party you dislike) agreeing to do that?

* America, being so big and all, has state as well as federal taxes. Some states do not levy an individual income tax, including Texas and Florida. Places where the Bush family have tended to hang out. Hmm.

NOTEWORTHY NUGGET

Today, Germany has one of the most complicated systems of taxation in the world. It's even been suggested that three-quarters of the world's literature about taxation refers to the German system.

RED FLAGS

- Don't confuse Bretton Woods with the Marshall Plan. Bretton Woods didn't solve the postwar imbalanced international economic situation: Europe was still broken and debt-ridden.

    * General George Marshall, after sorting out the Allied victory over Hitler, became the US Secretary of State (1947–1949) and recognized this problem.

    * Thus the United States set up the European Recovery Program—aka the Marshall Plan—to provide monetary support for rebuilding Europe largely through grants rather than loans, for four years starting in April 1948.

    * It wasn't an entirely selfless act on America's part; it was partly to prevent the spread of communism.

* It worked: By 1952, for all Marshall Plan recipients, output in 1951 was at least 35 percent higher than in 1938. Over the next two decades, Western Europe enjoyed unprecedented growth and prosperity. Some suggested that the only way to sort the recent Eurogeddon crisis was to have a new "Marshall Plan" to allow Europeans to get out of the debt hole they're currently in.

- It is dangerous to ignore history on taxation or you will be bound to repeat it.

  * Poll taxes, which every adult has to pay without their income or overall wealth being taken into account, have almost always been unpopular in England. From Richard II in the late fourteenth century on, their implementation contributed to revolts and such like. So what did Margaret Thatcher do? A decade after becoming prime minister, she decided to implement one. Cue riots in March 1990 and her resignation that November. The poll tax undoubtedly contributed to her downfall.

  * America got it right twice, with the two world wars. In 1918, the top rate of US federal income tax was increased to 77 percent (on income over $1,000,000) to finance World War I. During World War II, Franklin D. Roosevelt even tried to impose a 100 percent tax on all incomes over $25,000 to help with the war effort. Unfortunately President Bush II ignored his history books, cut the top marginal tax rate down to 35 percent in 2001, proceeded to wage two wars, and didn't pay for them. Throw in Medicare Part D and cue debt drama.

WISE WORDS

When I was young I thought that money was the most important thing in life; now that I am old I know that it is.

—Oscar Wilde

SOCIAL SURVIVAL STRATEGY

Argument: "Politicians who remain in power too long end up out of touch—look at Margaret Thatcher."
This is hard to disagree with and can be applied to almost everyone in office. Margaret Thatcher, the grocer's daughter, rose to power precisely because she wasn't a member of the traditional elite, liked debate (p. 33), and was in touch with the electorate. Ten years later, while she was surrounded by yes-men, the poll tax occurred, and within months she'd resigned.

Crisp Fact: "The world's largest bitcoin wallet holder is the US government."
The US government has its tentacles everywhere . . .

Pivot: "The winner always takes it all. That was a great ABBA song! Have you seen *Mamma Mia!*, or is the idea of a jukebox musical too horrific for you?"
It's hard not to have an opinion on jukebox musicals; unlike Wagnerian operas, everyone can understand the concept. Useful way to turn the chat to something all and sundry can contribute to and not come to blows about. Unless you're talking about *Jersey Boys*. There are some very serious *Jersey Boys* fans.

CHEAT SHEET 6—ECONOMISTS

The wisest words that an economist has ever uttered were those of the Canadian-American John Kenneth Galbraith (1908–2006). You should use them if anyone ever asks you about the economy.

> The only function of economic forecasting is to make astrology look respectable.

As we now know, all the money and learning in the world didn't make most economists (with a few notable exceptions such as Dr. Doom, Nouriel Roubini) any good at predicting financial Armageddon in 2008, did it?

Like astrology, the earliest discussions of economics date back to ancient times. Back then, and until the Industrial Revolution, economics was not a separate discipline but a part of philosophy. One might suggest it would have been better off remaining there, debated as an abstract notion rather than depended on for small stuff such as the security of nations.

For those who want to drop in a few historical names in

conversation, we now take a quick tour though times past via one of our trusty reference grids.

ERA	PHILOSOPHER/TERM	PHILOSOPHY
Ancient Greece	Aristotle and Company	Examined ideas about the "art" of wealth acquisition and questioned whether property is best left in private or public hands. Posited a natural and an unnatural kind of wealth getting, which we can all relate to. The natural referred to what it took to keep a household going—securing food and a roof over one's head (Main Streeters). Unnatural was the making of money for its own sake (Wall Streeters).
Medieval	Thomas Aquinas and other scholars	Argued that it was a moral obligation of businesses to sell goods at a just price.
Western Europe, sixteenth to late eighteenth centuries	Mercantilism (term was invented later by its critics)	A political and economic movement. It suggested governments should play a protectionist role in the economy by implementing masses of regulation. So began an argument that will probably be with us for the rest of time.
Eighteenth century	Capitalism (term coined later by its critics, primarily Karl Marx)	Spearheaded by the Scottish philosopher Adam Smith, often cited as the father of modern economics for his treatise *The Wealth of Nations* (1776). His vision of a free market economy, the opposite of mercantilism, was seriously helped by timing (as with everyone who is a success). *Wealth of Nations* coincided with: • The American Revolution. • The French Revolution (inspired by the American, and which caused Europe-wide upheavals). • The Industrial Revolution (the start of), which allowed more wealth to be created on a bigger scale than ever before.

ERA	PHILOSOPHER/TERM	PHILOSOPHY
Eighteenth century (*cont.*)	Capitalism (term coined later by its critics, primarily Karl Marx)	NB: It was a Frenchman, Vincent de Gournay (1712–1759), who is reputed to have asked why it was so hard to *laissez faire et laissez passer* (free enterprise, free trade).
Nineteenth century	Marxism	Karl Marx was, and in many ways still remains, the preeminent socialist economist; his ideas are credited as the foundation of modern communism. He led the backlash against the Smith school's "laissez-faire" attitudes, believing that capitalism contained the seeds of its own destruction. Marx thought that as wealth became more concentrated in the hands of a few capitalists, the ranks of an increasingly dissatisfied proletariat would swell, leading to bloody revolution and eventually a classless society.
Post– World War II	John Maynard Keynes	Advocated interventionist fiscal policy to stimulate economic demand and growth. What Democrats like doing now.
Twentieth century	Chicago School	What Republicans like doing now. Keynes was challenged by what came to be known as the Chicago school of econom-ics at the University of Chicago. They advocated "liberty" and "freedom," harking back to nineteenth-century-style noninterventionist governments. More University of Chicago academics have been awarded the Nobel Prize in Economics than those from any other university. But since Obama received one in 2009 for peace and Europe one in 2012 when it was trying to bankrupt the world, perhaps we shouldn't set too much store by this.

As already alluded to, but worth reiterating at every opportunity should someone try to tell you what the economy is going to do, the "profession" of economics is notoriously bad at predicting recessions. Your local "walk-ins welcome" psychic would probably be more reliable.

Thus most economists failed to predict the worst international economic crisis since the Great Depression of 1930s—our very own credit crunch.

WISE WORDS

If all economists were laid end to end, they would not reach a conclusion.

—George Bernard Shaw

SOCIAL SURVIVAL STRATEGY

Argument: "I'm with Galbraith, the only function of economic forecasting is to make astrology look respectable."
All "professionals" tend to be bluffing—nobody really has a clue when it comes down to it. This phrase is brilliant as it shuts up any blustering business buffoon.

Crisp Fact: "The term *capitalism* was actually coined by its critics, primarily Karl Marx."
It can take a critic to cement an idea in the mainstream—better to be talked about than not at all.

Pivot: "The 'profession' of economics is notoriously bad at predicting recessions. Know any good psychics? I'm trying to decide whether to invest in the markets or not."
Everyone has a stance on psychics. Some will think them fakes, some will blush (so you know they're ashamed to have one on speed dial), and others will be fishing out their phones to send you contact details for their favorites. A mischievous way to change the topic.

CHEAT SHEET 7—A QUICK GUIDE TO THE CREDIT CRUNCH (C. 2008) AND EUROGEDDON (STILL GOING)

BACKGROUND BRIEFING

A credit crunch is a reduction in the general availability of loans (or credit). Suddenly it gets very hard to meet the conditions required to get a bank loan. And we in the early twenty-first century had a crunch to call our very own. Warren Buffett, a man who we will see in Cheat Sheet 8 is normally proven right in all matters financial, called the crunch *poetic justice*.

Banks looked insolvent, credit availability declined, investors got freaked—so global stock markets crashed. International trade declined, economies across the globe slowed, and many countries went into recession. We looked financial Armageddon in the face. And although the sky hasn't fallen on our heads, arguably Europe still hasn't fundamentally recovered, and can American millennials really pay for the baby boomers' lengthy retirements and all their Social Security and Medicare? Are Americans entitled to entitlements and can they afford them?

A credit crunch is usually accompanied by a flight to quality by lenders and investors, as they seek less risky investments (often at the expense of small- to medium-size enterprises). Hence the subsequent strength of the dollar and gold at the end of the naughties. Yes, back to the United States (even though, as we shall see, that's where the problems started) and gold again.

The causes and effects of our credit crunch will be argued about for decades to come, especially by all the economists who failed to predict it (back to Galbraith's quote from earlier about economists and astrologers). However, there were basically two reasons for our gigantic mess.

CAUSE 1. THE US HOUSING BUBBLE

The crisis was triggered by the bursting of the United States housing bubble, which peaked in 2006. High default rates (people not paying up) on subprime (risky) loans and adjustable-rate mortgages (ARMs) began to increase quickly thereafter.

Borrowers had been encouraged to assume big mortgages in the belief that the housing market would continue to rise and that interest rates would remain low. When this began to change, defaults increased and the whole thing snowballed.

Basically, credit rating agencies and investors failed to accurately price the risk involved with mortgage-related financial products. And where America led, the rest of the world followed, because we now live in a global society, so bankers in Britain and beyond were busy extending credit to people who shouldn't have had it. The phrase to throw in at dinner parties and job interviews here is *global contagion*. That is why so many people around the world spent so much time worrying about the financial stability of Iceland, then the PIIGS (no, not about the supply of bacon for your BLT, but Portugal, Italy, Ireland, Greece, and Spain), and then the entirety of Europe and the world.

CAUSE 2. GOVERNMENTS

Now, you must note, as a well-read individual, that the crisis was not just Wall Street's fault. History has shown that markets are not self-correcting. Give a banker an inch, he'll take a mile, and boom and bust will follow. It's lawmakers' responsibility to rein these banksters in. That's the point of GOVERNING. Hence Glass-Steagall was invented.

KEY TERM: GLASS-STEAGALL

There are (or should be) two types of banks: investment banks (for gamblers—i.e., Gordon Gekko types) and commercial banks (where you have your checking and savings accounts). After the Wall Street crash of 1929 leading to the Great Depression of the 1930s, Congress put a firewall between investment and commercial banks: the Banking Act of 1933, or as it's commonly known, the Glass-Steagall Act. Gordon Gekko could lose everything and you wouldn't. This firewall helped to lead to the largest sustained period of economic growth in American history.

In 1980 Ronald Reagan was elected, which brought in a culture of deregulation culminating in the repeal of Glass-Steagall in 1999. To put it simply: Gordon Gekko was now allowed to use your cash to make bets. And yes, the repeal happened under Bill Clinton, a Democratic president. But you should always blame the tearing up of the rule books on Alan Greenspan (chairman of the US Federal Reserve, 1987–2006) instead of Clinton, as Greenspan was really the "brains" behind it. To make matters worse, the regulatory framework that governments (apart from Canada's) had for the financial markets did not keep pace with financial innovation, such as the increasing importance of the shadow banking system.

KEY TERM: THE SHADOW BANKING SYSTEM

- Like mercantilism and capitalism, this term was invented after the practice started.

- The shadow banking system consists of nonbank financial institutions that play an increasingly critical role in providing credit across the global financial system.

- Many institutions and vehicles resembling shadow banks emerged in American and European markets between 2000 and 2008.

- Famous examples of shadow institutions include private equity companies, hedge funds, and mortgage brokers such as Countrywide Financial. Countrywide Financial was naughty in many ways, including allegedly giving politicians favorable mortgage rates as well as in essence screwing its clients. In 2006 it was the US's biggest single mortgage lender, financing 20 percent of all mortgages. By 2008 it was failing miserably and was bought by Bank of America.

Shadow institutions were not subject to the same safety and soundness regulations as depository banks (which after the repeal of Glass-Steagall weren't that strong anyway). This is to say, shadow institutions didn't have to keep as much money in the metaphorical vault relative to what they borrowed and lent, what is known as *capital requirements*. Therefore they could have a very high level of financial leverage—a lot of debt relative to the liquid assets available to pay immediate claims. This is fine and means a lot of money can be made—unless there is a *Mary Poppins* moment, where the little boy in the bank screams, "Give me back my money!" and we all want our money back at the same time.

The shadow banking system has been blamed for aggravating the subprime mortgage crisis and helping to transform it into a global credit crunch. After Glass-Steagall was repealed and as the shadow banking system expanded to rival or even surpass conventional banking in importance, politicians and government officials should have realized that they were re-creating the kind of financial vulnerability that made the Great Depression possible. And they should have responded by extending regulations and the financial safety net to cover these new institutions.

But oh no, they didn't. Politicians encouraged financial vulnerability. The government wanted to give people the opportunity of home ownership, so (through Fannie Mae, Freddie Mac, etc.) it lowered the requirements to get a mortgage. Banks just followed their lead.

And then there was—and still is—Europe. The argument can certainly be made that Eurogeddon was started by the crisis in America. The United States sneezed and Europe caught a cold so bad that it threatened the whole world's financial well-being. Unfortunately the banking regulations in Europe were even looser than those in the United States, so while America produced most of the toxic mortgages and securities, they were bought by European institutions.

These institutions needed their own series of bailouts, and they didn't own up to the extent of their insolvency, which slowed Europe's recovery. There's also been the "small" problem of certain European governments' level of spending. Added to which, there's a fundamental problem in Europe. The euro. It is of flawed design.

The euro is a classic case of "marry in haste, repent at leisure." Economic union without political union can't work, so divorce is always in the background (for example, the Grexit—Greek exit).

NOTEWORTHY NUGGETS

- The European Union (EU) is comprised of twenty-eight member states, which when put together make the EU, with a population of around 500 million people, the largest economy in the world.

- At time of going to press, nineteen of those countries are members of the Eurozone, nations that use the euro.

- The Eurozone is the world's second largest economy, with a population of around 340 million.

- Euro coins and banknotes entered circulation on January 1, 2002.

- The euro is used daily by several hundred million Europeans. As of 2013, more than 210 million people around the world, including 182 million people in Africa, use currencies pegged to the euro.

Still at a loss? If at a highbrow drinks party, throw in the word *Greece* after Glass-Steagall and then take an elaborate sip of your beverage. People will nod and mutter and then focus on the nearest canapé.

WHY IT MATTERS TODAY

The best analogy of the crisis is a medical one.

When someone has a heart attack, there are two vital stages in saving them. The first is the initial lifesaving shock treatment. With this crisis, governments and central banks responded with unprecedented fiscal stimuli, monetary policy expansion, and institutional bailouts. It really did get all very dramatic; think, say, of an episode of the medical drama *ER* when George Clooney was still on it. On September 18, 2008, Federal Reserve chairman Ben Bernanke met with key US legislators to propose a $700 billion emergency bailout. He supposedly told them: "If we don't do this, we may not have an economy on Monday." Cue *TARP*.

KEY TERM: WHAT IS TARP?

- TARP is America's Emergency Economic Stabilization Act (also called the Troubled Asset Relief Program). Bernanke's bailout was signed into law on October 3, 2008.

- Note that TARP occurred under the Republicans' watch.

It is worth recalling in polite company that employment will lag behind the money markets. If they crash, unemployment will follow in time, and correspondingly, it will take time for employment to recover after the markets do. Therefore, after the crash in 1929 it was two years before unemployment reached its peak, and the same was true of our crunch.

The second stage of heart attack treatment is, once the patient is stable on life support, to determine at what point you take the tubes out and in which order. When do you decide "That's enough medicine"? If it's too soon, then that's another recession. If it's too late, then the resulting deficit is, as the US chairman of the Joint Chiefs put it, a threat to national security (China buying up American debt, which it now holds lots of, etc.). Europe went all out with austerity measures; America not so much.

What's the solution? There are some fundamental flaws in how America's politicians have ended up behaving. Financial regulations have been put in place since the crisis, such as the Volcker Rule (part of the Dodd-Frank Act), but as Senator Elizabeth Warren types are always reminding us, they are nowhere near as concrete as Glass-Steagall. There's also the world. We now live in a global economy. When the BRICS (Brazil, Russia, India, China, and South Africa), the emerging national economies, are unstable, it will have ripple effects. Also, of course, Europe.

Now, the problem for Europe is not the United States of Europe. It is the Disunited States of Europe. In Europe, the nineteen leaders of the Eurozone—and sometimes all twenty-eight leaders of the European Union—have to collectively come to an agreement on a decision. And then go home and sell that to nineteen—and sometimes twenty-eight—democracies. Europe literally and figuratively does not speak the same language. Thus these leaders were always behind instead of ahead of the crisis curve and always will be.

Compare that to the United States of America, which when there's a crisis like the credit crunch can come together. America also has a key weapon at its disposal: Not only is it the world's reserve currency (it can basically borrow money cheaply, as it's perceived as reliable) but the Fed can print as much money as is needed to finance its borrowing. The countries in the Eurozone do not have this power. Those that ran into big trouble, the PIIGS, do not have their own individual central banks that they can rely on to print money and buy their debts.

Why didn't the European Central Bank just print more money? Theoretically it could, but the Germans are very opposed to letting this happen. There are a multitude of reasons for this, from the historical—Weimar hyperinflation contributed to the rise of Hitler—to the belief that countries should not be bailed out for living beyond their means. This rankled within some European countries, especially Greece in 2015, for Germany received debt relief from foreign creditors after World War II. (Lack of debt relief after World War I helped contribute to the rise of Hitler in Germany.)

The irony in all this is that if you take the Eurozone as one entity, it does not lack for resources. The problem is political: Member states are reluctant to finance each other. There is a moral hazard issue. Why should a German be liable for Greek debt, but then have no say in how Greece runs its affairs and spends German money? Note that since 1945, the main point of the European project was never again to leave an aggrieved Germany isolated.

The euro is basically a political crisis that can be resolved only with greater fiscal and political union to complement the monetary union. However, getting countries to voluntarily give up their sovereignty is not exactly straightforward. Consumers, businesses, banks, and governments around the world are confidence players—that is to say, to get sustained economic growth they have to believe the system is solid. Can anyone truly say this about the Eurozone? This is where I stick my neck out and say that I'm not so sure.

WISE WORDS

Some day, following the example of the United States of America, there will be a United States of Europe.

—George Washington

TALKING POINTS

- When in doubt, just say "the markets don't like uncertainty." Nobody can argue with and everyone can understand that.

- Lehman Brothers, the fourth largest investment firm in America, was allowed to collapse in September 2008. There is still vigorous debate about this, with many believing it to have been a genuine error that played a huge part in the financial crisis playing out as it did.

- Let's look on the bright side of those predicting America's demise and China's rise. America's downfall has been prematurely predicted before, with the 1980s and Japan. Which didn't work out so well for the Japanese. Most countries (especially Europe) would love to have America's "decline." The USA's share of global GDP was about 25 percent in 1969—and according to the last figures your author was able to get her mitts on, still is. The Chinese government has to walk an increasingly fine line to maintain control in the here and now (globalization isn't exactly a dictator's friend—those within a closed society can compare their lot with other peoples'). And if China does end up ruling the world? They'll probably have to do so in English—it's way more rooted in global media and technology than Mandarin.

- Canada was the only G7 country (the G7 is an informal bloc of industrialized democracies—Canada, France, Germany, Italy, Japan, the United Kingdom, and the United States) to survive the financial crisis without a state bailout for its financial sector. This is because it had an uncomplicated and well-coordinated regulatory framework with capital requirements at its core that was innately suspicious of the rise of the shadow banking system.

  * Canada has had no systemic banking crises since 1840. The United States has had twelve.

  * There were some warning "flashes" about Canadian credit growing faster than it should be in 2014. But even if there's a crisis, historically it's still winning.

- In regards to the 2008 financial crisis, the powerful sacrificed taxpayers to the interests of the guilty (who didn't go to jail), full stop. Anyone who argues that this is incorrect is not someone you want to be hanging out with.

- The word on everyone's lips these days is inequality. The top 0.01 percent has seen their earnings rise exponentially, while everyone else has seen theirs stagnate. The American dream is inaccessible to too many millions. Pose the question, How does America level the playing field so that Main Street doesn't always come second to Wall Street?

- The monuments on euro notes are fictional so no country's national pride is offended.

- The euro is the world's second most traded currency in the world after the US dollar.

- As of 2014, with more than €995 billion in circulation, the euro has the highest combined value of banknotes and coins in circulation in the world, having surpassed the US dollar.

RED FLAGS

- Avoid an embarrassing schoolboy/girl error here. Note that the Enron scandal was way before the credit crunch—it occurred in October 2001.

  * Enron was an energy company based in Texas that had grown into one of the US's largest companies in just fifteen years. But its success was based on artificially inflated prof-

its and dodgy accounting. Enron became the largest bankruptcy reorganization in American history at that time and the biggest audit failure. The scandal also led to the dissolution of its auditor, longtime accounting firm Arthur Andersen.

- The long and the short of it, bulls and bears—don't mix them up:

  * "Going long" on an investment basically means betting its value will increase.

  * "Going short" on an investment basically means betting its value will decrease.

    —Hedge funds often take positions on both sides of an investment—like going to the horse races and hedging your bets by betting on most of the field. Hence the phrase *hedge funds* is certainly not the stupidest name banksters have ever come up with, although it may be one of the more unfortunate concepts.

  * A bull market is one in which prices are rising or are expected to rise; in contrast, a bear market is one in which prices are falling. So if you are bullish about the dollar's Forex rate against the pound, you think the dollar is going to strengthen against the pound, so you get more pounds for your dollars and that trip to London looks increasingly likely.

- Everyone agrees that the complicated US tax code, which hasn't been reformed since the Reagan era, needs to be sorted out and that loopholes must be closed. The problem? People have their own favorite loophole that they think should stay. It's a topic that you just go around in circles with, and as an interesting human being with a reputation to uphold, do you really want to talk about tax at all?

- Unless you want to cause a mass depression in polite company, refrain from pointing out that we live in a globalized economy. *Contagion* means what happens in Europe doesn't stay in Europe. Same goes for China or anywhere else for that matter.

- The UK with its pound is a member of the EU but not of the Eurozone. I was once on a US business network segment talking about Europe with someone who didn't know this. Seriously.

SOCIAL SURVIVAL STRATEGY

Argument: How can America level the playing field so that Main Street doesn't always come second to Wall Street?

Yes, this is a question, not an argument per se, but in polite company you are expected to pose it. Nobody actually knows the answer, although they might pretend that they do. Money isn't "trickling down" from the big earners to normal people fast enough, but forced redistribution of wealth is not the way America does things. Mention reforming the tax code and investing in education, and then blame DC. Even if you are talking to a politician from DC, they'll just blame someone else who lives there—it couldn't possibly be their fault, oh no.

Crisp Fact: "The monuments on euro notes are fictional so no country's national pride is offended."

The euro really is a classic case of "marry in haste, repent at leisure"—utilize this gem if you want to look knowledgeable in a discussion about finance . . . or divorce.

Pivot: "What's your favorite European city/where in Europe would you like to visit?"

Almost everyone will be able to wax lyrical on this topic—travel is always an excellent cocktail party conversation topic.

CHEAT SHEET 8—AMERICAN DREAMERS—THE GOOD, THE BAD, AND THE AHA!

We are now going to briefly profile three quintessential American dreamers: Warren Buffett, Bernie Madoff, and Oprah Winfrey. From them, we will glean some lessons on how to hopefully, as long as our governments don't screw us over, end up more like Buffett and Oprah than Madoff.

CASE STUDY 1. THE GOOD—WARREN BUFFETT

Warren Buffett, the "Oracle of Omaha," who was born in 1930, is the chairman, CEO, and largest shareholder of Berkshire Hathaway, and one of the most successful investors on the planet.

TIP 1

An oft-quoted Buffettism is: "The first rule of investing is don't lose money; the second rule is, don't forget Rule No. 1."

Rejected by Harvard (successful people always encounter failure—it is the making of them; success is about not giving up), Buffett then enrolled in and graduated from Columbia Business School. He subsequently returned to Omaha and worked as a stockbroker while taking a Dale Carnegie public speaking course.

SUGGESTED READING

Warren Buffett called Dale Carnegie's *How to Win Friends and Influence People* the most important book he's ever read. Once you get past the fact that the chapter titles tend to state the obvious—for instance, "If You're Wrong, Admit It," "Give a Dog a Good Name"— it is a worthwhile read. Forgetting or ignoring the obvious is usually the root cause of any pickles we find ourselves in.

Buffett invests only in "something that I can understand to start with; there are all kinds of businesses I don't understand." Buffett has thus made investments over the years in companies like Coca-Cola, the *Washington Post,* and Gillette, but avoided taking part in the dot-com boom in the 1990s. Buffett was dismissed as having lost touch but had his "I told you so" moment when the technology market bubble burst.

TIP 2

Invest only in what you understand.

Buffett is famous for not flashing his cash; he lives in the same house in Omaha that he bought in 1958 for $31,500 (last assessed in 2003 at $700,000). Possibly the most noteworthy aspect about his domestic setup was a slightly unconventional arrangement with the women in his life. There was his first wife Susan, whom Buffett had three children by. In 1977, Susan went off to San Francisco to pursue a singing career and introduced him to Astrid Menks, who became his longtime companion. Buffet remained married to Susan until she died in 2004, and he married Astrid in 2006. Holiday cards to friends were signed "Warren, Susie, and Astrid." If that wasn't remarkable enough, he's pledged to give away his fortune to charity, with over 80 percent of it going to the Bill & Melinda Gates Foundation.

CASE STUDY 2. THE BAD—BERNARD MADOFF

Bernard Lawrence "Bernie" Madoff, born in 1938, is the former chairman of the NASDAQ stock exchange and the admitted operator of a Ponzi scheme.

KEY TERM: PONZI SCHEME

- A **Ponzi scheme** is a bogus investment operation. It pays returns to investors either from their own money or from that of later investors, rather than from any actual profits on real investments.

- It lures investors in by offering short-term returns that are either strangely high or unusually regular.

- The system is destined to collapse because the earnings, if any, are less than the payments to investors.

- The scheme is named after Italian-American immigrant Charles Ponzi, who became notorious for using the technique in 1920, although he did not invent the tactic. Charles Dickens's 1844 novel *Martin Chuzzlewit* and 1857 novel *Little Dorrit* each describe such a plot decades before Ponzi was born.

Madoff founded his Wall Street firm Bernard L. Madoff Investment Securities LLC in 1960, with money he had earned working as a lifeguard and sprinkler installer. He was its chairman until his arrest on December 11, 2008. In order to compete with firms that were members of the New York Stock Exchange trading on the stock exchange's floor, his company began using cutting-edge computer information technology to circulate its quotes. After a trial run, the technology that the firm helped develop became the NASDAQ (National Association of Securities Dealers Automated Quotations).

There was, initially, something of merit about Madoff. NASDAQ became the largest electronic-screen-based equity securities trading market in the USA. It now has more trading volume than any other stock exchange in the world. There is controversy over when Madoff's asset management firm turned into a Ponzi scheme. According to him, he began the Ponzi scheme in the early 1990s. However, federal investigators believe the fraud began as early as the 1980s, and the investment operation may never have been legitimate. Finally, in December 2008, Madoff's sons told authorities that their father had just confessed to them that the asset management arm of his firm was a massive Ponzi scheme, and quoting him as saying it was "one big lie."

TIP 3

Keep it legal.

In March 2009, Madoff pleaded guilty to eleven felonies and admitted to turning his wealth management business into a massive Ponzi scheme that defrauded thousands of investors of billions of dollars. The amount missing from client accounts, including fabricated gains, was almost $65 billion. On trial, Madoff refused to name any coconspirators and pleaded guilty to all charges, so in June 2009 he was sentenced to 150 years in prison, the maximum allowed. Definitely, defiantly bad, Madoff's Ponzi scheme preyed heavily on his fellow Jews, destroying the fortunes of numerous Jewish charities and institutions, including Steven Spielberg's Wunderkinder Foundation.

CASE STUDY 3. THE AHA!—OPRAH WINFREY

Oprah Gail Winfrey is the epitome of the multi-hyphenate. Talk show host, television producer, publisher, philanthropist, and actress, she was the wealthiest African-American of the twentieth century and the only black billionaire on the planet for three years running. An inspiration to millions, Oprah has been called the most powerful woman in the world.

Born on January 29, 1954, in the very rural Kosciusko, Mississippi, on her birth certificate she was actually called Orpah, from the Hebrew Bible's Book of Ruth. However, everybody mispronounced it, so she ended up with Oprah. (And since she's mononymously known as that, we will continue to refer to her by her first name.) She had an incredibly tough upbringing and has revealed that she survived a brutal rape at the age of nine and continued sexual molestation between the ages of ten and fourteen. At fourteen, Oprah gave birth to a son, who died in infancy. To survive the trauma, she is on record as saying she had to believe in a "power greater than herself" and that these experiences later inspired her need to empathize with people in her daily life.

TIP 4

From Oprah herself, naturally: **Turn your wounds into wisdom.**

A troubled Oprah eventually ended up getting stability and structure when she moved to live with her dad in Nashville. In 1971 she entered Tennessee State University. She kicked off her broadcast career in Nashville, then in 1976 hosted *People Are Talking*, a Baltimore chat show that became a hit. A Chicago TV station brought her in to host *A.M. Chicago* and Oprah swiftly went on to do what had been considered improbable—beat competitor Phil Donahue in her time slot.

Cue a call from Steven Spielberg, a role in 1985's *The Color Purple*, and an Oscar nomination for Best Actress in a Supporting Role for her performance as Sofia.

TIP 5

Still from Oprah herself: **Every time you state what you want or believe, you're the first to hear it. It's a message to both you and others about what you think is possible. Don't put a ceiling on yourself.**

You know the rest—she earned worldwide domination from her natural style of emotional ad-libbing through group therapy sessions. In 1986 she launched *The Oprah Winfrey Show*, which was nationally syndicated and ran through 2011. She swiftly took control of the show from ABC and made it through her own production company, Harpo (Oprah backwards). Other notable Oprah activities include her book club, *O Magazine*, the cofounding of Oxygen Media, and philanthropy through the Oprah Angel Network. The *Wall Street Journal* coined the term *Oprahfication*—public confession as form of therapy. And then there was the Oprah Effect: When Oprah endorses something or someone—perhaps most notably Barack Obama—people listen.

On a personal level, she has been with her boyfriend Stedman Graham since 1986 and met her BFF Gayle King when they were in their early twenties.

TIP 6

Seriously, why would it be from anyone but Oprah herself?: **Every one of us gets through the tough times because somebody is there, standing in the gap to close it for us.**

Arguably we all emote more—from politicians to television anchors to people next to us in the office—because of Oprah. In 2012 she even made it into the dictionary with her catchphrase "aha! moment," the official definition from *Merriam-Webster* being: "a moment of sudden realization, inspiration, insight, recognition, or comprehension."

On January 1, 2011, OWN, the Oprah Winfrey Network, launched. Yes, it may have had its teething problems, but Oprah will always be adored, literally and figuratively, through thick and thin. And she has uttered what are quite possibly the wisest words on which to end a finance chapter: "Though I am grateful for the blessings of wealth, it hasn't changed who I am. My feet are still on the ground. I'm just wearing better shoes."

We now turn to religion, which unlike the "Church of Oprah" has left too many parts of the world in ruins far too often.

WISE WORDS

Success is not final, failure is not fatal: It is the courage to continue that counts.

—Winston Churchill

SOCIAL SURVIVAL STRATEGY

Argument: "Invest only in what you understand."
Financial "advisors" may try to make you feel inferior with their "superior" knowledge, but remember how well most of them didn't predict the financial crisis? Ignore them and follow one of the most successful investors ever, Buffett—put your money only in what you understand.

Crisp Fact: "There were at least six botched investigations of Madoff by the financial authorities. Muppets."
Those in charge can and do have the wool pulled over their eyes

just as much as the rest of us. Something that is too good to be true always is.

Pivot: "*The Oprah Winfrey Show* was my daytime TV guilty pleasure back in the day. I'm not sure I have one now, although I am partial to *Saved by the Bell* reruns. You?"

Nobody you want to speak to for any length of time wishes to dwell on finance; everyone has at some point played hooky from school or work and can wax lyrical about their secret daytime TV favorite.

SUBJECT THREE—RELIGION

RELIGION SUMMARY

The key theme to keep in mind when discussing this subject—apart from appreciating at the start that you are walking on eggshells—is how similar religions are. Really. Judaism, Christianity, and Islam are Abrahamic. Hinduism, Buddhism, and Sikhism are Dharmic. All the main religions use the lunar calendar to varying degrees, so their big dates tend to shift on the Gregorian, aka Western, calendar. Arguably the great tragedy of mankind is that so much strife has come from them. But you do not want to focus on catastrophe over cocktails, so a fun crisp fact to throw out there—it will upset Fox News viewers if you're with some, but they will (hopefully) take it in seasonal spirit—is that Christmas can be linked with paganism, so much so the Puritans canceled it in 1644. And that's the type of Puritan that originally turned up in America; thus it's the ultimate American tradition to wage war on Christmas, despite Fox's arguing to the contrary every year. A good pivot out of the whole quagmire that is a religious deliberation, especially if it's ended up on anything to do with the "war on terror," is to remark that there exists a debatable myth that the word *assassin* is derived from the Arabic word for hashish user from the Middle Ages. You can then inquire where your companion stands on legalizing pot. The strait-laced especially may surprise you.

You do not have to be one of the 1.1 billion a-religious types in the world to agree to a degree with a certain Roman Stoic philosopher. For the other 6 billion or so worshipers in the world, there are about 4,200 religions. Nobody can escape faith; it is something that has an impact on all our lives on a daily basis.

This series of Cheat Sheets encompasses descriptions of the main beliefs and practices of over 2 billion Christians, well over 1.5 billion Muslims, possibly more than 1.5 billion Buddhists, a billion Hindus, and 14 million Jews, almost half of whom live in America (compared to around 2.6 million Muslims). Judaism may be only the twelfth largest religion and Yasser Arafat, former chairman of the Palestine Liberation Organization, may have claimed that his strongest weapon was the womb of the Arab woman, but Judaism began in the Middle East over 3,500 years ago. It is thus the original of the three Abrahamic faiths, the others being Christianity and Islam. Judaism will forever remain one of the world's great religions.

It is important to pause here, and we return to this when we discuss the Middle East in Cheat Sheet 17. Judaism, Christianity, and Islam all trace themselves back to Abraham. More than half the world thinks themselves as part of these religions, grounded in faith, charity, and obedience with a final goal of heaven/hell. Just under a third of the world worship through Dharmic religions (such as Hinduism, Buddhism, and Sikhism), which focus on honing one's consciousness. We are more similar than we sometimes give ourselves credit for.

The problem with religion has often enough been one of ignorance

of other types of faith, which considering the degree of interrela-
tion between many of them is perhaps a little surprising. Followers
of Islam describe themselves as believing in the same Abrahamic
God as Jews and Christians. Jesus is one of Islam's prophets, after
all—which I admit that I didn't know, or had forgotten, until 2013.
Neither did three people I got drunk with while discussing the subject, including the CEO of a major NYLON company and a journalist
at one of Rupert Murdoch's more reputable publications. Yes, a few
do exist. In fact, Jesus Christ is mentioned five times more often than
Muhammad in the Qur'an.

These next Cheat Sheets will ensure that you make no clanging
errors on the matter of religion. But if it comes up, obviously use
your common sense. Religion can be such a sensitive subject that to
dwell or debate on it can end only in tears. And that's on a good day.
We begin with Cheat Sheet 9, a reference grid of religions containing pertinent points that will be forever useful to have up your
sleeve. Cheat Sheet 10 is an overview of big religious holidays so you
don't look like an insensitive oaf when dealing with people of different faiths throughout the year. Our final Cheat Sheet on this subject will look at two areas where religion has been erroneously used
as an excuse for bad behavior—as an argument against homosexuality and as justification for terrorism.

Recent studies suggest that the fastest-growing religious denom-
ination in America is the religiously unaffiliated, the "nones." After
penning this section, I found it easy to see why.

CHEAT SHEET 9—RELIGIONS

RELIGION/ SUBSECTIONS	FOLLOWER COUNT	BASIC BELIEF	SCRIPTURES/ BASIC WORSHIP
Christianity Abrahamic Three largest subsections: • Catholics • Eastern Orthodox (split from Catholics in eleventh century) • Protestantism (split from Catholics in sixteenth century, endless denominations since then).	Biggest religion, if include all subsections: 2.1 billion, c. 33 percent of world. Catholics make up 1.2 billion of those. In 1910, about two-thirds of the world's Christians lived in Europe; now only about a quarter do. More than a third are in the Americas and one in four in sub-Saharan Africa.	• 2,000 years old. • One God but three elements to God: the Father, the Son, the Holy Spirit. • Began as Jewish sect. • Based on teachings of Jesus Christ (a Jew and the Messiah promised in the Old Testament). • Jesus, son of God, was sent to save us from our sins. Died for us (Crucifixion), rose from dead three days later (Resurrection).	• The Bible, inspired word of God, consists of the Old Testament (original Hebrew Bible of thirty-nine books, also the sacred scriptures of the Jewish faith, written between 1200–165 BC) and the New Testament (twenty-seven books, making up the Gospels and the Letters/Epistles, written in first century AD). • Endless debate between the subsections on the specific rules. • Worship in church. • Eucharist, aka Holy Communion (bread/wine in service) reenacts the Lord's Supper, just before Jesus sacrificed himself for us.

DIET	CIRCUMCISION, CONTRACEPTION, ABORTION, GAYS, MARRIAGE	LIFE-AFTER-DEATH PLAN	CELEBRITY ENDORSEMENT
Strict Roman Catholics and worshipers of the Russian Orthodox faith follow a number of fasting rules, especially during Lent. Most Christians you will come across have a distinct lack of dietary requirements and holidays that usually involve eating.	Circumcision not a requirement, some even against (though Jesus would have been snipped). Catholics say no to abortion, contraception, same-sex marriage, though men and women can pick whom they marry. Other subsections more forgiving.	Most believe in heaven. Some believe in hell. Reasonable people the world over believe that there is a special place reserved in the latter for child molesters, cc the Vatican.	• American politicians. Endlessly. Separation of church and state? #NotSoMuch • Queen holds the title "Defender of the Faith and Supreme Governor of the Church of England." Charles would like to be "defender of all faiths."

RELIGION/ SUBSECTIONS	FOLLOWER COUNT	BASIC BELIEF	SCRIPTURES/ BASIC WORSHIP
Islam Abrahamic Two main denominations, split stemming from disagreement over who would lead Muslims after the Prophet Muhammad's death in 632 AD: • Sunni (75–90 percent) • Shia (10–20 percent) • NB: Sufism, Islamic mysticism, can be found in both Sunni and Shia groups.	World's second largest religion: 1.6 billion+Muslims. C. 23 percent of world. 25 percent live in South Asia, 13 percent in Indonesia (largest Muslim majority country), 20 percent in the Middle East, and 15 percent in sub-Saharan Africa.	• Islam has always existed but was revealed to humanity by the (final) Prophet Muhammad over 1,400 years ago in Mecca, Arabia. • Six main beliefs are: There is only one God (*Allah* is God in Arabic); angels; holy books; prophets; day of judgment; and predestination (Allah has the knowledge of all that will happen, although this doesn't stop human beings from making free choices). • Five Pillars of Islam: belief, praying five times a day, giving money to charity, fasting during Ramadan, and at least one pilgrimage to Mecca.	• The Qur'an. The verses of the holy book were revealed to Muhammad by God through the Archangel Gabriel over 23 years. • The Sunnah is the practical example of Prophet Muhammad. • Worship in a mosque. • Islamic leaders are imams, clerics, and mullahs. • Sharia "road to a watering place" law regulates all human actions—the water source symbolizes God. Comprised of a number of sources including the Qur'an and fatwas (the rulings of Islamic scholars, what the author Salman Rushdie had a few issues with). Hard to enforce in a mixed religious society.

DIET	CIRCUMCISION, CONTRACEPTION, ABORTION, GAYS, MARRIAGE	LIFE-AFTER-DEATH PLAN	CELEBRITY ENDORSEMENT
• Haram (banned): alcohol, no food sacrificed to idols, no pork or flesh with undrained blood. • Halal (allowed): all vegetable, fruit, grain, and seafood. Kindly killed (and slaughtered in name of God by a Muslim or Christian or Jew—so kosher okay) meat from herbivorous animal. Game one has hunted/killed oneself. • Supposed to use only right hand for eating and drinking. • Fast from dawn to dusk during the month of Ramadan.	Almost all circumcised; debate over whether a religious requirement. Forced marriage against Sharia; arranged marriage allowed. Men can in principle have four wives. Sharia does *not* require women to wear a burka, but they are required to dress modestly. Hijab implies covered and is not obligatory in front of relatives or other Muslim women. Everyone else a no—implies lack of respect and discipline.	Heaven exists, the reward for good deeds including kindness to animals, prayer, and charity. Lying and disbelief in God will land you in hell, but if you repent you might be forgiven.	• Muhammad Ali. • Iman, supermodel who was married to the late David Bowie.

RELIGION/ SUBSECTIONS	FOLLOWER COUNT	BASIC BELIEF	SCRIPTURES/ BASIC WORSHIP
Buddhism Dharmic Multiple schools. Two main: • Theravada • Mahayana	376 million to 1.7 billion, at least 7 percent of world's population. Most popular within Asia. One of the fastest-growing religions in the world	• 2,500 years old—arose c. the sixth century BC from the quest for enlightenment of a member of Nepal's royal family, Siddhartha Gautama (aka the Buddha, aka the Awakened One). • No belief in personal God— nothing is fixed or permanent and change is always possible • All schools aim to aid followers on path to enlighten- ment, reaching a state of nirvana.	• Buddhist schools differ on path and significance of various scriptures. • Three jewels symbolize the foun- dations of tradition and practice: the Buddha, the Dharma (the teach- ings), and the San- gha (the community). • Fundamental to its doctrine are the Four Noble Truths, which explain the causes of and how to overcome dukkha (suffering). • Buddhists can worship at home or at a temple.

DIET	CIRCUMCISION, CONTRACEPTION, ABORTION, GAYS, MARRIAGE	LIFE-AFTER-DEATH PLAN	CELEBRITY ENDORSEMENT
No set dietary laws, much diversity in practice. First Precept is often interpreted as "do not harm," so many choose to be vegetarian. If you believe in reincarnation you could be eating a reincarnated human, after all. Killing animals thus could also be bad karma.	Buddhists are expected to take full personal responsibility for everything they do and for the consequences that follow. Wrong to kill for any reason, so contraception that prevents conception okay, but those stopping development of fertilized egg wrong (e.g., IUD). Buddhism not strongly pro-family and does not regard having children as a religious duty. Homosexuality pretty much okay. There is no single Buddhist view on abortion.	Existence is endless because of reincarnation. Karma drives the cycle of suffering and rebirth for each being. Some controversial debate about disabled people and animals coming back because of past misdeeds.	• The Dalai Lama: head monk of Tibetan Buddhism, until Chinese government took control in 1959 was responsible for the governing of Tibet. • Tina Turner.

RELIGION/ SUBSECTIONS	FOLLOWER COUNT	BASIC BELIEF	SCRIPTURES/ BASIC WORSHIP
Hinduism Dharmic Incorporates numerous traditions, so sometimes labeled a "family of religions" rather than a single one. Includes: • Shaivism • Vaishnavism • Śrauta	1 billion. Possibly the world's third largest religion, c. 14 percent of world's population. 950 million are in India.	• Arguably oldest living religion, originated in modern-day Pakistan. • Hard to define—has no single founder or scripture, no rigidly agreed-upon teachings; formed of many traditions and includes many practices and beliefs. • Most Hindus draw on dharma, a common system of values, believe in a Supreme God and that existence is a cycle of birth, death, and rebirth, governed by karma.	• Multiple key figures, philosophies, and holy books. • Main sacred texts most Hindus revere come from the traditions of Shruti (heard, include the Vedas) and Smriti (remembered). • The *Kama Sutra* is an ancient Indian Hindu text in Sanskrit. It is not merely a sex manual—more of a guide to aspects of love.

DIET	CIRCUMCISION, CONTRACEPTION, ABORTION, GAYS, MARRIAGE	LIFE-AFTER-DEATH PLAN	CELEBRITY ENDORSEMENT
Hindus all about nonviolence, so many are lacto-vegetarians. If meat eaten, very seldom beef, as the cow is a symbol of unselfish giving. Cow slaughter is legally banned in almost all states of India.	No ban on birth control. Abortion considered a course of action if causes least harm to all involved—i.e., mom, dad, fetus, and society. BUT since nonviolent, generally opposed. Production of offspring a public duty. Homo-sexuality—diverse views but same-sex relations and gender variance has been represented within Hinduism from Vedic times to now. Is okay in the *Kama Sutra*, after all . . .	The doctrine of reincarnation, which sees life as a repeating cycle of birth, death, and rebirth, is basic to Hindu thinking.	J. D. Salinger.

RELIGION/ SUBSECTIONS	FOLLOWER COUNT	BASIC BELIEF	SCRIPTURES/ BASIC WORSHIP
Judaism Abrahamic	14 million, c. 0.22 percent of the world's population. Around 6 million in America, 6 million in Israel. Some 6 million Jews were murdered in the Holocaust.	• Judaism originated in the Middle East over 3,500 years ago. Was founded by Moses, although Jews trace their history back to Abraham. • Believe in a single God, who created the universe and with whom they have a covenant. In exchange for the good deeds that God has done and continues to do for the Jewish people, Jews keep God's laws and seek to bring holiness into all aspects of their lives—it's what you do that counts. God appointed the Jews to be his chosen people in order to set an example of holiness and ethical behavior to the world. • A Jew is someone who has a Jewish mother. Can't technically lose the status by adopting another faith. Hard to convert to, especially if you're husband hunting, as it's through the female line. Sigh. Sob.	• Most important text is the Torah, written in Hebrew (the five books of Moses, dictated to him by God on Mount Sinai fifty days after their exodus from Egyptian slavery). • The Torah is the first section or first five books of the Jewish Bible, though the word can be used in a more general sense to incorporate Judaism's written and oral law. • Leaders are called rabbis, worship done in synagogues.

DIET	CIRCUMCISION, CONTRACEPTION, ABORTION, GAYS, MARRIAGE	LIFE-AFTER-DEATH PLAN	CELEBRITY ENDORSEMENT
Kashruth—Jewish dietary laws. Food that can be consumed is kosher, meaning fit. Includes no unclean animals—e.g., pigs and shellfish. Some food can/can't be consumed on various holidays.	Contraception pretty much okay; female ones preferred, as men are not supposed to "waste seed," which they do when using a condom. (Convenient for Jewish men, anyone?) Orthodox Jews don't permit sex in the presence of blood. Does not forbid abortion, but permitted only for serious reasons. Family faith. Jewish baby boy circumcised at eight days old, following the instructions that God gave to Abraham around 4,000 years ago.	Vague—Jewish sacred texts and literature don't expand as much as other faiths on life after death.	New York City. Hollywood.

SOCIAL SURVIVAL STRATEGY

Argument: "Judaism, Christianity, and Islam are Abrahamic. Hinduism, Buddhism, and Sikhism are Dharmic. It's naive, but why can't we all just get along? Really, why can't we?"

Use this when someone is focusing on the dissimilarities of people around the world and you feel the need to point out that we are all human beings—tragedy comes when we forget that.

Crisp Fact: "Hinduism is arguably the oldest living religion. It originated in modern-day Pakistan."

We live in a very young country—this is useful when it's worth contemplating the greater scheme of things.

Pivot: "That whole Charlotte's happily converting to Judaism, *Sex in the City* story line? Do you know of anyone who that's actually worked for? Seems to me more farfetched than a freelance writer being able to buy Blahniks. Incidentally, I love your shoes/socks/ earrings, where did you get them from?"

Fluffy, yes, but guiding conversation toward fashion is far less dangerous terrain, unless you've been sat next to Anna Wintour.

CHEAT SHEET 10—RELIGIOUS HOLIDAYS

BACKGROUND BRIEFING . . . AND WHY IT MATTERS TODAY

I am nominally a Christian. That didn't stop me one Wednesday in February suggesting to a coworker that he wipe the black mark off his forehead. Well, Ash Wednesday wasn't a big deal in my household. At least I've never asked a Muslim what new fad diet they're on during Ramadan.

This Cheat Sheet will help you avoid such faux pas, but do bear in mind that this is only the tip of the iceberg on the festivals of the major religions. In Hinduism alone, it's apparently an understatement to claim that there is a holiday for every day of the year. Thus Cheat Sheet 10 is comprised of a few notable talking points and red flags with a quick look at the main religious holidays, which will insert a basic sensitivity chip into you.

To add to the general confusion, all the main religions use the lunar calendar to a varying extent, so their big dates tend to shift on the Gregorian, aka Western, calendar, which is a solar calendar. Easter is the first Sunday after the first full moon following March 21. The months of the Islamic calendar are based on the sighting of the new moon, which leaves room for much debate about precisely when that is. Each month of the Jewish calendar also begins with the new moon, and there's sometimes an extra month to keep the calendar synchronized with the solar year. Meanwhile, with the exception of the Japanese, Buddhists use the lunar calendar, and the dates of their festivals are different depending on the country and the particular Buddhist tradition. The cycle of nature dictates a significant number of the Hindu holidays.

Upshot? If you hadn't realized already, with anyone orthodox, you need to eggshell tread throughout the year. Although if a Christian gets too antsy with you around Easter, you can point out that it's an amalgamation of holidays: The history of eggs can be traced back to ancient Greece, and the Easter bunny is pagan.

> ## NOTEWORTHY NUGGET
>
> The period of forty days is of deep significance to both Jews and Christians. Figures it crops up for in scripture include Moses and Jesus, who both fasted for forty days before receiving the Ten Commandments and taking on his ministry, respectively.

TALKING POINTS

- There are only two Muslim festivals in Islamic law, Eid al-Fitr and Eid al-Adha. A number of Muslims actually frown upon celebrating the Prophet's birthday, Eid Milad un-Nabi, seeing it as contrary to Islamic law.

- Fox News is arguably incorrect with its annual December decree that there is a "war on Christmas," for the simple fact it's so pagan that Puritans (them) at one point banned it. Read on . . .

  * Numerous historical studies link Christianity with paganism, and many Christian festivals can trace their roots back to Babylon. Jesus probably wasn't born on December 25. The gospels don't mention the date, and from them, scholars have deduced it was too cold, compared to what else was going on at the time (shepherds outside with their flocks, etc.). How-

ever, at that time of year the Babylonian Queen of Heaven had a son.

* Christmas also stems from ancient Greek festivals, Druidic beliefs, and Hanukkah. It was Pope Julius I in the fourth century AD who set the date for Christmas as December 25, to link together Christian and other celebrations at the time, including various Roman holidays celebrating the winter solstice.

* The majority of Christmas customs don't come from the church. Mistletoe was a pagan fertility plant. Thus in 1644 the Puritans canceled Christmas in England because the celebrations were pagan/heretical/superstitious and not really all that Christian. And it was this type of Puritan that originally turned up in America, so it's the ultimate American tradition to wage war on Christmas. Which is what you tell Bill O'Reilly if you ever meet him at a "holiday" party in December.

• At a Halloween party trying to chat up someone in S&M gear? You could note that between the Celts (who called it Samhain), the Anglo-Saxons, and the Illuminati, Halloween is basically a Dan Brown novel on steroids. Then again . . .

RED FLAGS

• Thanks to globalization, many of us regularly do deals with people of different religions. If you're trying to impress/elicit something out of them, it is probably best not to send a rude e-mail asking why they haven't replied to one of yours on their Sabbath. So note the following:

* Christian—Sunday is the Lord's Day throughout the year, as it's the day Christ rose from the dead.

* Islam—Friday.

* Buddhism—changes depending on the lunar cycle.

* Hinduism—tends to be Saturday.

* Judaism—Saturday (the Sabbath or Shabbat). Note that the Jewish day begins at sunset, which means that all Jewish holidays begin the evening before their Western date. Occasionally they are moved around, as sometimes the Sabbath is not supposed to be the same day as certain festivals.

• Someone defending racial profiling of Muslims or the banning of building a mosque? If you're on a Fox Business show that you have had a regular spot on, don't say, "Have you ever heard of the phrase 'to kill with kindness'?" You will never be invited to return to the aforementioned show.

• If a Jewish former business partner/ boyfriend/girlfriend should apologize for their misbehavior to you in the ten days after Rosh Hashanah, be gracious about it and don't rub it in that they're doing it because God's currently deciding what the next year is bringing them. It is also deeply manipulative of you to go after them for an apology during that time. I've never done that, obviously—oh no. Of course if your gripe is a result of lack of condom usage (see Cheat Sheet 9 on Jews and birth control), I'd say fair game.

> ## WISE WORDS
>
> We build too many walls and not enough bridges.
>
> —Isaac Newton

IMPORTANT HOLIDAYS

CHRISTIANITY

SHROVE TUESDAY AKA PANCAKE DAY AKA MARDI GRAS (French for Fat Tuesday). Occurs in February or March and is supposed to use up foods that Christians wouldn't eat during Lent. But now many consume those foods throughout Lent anyway.

ASH WEDNESDAY, START OF LENT (means lengthen, days are getting longer—i.e., it's spring). The Wednesday after Shrove Tuesday. If people have a mark on their forehead, they've been to church so they can carry the sign of the cross out in the world.

PALM SUNDAY. Sunday before Easter, which takes place in March or April. Marks Jesus turning up in Jerusalem and is the beginning of Holy Week. Cue triumphant-type services with palm leaves that are then burned to ashes for the following year's Ash Wednesday.

MAUNDY THURSDAY AKA HOLY THURSDAY. Thursday before Easter. Marks the Last Supper, where Judas betrayed Jesus. Busy for the queen—gives out Maundy Money to deserving seniors. Tradition dates back to King John in 1213.

GOOD FRIDAY. Friday before Easter. Crucifixion of Jesus.

EASTER SUNDAY. Resurrection of Jesus Christ. Most important day for Christians.

DECEMBER 25, CHRISTMAS, JESUS CHRIST'S BIRTH AKA THE NATIVITY. As established previously, it's the ultimate American tradition to cancel it. Also notable as unlike all of the holidays above, it doesn't move.

ISLAM

EID MILAD UN-NABI. Birthday of the Prophet. Some Muslims celebrate; some frown upon it.

RAMADAN. Ninth month of the Islamic calendar, compulsory fasting (no food or drink or medications) during daylight for every able Muslim. Qur'an was revealed during this month (mosques tend to recite a thirtieth of the Qur'an each night) and it is a period blessed by Allah, so actions are more powerful. Obviously far harder to do in the summer months—days are longer and hotter. For countries, indeed places, that are predominantly Muslim and are undergoing unrest, the impact of Ramadan must always be considered.

LAYLAT AL-QADR, THE NIGHT OF POWER. Falls on one of the last ten days of Ramadan, the holiest night of the year, the night the Qur'an was first revealed. Considered better than a thousand months, so if you worship on that night, worship is equal to a thousand months.

EID AL-FITR, THE FESTIVAL OF BREAKING THE FAST. Thanking Allah for getting them through Ramadan and celebrating its end. People dress in their best clothes, decorate their homes, give treats to children, and spend time with family.

EID AL-ADHA, THE FEAST OF SACRIFICE. One of the two most important Islamic festivals, it commemorates the prophet Abraham's willingness to obey Allah by sacrificing his son Ishmael. Just before Abraham sacrificed his son, Allah replaced Ishmael with a ram. Lasts for three days and occurs at the conclusion of the annual pilgrimage to Mecca (Hajj). A lamb or other animal is sacrificed and the meat distributed to loved ones and the poor.

BUDDHISM

SANGHA DAY, AKA FOURFOLD ASSEMBLY, AKA MAGHA PUJA DAY. Typically in February. Second most important Buddhist festival, celebrating the Buddhist community. Celebrations vary, but a traditional time for gift exchange.

NIRVANA DAY. Occurs on February 8 or 15 and marks the anniversary of Buddha's death. Used to reflect on the death of loved ones and one's future death. Nirvana isn't just a rock band.

BUDDHA DAY, AKA VESAK, AKA WESAK, AKA VISAKHA PUJA. Every May on the night of the full moon. Most significant Buddhist celebration. Celebrates birth, enlightenment, and death of the Buddha.

BODHI DAY. This one has the secular date of December 8 in Japan, so in our horribly simplistic manner we'll focus on that. Some Buddhists celebrate Gautama's attainment of enlightenment under the Bodhi tree at Bodh Gaya, India.

HINDUISM

HOLI, THE FESTIVAL OF COLORS. Normally celebrated in March, this is one of the two main Hindu festivals. There are street parties, dancing, and singing. People smear each other with paint and throw colored powder and water around.

DIWALI, THE FESTIVAL OF LIGHTS. Celebrated at some point between mid-October and mid-November. A national holiday in India. Involves lights, fireworks, gift exchange, gambling, and new clothes. If you're doing business with India, take note—people regard it as favorable day to start a new accounting year, as for many it honors Lakshmi, the goddess of wealth. Festival lasts five days.

JUDAISM

PASSOVER, AKA PESACH. Typically in March or April. One of the most important Jewish festivals, remembering the Israelites' liberation from Egyptian slavery. God set ten plagues on the Egyptians, the final one killing the firstborn of all households apart from the Jews', who had been told to sacrifice lambs and mark their doors with the blood to escape this fate. The lambs were eaten with bitter herbs and unleavened bread; hence they're included in the Seder, the meal Jews eat on the first two nights of Passover.

ROSH HASHANAH. The Jewish New Year falls at some point between September 5 and October 5. Jews believe God decides what will happen in the year ahead and judge a person's good vs. bad deeds. Begins the ten "Days of Awe"—when Jews are expected to find all the people they have hurt during the previous year and apologize to them. Deadline: Yom Kippur.

YOM KIPPUR, DAY OF ATONEMENT. Occurs between September 14 and October 14. Sacred, solemn, important to attend synagogue. Fast from sundown to sundown, acknowledgment of personal and communal sin and wrongdoing. Jews believe God makes the final decision on who will live, die, prosper, and fail during the next year, and seals his judgment in the Book of Life.

SUKKOT, THE FEAST OF TABERNACLES. Also falls in September/ October. Commemorates the years the Israelites spent journeying to the Promised Land and living in temporary dwellings—hence four types of plant involved.

HANUKKAH. Occurs any time between late November and late December. Marks the story of the "miracle of oil" in 164 BC. A group of Jews recaptured Jerusalem from Syrian Greeks. They had only enough sacred oil to light the seven-branched candlestick (menorah) for a day, but it stayed lit for eight days. During Hanukkah they light an extra candle on a nine-branched menorah every night, say prayers, and eat fried foods to remind them of oil. Some gifts exchanged.

SOCIAL SURVIVAL STRATEGY

Argument: "All the main religions use the lunar calendar to a varying extent, so their big dates tend to shift on the Gregorian aka Western aka solar calendar. Why can't we all get along again?"
The eternal question: We are all human beings—why on earth do we let religion be the root cause of all trouble and strife?

Crisp Fact: "Christmas can be linked with paganism. So much so the Puritans canceled it in 1644. And that's the type of Puritan that originally turned up in America, so it's the ultimate American tradition to wage war on Christmas, Mr. Bill O'Reilly and Fox News."

This can be a fun one during the Yuletide season—FNC watchers' faces are a picture if you have this debate, while non-FNC viewers will have much fun agreeing with you. Make sure the discussion doesn't degenerate into too much animosity, though—it is Christmas, after all.

Pivot: "As Isaac Newton said, 'We build too many walls and not enough bridges.' What's your favorite bridge, by the way? I think everyone should have one."

Nobody can argue against the fact that we spend too much time arguing with each other; this is as good a pivot out as any.

CHEAT SHEET 11—RELIGION IS NO EXCUSE

CASE STUDY 1. CHRISTIANITY . . . AND HOMOSEXUALITY

You need do no more than quote Aaron Sorkin's *The West Wing* on this one. Simply recall President Bartlet's perfect response to a talk-show host labeling homosexuality as an "abomination" because of Leviticus 18:22: "You shall not lie with a male as with a woman; it is an abomination."

I'm interested in selling my youngest daughter into slavery as sanctioned in Exodus 21:7. She's a Georgetown sophomore, speaks fluent Italian, always cleaned the table when it was her turn. What would a good price for her be?

My chief of staff, Leo McGarry, insists on working on the Sabbath. Exodus 35:2 clearly says he should be put to death. Am I morally obligated to kill him myself or is it okay to call the police?

Here's one that's really important cause we've got a lot of sports fans in this town: touching the skin of a dead pig makes one unclean. Leviticus 11:7. If they promise to wear gloves, can the

Washington Redskins still play football? Can Notre Dame? Can West Point?

Does the whole town really have to be together to stone my brother, John, for planting different crops side by side? Can I burn my mother in a small family gathering for wearing garments made from two different threads?

Ergo, not everything that is written in scripture is appropriate to follow in the twenty-first century. Shrimp are referred to as an abomination four times more than homosexuality in the Bible, but that hasn't stopped the rise of the artery-clogging "delicacy" that is popcorn shrimp. Marriage, the love of two people, is a conservative tradition. We discuss this further in Cheat Sheet 26.

CASE STUDY 2. RELIGION . . . AND TERRORISM

It's not just extremist Islamic groups that radically interpret scripture to an intolerant degree. Believers in all the world's big religions can choose from both violent and peaceful messages to justify their behavior.

NOTEWORTHY NUGGETS: VIOLENCE

- Integral to Buddhist thought is the edict not to kill or inflict pain on others, but Buddhist monks have been guilty of precisely that in Sri Lanka.
- However many messages of love and peace that Judaism and Christianity may contain, they have not prevented the existence of Zionist militants or for Christianity, any number of attacks from the fifteenth-century Spanish Inquisition to those on abortion providers today.
- Gandhi, a Hindu, was assassinated by . . . a Hindu.

And then we come to Islam. As with Christianity and Judaism, Islam's texts include peaceful and warring messages.

NOTEWORTHY NUGGET: ASSASSIN

There exists a debatable myth you should be aware of that the word *assassin* is derived from the Arabic word for hashish user from the Middle Ages.

Islamic terrorism has multiple motivations; religion is only one of many factors. The relationship between the Arab world and the West is challenging thanks to culture, societies, ideology, history, and Western imperialist foreign policy (see Cheat Sheets 14, 16, and 17). Then there's political and economic hardship within Arab countries.

The majority of specialists believe that Islamic law bans terrorism and that it is a violation of key Islamic principles. Osama bin Laden was not a graduate of an Islamic university and ignored fourteen centuries of Muslim scholarship. Instead he was inspired by Sayyid Qutb, someone President Gamal Abdel Nasser, the second president of Egypt, executed in 1966. Qutb himself became radicalized because he was imprisoned and tortured in one of Nasser's concentration camps for fifteen years.

KEY TERM: JIHAD

- *Jihad* means struggle or effort. It's not necessarily violent and it can be applied to secular fights—for instance, it has been to women's liberation.
- The greater jihad is the inner struggle to fulfill God's high standards in the way lives are lived.
- The lesser jihad is the outer struggle against Islam's enemies.
- All Muslims thus see jihad as a treasured spiritual value.

Most experts agree that the laws of jihad ban malevolent and undiscriminating murder unless it is for self-defense. It is not to be used to conquer, colonize, and convert other nations to Islam. Even if engaged in a holy war, Muslims are urged not to harm noncombatants, women, and children—or property. Thus the activities of al-Qaeda, ISIS, and Boko Haram are viewed by the vast majority of Muslims as completely unacceptable, and there have been numerous fatwas (rulings) condemning and forbidding terrorism. A few terrorists grab the headlines, but this minuscule minority does not define a diverse and complex religion of 1.6 billion followers.

KEY TERMS: ISIS AND BOKO HARAM

- ISIS, the Islamic State of Iraq and Syria (also known as ISIL, the Islamic State of Iraq and the Levant). Number of members hard to estimate, but thought to be less than 50,000. Just under 4,000 are from the West, with around 200 from the US.

  * ISIS is predominantly made up of Sunni Muslims (the Iraqi government and military is mostly Shia) and has its roots in the Iraqi faction of al-Qaeda.

  * Its influence rose as a result of the power vacuum created by the Syrian conflict (from 2011) and it fell out with al-Qaeda in 2013.

  * ISIS got a lot of its initial funding through kidnapping. Note the US, UK, and Poland don't pay ransom money; the US and UK often try to get their citizens back militarily.

- Boko Haram is a terrorist group that mostly operates in northeast Nigeria. It has links to al-Qaeda and has pledged support to ISIS. You'll have heard of them because in 2014 they targeted a girl's school. A girl's school being the scariest possible concept for a fanatic; it's why the Pakistani Taliban shot then fifteen-year-old Malala Yousafzai in the head.

There was a big argument in 2015 on the semantics of whether the US government should call ISIS Islamic terrorists. The reason there is caution is that the label helps extremists depict their cause as a religious crusade between Islam and the West. There is the risk that not every Muslim, especially since the US recently invaded two Muslim countries, will be able to differentiate that a war against Islamic terrorists is not a war against Islam. In the same way it would be incorrect to label the IRA bombings "Catholic terrorism," the term "Islamic terrorism" could be unhelpful and risks turning friends into enemies. As we discuss in Cheat Sheet 17, this is an intra-Muslim battle, not a Christian-Muslim one, and Muslims are the primary victims of this terrorism. Also keep in mind that nationalism is often disguised as fundamentalism; religion is used as cover for the political, for gaining power.

We now turn to history. For without understanding our past, we have no chance of getting a grip on our present.

WISE WORDS

What is tolerance? It is the consequence of humanity. We are all formed of frailty and error; let us pardon reciprocally each other's folly—that is the first law of nature.

—Voltaire

SOCIAL SURVIVAL STRATEGY

Argument: "Nationalism is often disguised as fundamentalism."
Religion is often used as a cover for those trying to gain political power. This topic is always complex, and if it arises, it is one of those times that if you're not a specialist and not learning from one, be aware of how little you probably know.

Crisp Fact: "Shrimp are referred to as an abomination four times more than homosexuality in the Bible."
This fact's an oldie, but it's still a goodie. We all know that bits of the Bible shouldn't be taken at face value, but this is a handy nugget to have in your brain.

Pivot: "I'm sure I saw this topic done well on *The West Wing*. Why is it that Aaron Sorkin had only one TV series that worked? What was it about *Studio 60 on the Sunset Strip* and *The Newsroom* that didn't quite hit the mark? And *Sports Night* lasted only two seasons."

Anyone who owns a TV set probably has an opinion on Aaron Sorkin. Even if you're with a Republican annoyed by Sorkin's liberal sensitivities, you can swiftly shift the tête-à-tête to the logistical challenges they must have faced when they shot the infamous long "walk and talk" scenes in *The West Wing*.

SUBJECT FOUR—HISTORY

HISTORY SUMMARY

The key theme to think about when discussing anything related to history is that you can probably blame the British, as the reason it is coming up in conversation now will be as a result of an impolite move the Brits made in times gone by. For instance, in regards to the Middle East, the post–World War I boundaries made no sense on religious or ethnic grounds, and we're paying for that today. And who can be blamed for the decision? For all intents and purposes, the Brits. A startling fact to bring up is that Henry Hudson sailed up the New York river that would later bear his name on September 11, 1609. And needing to get out of a cantankerous confab? Remark that Qatar was originally set to host the FIFA World Cup in 2022, the first Arab country to do so, and inquire if the person you're speaking to is a soccer fan. It is the world's most popular sport, after all.

The important thing to remember about history is that it is written by the winners. Fair and balanced when you read all about it? Not so much.

History comes from the Latin *historia* (which in turn was borrowed from the Greek). It is infinite. You can never stop learning about it. It is my passion, what I *read,* as we Brits call *majoring in,* at university. Thus to me, this subject was by far the most daunting. What to leave out? In my view everything is relevant.

I moved to America on February 1, 2010. This subject contains a soupçon of all I have needed to know about to get by in this country. On air, at parties, and meeting boyfriends' parents. Hopefully this will serve you in good stead.

Along with most immigrants I've spoken to on the topic, I always feel guilty that my grasp of American history is a bit shaky. This is because wherever one is brought up, the history one is taught tends to be of that country. If we do study America, it's normally about the impact it had on our own lands when it hit superpower status. Many an immigrant finds it startling to learn quite how long and how large slavery loomed and of the subsequent institutionalized racism that African-Americans have had to fight in the land of the free. The more I read, the more I see the history of civil rights—from the fight for freedom from Britain, then against slavery, then for equality of the races and sexes—as the history of America. If you're American, Cheat Sheet 12 concerning basic American beginnings may contain information that is so obvious to you, you end up skipping it. But around 13 percent of your nation's population are immigrants. And what's contained in 12 isn't so ingrained in us, so I've written it for us foreign types. It is also for those Americans who ask us foreigners how we celebrate Thanksgiving in our native lands.

We follow this up in Cheat Sheet 13 with a grid of American presidents. There have been forty-four presidential administrations but only forty-three presidents—Grover Cleveland served two nonconsecutive terms. You've got to feel sorry for the commanders in chief. The nation wants its presidents to be grandfatherly figures that solve all of America's problems, which of course is an unrealistic expectation at the outset. There is more to leadership than rhetoric, but that's often all these men have been left with apart from in the area of foreign policy, thanks to the separation of powers. Interestingly, America wasn't always headed the presidential route. Some wanted George Washington to wear a crown. However, he and the framers of the Constitution refused. What is the one thing the White House lacks? A throne. Two gentle reminders: Mount Rushmore, near Keystone, South Dakota, features George Washington, Thomas Jefferson, Theodore Roosevelt, and Abraham Lincoln. It wasn't their idea: Their faces were completed in 1941. And a reminder: If you're going to say Obama is worse than Nixon in relation to the media, you might acknowledge that Nixon officials discussed murdering a reporter. What this Cheat Sheet will really do for you is to help you in playing quizzes on your smartphone and in being generally smug.

That smugness will probably disappear when you read Cheat Sheet 14 on American imperialism. Don't pretend you don't know what I'm talking about. By 1900, America had gotten big. It reached from the Atlantic to the Pacific. It had the world's largest economy. The USA established itself as a world military power with the Spanish-American War and its late entrance into World War I. Yes, there has always been a bit of an interventionist vs. isolationist (non-interventionist) debate going on within the United States. But face facts: The first nation to have nuclear weapons and the only one ever to deploy them, America is cemented into the status of superpower. America just needs to remember two things: that it should regularly remind its politicians that this doesn't mean the nation *has* super-powers and that it needs to keep a close eye on its presidents, since foreign policy is where they have most jurisdiction. Every president, whatever his or her views coming into office, always comes to depend on the intelligence agencies. No president is going to give up the CIA, a secret service founded after World War II that has one client. When in doubt in international chat? Proclaim that in this interconnected age, national solutions are not enough; global solutions are required. (That was one of my favorites at MSNBC. Incredibly difficult to make happen, of course.)

My home territory and what I'm probably best known for on

American TV is next. The royals. Indeed I am PEOPLE Now's Royals correspondent. Yes, the monarchy is a historic anomaly. Yes, there is a fundamental ambiguity in having a hereditary monarchy head a parliamentary democracy. But it works. And as we Brits say, "If it ain't broke, don't fix it." It may seem antiquated, but the queen is still a figurehead to two billion people, a third of the world. The monarchy is there to be above politics. It represents stability and continuity and shines a spotlight on good causes. For Brits, the monarch is a focus for national identity, unity, and pride. The monarch has two selves, the mortal personal one, which may not always be lovable, and the immortal spiritual side. The latter represents that there will always be an England. Why the interest in America concerning the British royals? Throughout history, even in republics, we have irrationally elevated certain individuals. Americans have political dynasties. And celebrity culture exists. Prince Harry on the front lines for his country versus the reality TV prince du jour? Actually, which one is better to talk about? And who doesn't love a wedding or a birth, the distraction of a fairy tale in this age of relentless bad news?

Because I thought you'd appreciate the irony, Cheat Sheet 15 is a grid of the kings and queens of England from 1066, when William the Conqueror created a nation. The ironic part? We've had fewer monarchs since then than America has ever had presidents. If you're really keen to beat British friends at trivia, there's even a rhyme to remember the kings and queens of England since William I (the Conqueror), which it is unlikely they'll ever have bothered to learn:

> *Willie, Willie, Harry, Steve,*
> *Harry, Dick, John, Harry Three.*
> *Edward One, Two, Three, Dick Two,*
> *Henry Four, Five, Six, then who?*
> *Edward Four, Five, Dick the Bad*
> *Harrys twain and Ned, the lad.*

Mary, Lizzie, James the Vain,
Charlie, Charlie, James again.
William and Mary, Anne o'Gloria,
Four Georges, William and Victoria,
Edward Seven, Georgie Five,
Edward, George, and Liz (alive).

I'm probably most proud of Cheat Sheet 16. We cover World War I, World War II, and the cold war in it. Please read 16 just for me. Take from it that brinkmanship is always a part of international relations, but it is also vital to understand the opposition's motives and legitimate interests. That a nation should never go to war believing it will be quick and cheap and all its consequences controlled. And if the peace is not secure, war is liable to occur again.

The final Cheat Sheet on this subject, 17, covers the Middle East. You need to read it. You know you do. We look into the history of the hottest hot spots. We touch on terrorism. Explain the concept of the two-state solution, which you may come away believing is an illusion. And find out why there's one thing that at least everyone can agree on about the region: Blame the British.

There's a thought that I want to leave you with, as you'll be using this subject primarily in discussions about the state of the world today. In my final year at Cambridge I was lucky enough to study under Professor Christopher Andrew, who changed my view of the world so completely, so utterly, that I've never looked at anything the same since. The subject?

The secret world and international relations. Spies.

Whenever modern international relations come up, this is your get-out-of-jail-free card. Pundits can and do try their level best on air and in "ink" to provide us with enlightening commentary. But by definition, they are making comments with often very little knowledge of what is actually going on.

For they lack key information from one crucial source: the second oldest profession. Spies. As Sun Tzu, the ancient Chinese strategist, philosopher, and military general, wrote: "It is only the enlightened ruler and the wise general who will use the highest intelligence of the army for the purposes of spying, and thereby they achieve great results."

One must never underestimate the impact the intelligence communities, the secret world, is having on international relations. While I was studying with the masterful Andrew, it was drummed into me that contemporary commentators tend to make at best incomplete and at worst incorrect assumptions about the topics of the day.

Take World War II. Perspective on it was turned on its head in the 1970s, when the high-level intelligence produced by the code breakers at Bletchley Park in the UK was revealed. (Homework: See *The Imitation Game*. It stars male perfection personified, Benedict Cumberbatch, so hardly an arduous task.) Winston Churchill referred to the code breakers as "the geese that laid the golden eggs and never cackled." The intelligence, code-named Ultra, provided such crucial assistance to the Allied war effort that according to General Dwight D. Eisenhower, it "saved thousands of British and American lives and, in no small way, contributed to the speed with which the enemy was routed and eventually forced to surrender." Ultra certainly quickened the arrival of VE Day, and consequently the first nuclear bomb went off over Japan, not Germany. Since the end of World War II, intelligence has played a key role; the CIA was formed right after it to monitor the potential threat of communist countries and isn't going anywhere.

It is simply impossible—and illegal—for anyone to paint a full picture of present foreign policy for public consumption. Journalists can speculate in leading fashion, but they cannot know or reveal for sure. Take Strobe Talbott, former diplomatic correspondent of *Time*. He noted in February 1984 that he was struck by how "extraordinarily conciliatory" Ronald Reagan's comments on the death of Yuri Andropov and his succession by Konstantin Chernenko were.

It later came to light that Ronald Reagan's almost overnight abandonment of his "evil empire" rhetoric against the Soviets in the 1980s was in no small part due to the secret world. Intelligence, including that provided by the British double agent Oleg Gordievsky, helped convince Reagan to change course. Thanks to the American president's incendiary words combined with Soviet paranoia (the Russians were notoriously bad at listening to any sensible intelligence coming their way, Stalin being a classic example before his death in 1953—he had ignored the warnings about Barbarossa, that Hitler was going to invade the USSR, so got taken by surprise), a NATO exercise in 1983 was misinterpreted by the Soviets as a potential first strike. The world had come closer to nuclear war than at any time since the Cuban Missile Crisis in 1962. Reagan wrote in his memoirs: "I feel the Soviets . . . are so paranoid about being attacked that without in any way being soft on them, we ought to tell them no one here has any intention of doing anything like that."

We know that secret contact with the Iranians has been a hallmark of the West's foreign policy with Iran for decades, from the covert action in Iran during the Truman years—operations designed to diminish Soviet and Communist influence—to 1953's fake Tudeh crowds organized by the CIA under Eisenhower. And of course Iran-Contra. More recently, the West has been involved in a covert war with Iran in an attempt to head off an overt one. The Stuxnet computer virus that set back Iran's nuclear program. The killing of several Iranian nuclear scientists on Iranian soil.

The only certainty we have in the public discourse in regard to any of the world's hot spots is that we are dealing with smoke and mirrors with every player. Politicians are involved in rhetorical posturing to their bases, but are quite probably of other views behind the electioneering scenes. History will be their eventual judge. Obama's administration publicly found itself in trouble because of its "spying" on friendly European nations. Most nations, apart from possibly Britain and America, spy on each other (the Brits and Yanks are besties, with Britain telling the Americans almost everything). Europe just has a case of spy envy. After it vociferously denounced the United States for spying on it, what happened to Germany? They were caught consistently spying on Turkey, its NATO ally— and had even by mistake "accidentally" intercepted phone calls between Hillary Clinton and John Kerry. Europe wishes that their spying was as advanced as the Americans', but that doesn't mean they were surprised by it and didn't have their own programs. I have an iota of sympathy for the intelligence agencies, I must admit. Their successes are rarely celebrated publicly, but their mistakes are usually exposed to the world to see, and they make many.

I was barred from a certain Fox host's show, which I used to appear on weekly, after bringing the intelligence element into a debate over Benghazi, right before the 2012 presidential election. The September 11, 2012, attack, in which the American ambassador to Libya ended up losing his life, was the subject of accusations of inaccuracies and cover-ups. I was not prepared to place the blame solely on the president's administration. I said on air that a key factor in the subsequent confusion of what went into the public domain was that the secret world has always had an uneasy relationship with the press, and especially in the age of the twenty-four-hour news cycle. The CIA had a facility in Benghazi that was undeniably impacting the information flow the media had been receiving and which Congress's hyper-partisan hearings exposed. I later discovered that the host took exception to my bringing something up that showed him up. Despite the insistence of a member of his team that I was right to do so and should be invited back, I was never booked on his show again. At least Hannity spent years asking me to return for another round.

It is vital that we have a vigorous public discussion about international relations and also intelligence agencies. But we won't know everything and we should always remember how these are inextricably intertwined. So if someone is being belligerent about foreign policy and you want to shut them down, say this: The best we can hope for is that the secret world is providing our leaders with accurate intelligence—and that they are listening to it.

Now to the Cheat Sheets.

CHEAT SHEET 12—BASIC AMERICAN BEGINNINGS

BACKGROUND BRIEFING

A million (legal) immigrants a year come to this country. This cheat sheet is for them. We're not usually taught in our home nations why you eat turkey at Thanksgiving. Only if you're one of *those* Americans who ask us why we don't partake of the bird do I suggest that this section is compulsory reading for you!

It's inaccurate and somewhat offensive to call America a young country. People have inhabited every part of the area for at least 12,000 years. Current wisdom suggests that Paleoindians probably came from Eurasia via Siberia, which was still joined with Alaska until around 10,000 years ago, and then headed south. The multiple Native American Indian tribes were and are hugely diverse, speaking many completely different languages.

There is a prevailing theme throughout our examination of history. For centuries Europeans would arrive somewhere and disrupt ways of life to the detriment of those already in residence. Some would argue that Uncle Sam subsequently took up where those predecessors left off.

Christopher Columbus collided with the Bahamas in 1492, kick-starting adventurous Europeans traveling to America to seek their fortunes and/or religious freedom. Well, mostly. Australia wasn't the only place the Brits shipped convicts to.

However, it's important not to be too England-centric here. There was an influx of Europeans in general to America. The Spanish were front and center to the whole experience in the sixteenth century. They were the first to the Grand Canyon, and some settled in what is now Texas and California. The French were all over the Rocky Mountains and more. In the early seventeenth century, New York was actually called New Netherland and belonged to the Dutch, although to be fair it was the English Henry Hudson who brought their attention to it by sailing up the river that would later bear his name on September 11, 1609.

A pause as we look at that date.

NOTEWORTHY NUGGET: THE ROANOKE COLONY, AKA THE LOST COLONY

This tale can get very long and complicated, but basically, Roanoke was the first English settlement in America (in what is now North Carolina), and it vanished. In 1587, explorer John White led 116 settlers there. When he got back in 1590, they'd disappeared. Cue endless conspiracy theories—if someone knows about Roanoke, they will have one, so are likely to be thrilled if you ask for it. You might be less thrilled to hear about it.

The Dutch lost New York to the Brits by the end of the seventeenth century. The Brits were actually rather late in the day on the whole America thing. The year 1607 saw the start of the first Brit colony to succeed—in Jamestown, Virginia, named after King James I.

NOTEWORTHY NUGGET: TOBACCO

Native Americans taught the Spanish how to smoke tobacco and they then brought it to Europe.

Virginia wasn't good for gold, as hoped, but it was excellent for tobacco. By 1630 a million and a half pounds of the stuff a year was being exported from Jamestown.

KEY TERMS: THE *MAYFLOWER*, PILGRIMS, AND THANKSGIVING

- The *Mayflower* was a merchant ship that set sail from England in 1620 with 102 people on board. Less than a third of them were Protestant Separatists, who called themselves "Saints" and whom we label "Pilgrims." The other colonists were your typical immigrant/adventurer/speculator sorts. Must have made for an interesting trip.

- They signed the Mayflower Compact on board, the first example of a written constitution in North America. It pledged loyalty to the king but also stated they'd rule themselves based on a majority.

- They were headed to Jamestown. The wind took them to Cape Cod, New England, Massachusetts.

- Only 44 of the *Mayflower* passengers survived; they were much aided by the Native Americans.

- By the time of the English harvest festival in the following fall of 1621, the Pilgrims had an awful lot to be thankful for. They ate turkey, cornbread—and more. And continued the tradition every year.

- Thanksgiving was declared a national holiday by President Lincoln in 1863.

America's expansion toward the west, the American frontier, began. Fast-forward to the 1770s. There were thirteen flourishing British colonies in America, population of about two and a half million. Mercantilism dictated that the Brits wanted more money off the Americans (spot another recurring theme throughout the book: It's always about the cash). There was a sort of fair-share argument coming from my native land. Mainland English citizens paid higher taxes than Americans. The revenue from the Americans was used to pay for American defense—and the receipts covered only about a third of the cost of maintaining British garrisons in the colonies. The Americans' argument was that they no longer required Brit military might against France and Spain. And the whole taxation/representation thing—Americans didn't get to vote for the British parliament. One of the more considerable commotions came over the Brits' 1765 Stamp Act. Although it was repealed, the truce in its aftermath was uneasy.

KEY TERMS: THE BOSTON TEA PARTY AND THE BOSTON MASSACRE

- Patriots (anti-British rule) were in every one of the thirteen colonies, but were especially vocal and plentiful in Boston.

- The Boston Massacre was a small incident that literally began with snowballs and, well, snowballed. Bostonians, annoyed with British attempts to raise revenue, threw snowballs at a few British soldiers in March 1770.

- Although they were supposed not to open fire, the soldiers did. Five colonists were killed, including the former slave Crispus Attucks—the first African-American to die for the revolution.

- The Boston Tea Party came about because of a convoluted British brainwave involving a monopoly to the East India Company (an English company), cheaper tea for colonialists, and tax. On December 16, 1773, a group of annoyed Patriots stormed three ships and chucked 342 chests of tea into Boston harbor. So that's why Americans drink coffee—it's all becoming clearer now.

You could label the American Revolution an antitax movement. Armed conflict between the Patriots (American rebels) and the Loyalists (pro-Brits) kicked off in April 1775. (Side note: the ones who wore Redcoats were members of the British army.) The next summer, Thomas Jefferson penned the colonies' landmark Declaration of Independence, which was ratified on July 4, 1776. The United States of America was born and the war was full-on, with General George Washington leading the Patriots' Continental Army. The Patriots had some powerful allies—the French sent men and supplies. Meanwhile the Spanish and Dutch attacked British ships so their supplies couldn't arrive. Distance was definitely not on the Brits' side; communication-wise, the situation was a nightmare. Plus the people in my home nation were unconvinced as to why on earth they should be paying all this money to be at war. In fact there were pro-Americans within the British parliament. And then there were all those Enlightenment ideas floating around at the time. The Age of Reason and all that. The Americans had a point with their case for rights, liberty, and independence. We weren't stupid back in Blighty.

The Brits surrendered at Yorktown, Virginia, in 1781. Independence had basically been won, although officially the fighting ended in 1783. For the first time ever, a European power had been defeated in a colonial war.

The aforementioned George Washington became the first president. Alexander Hamilton made for a dynamic secretary of the treasury and established the Federalist Party (and is now the subject of the hit Broadway musical *Hamilton*). James Madison and Thomas Jefferson formed what is now labeled the Democratic-Republican Party in opposition. And some very gifted men set about writing the Constitution—see Cheat Sheet 18.

KEY TERM: THE LOUISIANA PURCHASE

- President Thomas Jefferson bought the Louisiana Territory off France in 1803, doubling the republic's holdings.
- Hence all the French influences still in what was the Louisiana Territory. Cajun and Creole food, anyone?

Americans had one more war with the Brits (aided by Canadian and Native American troops), the War of 1812. Causes included arguments about territory and trade. Note this is the war when Brits set fire to Washington, DC—including the White House.

The Federalists were against the 1812 war, which officially ended in 1815, and with it the Federalist Party. America briefly had a one-party period, the "Era of Good Feelings," but that didn't last long. After the 1824 presidential election the Democratic-Republicans split into two parties, and the rest, as they say, is history. The modern-day Democratic Party was formed circa 1828; the Republican Party was established in 1854.

Life, liberty, and the pursuit of happiness was a concept that of course did not equally immediately extend to slaves or women. It did, however, give both inspiration. The abolitionist movement was sparked in the United States, it being blatantly hypocritical to have inalienable rights . . . except for those living in human bondage.

There was no modern machinery for cultivation, so in the 1600s there had been indentured servants, white slaves under contract who would have their travel paid for to the colonies, work a certain number of years, and then get their freedom dues. However, this was not the rosy future that many indentured servants envisaged—only 40 percent survived their contracts. If by chance indentured servants managed to outlive their contracts, they were awarded the worst land. This led to a class of poor, furious farmers, so after the 1676 Bacon's Rebellion, planters preferred African slavery.

Georgia was briefly an exception. Founded by enlightened thinkers in 1733, it was a utopian experiment, which included no slavery. Alas, seventeen years later went the freedom for all who lived on its soil.

KEY TERMS: MIDDLE PASSAGE, LOOSE PACKING, TIGHT PACKING

- **Middle Passage**—the transatlantic sea journey of slave ships from West Africa to the West Indies. It took three weeks or more depending on the weather and on average claimed the lives of 50 percent or more of the slaves on the ships.
- **Loose Packing**—fewer slaves per ship in view that a larger percentage would arrive alive.
- **Tight Packing**—more slaves, although more died.

This brutal method brought between ten and twenty million Africans to the New World.

Every colony in America had slaves, even those in the North. But the populations in the North were smaller, and those African-Americans who were free gravitated toward urban centers.

KEY TERM: MANUMISSION

Manumission meant the voluntary freeing of a slave by the master. Masters did occasionally free their own slaves. Horrifically, these freed slaves were at risk of being kidnapped by slave catchers, who would force them back into slavery. They had no recourse. Owing to the laws concerning slaves, blacks were not allowed to testify against whites. If you've not seen *12 Years a Slave*, do so.

Throughout the nineteenth century the abolitionist movement grew. By 1804, all states north of the Mason-Dixon Line had abolished slavery. However, the number of slaves burgeoned. In 1790 there were almost 700,000; by 1860, almost 4 million. In the southern states, slavery was still very much entrenched in the plantation economy way of life.

The trigger to a slavery showdown was a certain President Lincoln.

Revolutions tend to go hand in hand with civil war. America got its between 1861 and 1865. Decades of rumbling frictions between the northern and southern states on matters including slavery, westward expansion, and federal authority came to a head.

After the election of the Republican—and antislavery—President Abraham Lincoln in 1860, seven southern states seceded from the Union to form the Confederate States of America. Once the Civil War began, four more joined. During the war, 2.4 million Americans fought, around 2.5 percent of the population died, and the South was pretty much decimated. If you feel you're enough of an expert on the subject and an independent observer has remarked that you have a talent for delicate debate, at this point you could float the idea that on some levels, the South is still recovering. In the likely event you're not (why would you even be in this Cheat Sheet otherwise?), take away the following: Yankees fought for the Union against the Confederates. Because the Confederates were proslavery, there has been a long-standing debate over whether their flag now stands for heritage or hate. In 2015 the tide decisively turned toward the latter. Also although many foreigners call Americans *Yanks,* the word actually applies to northern and not southern Americans, so if you're anything like me you've spent years getting it wrong.

President Lincoln and his commanding general Ulysses S. Grant prevailed. So began the Reconstruction Era, which refers to the period immediately after the Civil War in which the issues of slavery and readmission to the Union of the eleven states that had seceded were addressed.

KEY TERMS: BATTLE OF GETTYSBURG AND GETTYSBURG ADDRESS

- **Battle of Gettysburg.** Fought in July 1863 in Pennsylvania, it was one of the bloodiest and most decisive points in the Civil

War. The Union side beat the Confederate, finishing the Confederate invasion of the North.

- In November 1863, Lincoln spoke 273 words at the dedication ceremony for the National Cemetery of Gettysburg. He wasn't even the featured orator for the day, but his Gettysburg Address became one of the most famous speeches in history.

WHY IT MATTERS TODAY

We are our history. In 1863, during the American Civil War, Lincoln (reminder, Republican) issued the Emancipation Proclamation, which proclaimed the freedom of all slaves in the states in rebellion, thus making slavery's eradication a clear aim of the war. With its end came the Thirteenth Amendment ending slavery, the Fourteenth granting African-Americans citizenship, and the Fifteenth permitting African-American males the right to vote. Of course, discrimination against African-Americans didn't end there. The white supremacist Ku Klux Klan materialized in 1867, and as we know, despite President Ulysses S. Grant's closing them down in 1870, it wasn't the end of them—or of the fight for equal rights for African-Americans.

Civil rights comes from the Latin *ius civis,* and the concept that an individual has rights dates back to Roman times. To me, the fact that an individual's freedoms are protected is what America is all about, what it has always fought for, first from Britain and then internally, for equal rights for all whatever your race, sex (we look at feminism in Cheat Sheet 25), or financial situation. Naturally, in different eras and places, the phrase has been used for different causes and cases. In Britain, for instance, in the nineteenth century *civil rights* referred to the discrimination Catholics faced. Across the pond, in America come the 1860s, the phrase was used for the recently freed African-Americans.

But almost a hundred years later, African-Americans in southern states still suffered from entrenched racism; little wonder the Great Migration occurred, in which almost 7 million blacks emigrated to the North and West, where their situation was a little better. From the 1880s, laws named after Jim Crow, a black character in minstrel shows, had legally enforced state-sanctioned discrimination, including voter suppression. And please keep this in mind: White Southern Democrats were very much to blame, along with their Republican counterparts. That didn't stop African-Americans from being required to fight and die for their country; two world wars later, they finally won integration in the military when President Harry Truman issued an executive order in 1948.

The NAACP, the National Association for the Advancement of Colored People, was founded in 1909. Their concerted efforts finally yielded a big breakthrough with the 1954 *Brown v. Board of Education* decision, in which the Supreme Court struck down the "separate but equal" doctrine by rejecting separate colored and white school systems. The next fifteen years saw the civil rights movement really take hold. I cannot begin to do it justice here, so please forgive me as I touch on topics many of us immigrants need to know more about.

On December 1, 1955, Rosa Parks of Montgomery, Alabama, refused to give up her bus seat to a white male rider. Protests and boycotts followed. The civil rights movement as we know it began in earnest. In 1957 President Eisenhower (a Republican) federalized Arkansas's National Guard, sent them back to their barracks, and deployed the 101st Airborne Division to escort the Little Rock Nine, black students, to study at the all-white Little Rock Central High School. The students still suffered massive abuse. In 1960 in North Carolina's Greensboro, black college students sat at a whites-only restaurant counter, which sparked many other similar protests, known as sit-ins. Freedom Riders put the rule that segregation for interstate travel was illegal to the test, journeying on interstate buses.

Martin Luther King, Jr., emerged, a proponent of the nonviolent tactics used by Gandhi. Confrontations between peaceful protesters and police in Birmingham prompted President John F. Kennedy—who had a passionate little brother, Robert, pushing him on the civil rights issue—to work for new civil rights legislation. On August 28, 1963, over 250,000 took part in the march on Washington and saw King give his "I Have a Dream" speech from the steps of the Lincoln Memorial. Those famous four words, "I have a dream," weren't in the original text, by the way. He added the phrase in off the cuff.

The Civil Rights Act had been having a tricky time under JFK, with Congress squabbling away. Poignantly, Kennedy's assassination facilitated its passing, and less compromise occurred, as what kind of person could reject a murdered president's big wish? With President Lyndon B. Johnson pushing it through in a manner that Kevin Spacey later channeled for *House of Cards,* the 1964 act passed and segregation was forbidden in public facilities, racial discrimination in employment was outlawed, and the way was paved for future antidiscrimination legislation, including the Voting Rights Act the following year. Of course, the civil rights war wasn't won, and battles continue to this day. The 1968 assassination of Martin Luther King shocked America. It also coincided with the rise of the Black Power Movement, the epitome of which was the Black Panther Party, which feuded with the existing black leadership regarding its policies of nonviolence and cooperation.

Yes, there have been high points. By the 1980s Reverend Jesse Jackson was campaigning for the Democratic nomination for president of the United States, and in 2008 Senator Barack Obama was elected to lead the free world. However, we are all aware that despite the gains in civil rights, deep inequality remains in this great nation. From Trayvon Martin to the unrest in Ferguson, Missouri, to Eric Garner's last words, "I can't breathe," becoming a rallying cry, to a white gunman murdering nine African-American during Bible study at a South Carolina church, we are continually reminded of it. Not every American has the same opportunity to live the American dream.

But it is still a dream, in my humble view as one of the million immigrants to this country a year, that drives this nation—we haven't given up on you figuring your way through. Uncle Sam just has so much going for him.

Why are we here? After the American Civil War, the foundations of America today emerged. In the late nineteenth century came the Gilded Age—America got rich.

KEY TERM: MANIFEST DESTINY

- The American expansion westward in the nineteenth century. The frontier, the Wild West, and all that.

- Term was coined in 1845 to describe the mind-set. All about individualism, innovation, conquest, persistence, boldness, violence.

- California Gold Rush, 1848, anyone? A total of $2 billion worth of precious metal was extracted from the Sacramento Valley area during the spell.

- Further game changers: In 1861, the first transcontinental telegraph, and in 1869, the first transcontinental railroad, which was much comfier—not to say quicker—than traveling in a wagon.

Immigrants came to stay with Uncle Sam—between 1880 and 1914, more than 22 million of them. With them, industrialization sped up. Later, of course, this was a factor in the Progressive Era—in 1914 alone, 35,000 workers died in industrial accidents. There was a reason for unions.

By 1890, American industrial production was greater and per capita income was higher than those of every other country on earth.

Yes there have been economic blips. There was one in 1893. But you know what? By 1900 the United States had the most robust economy on the planet. And despite the recessions of 1907, 1920, and the big crash of 1929, America was big. In the nineteenth and twentieth centuries, thirty-seven new states were added in the coast-to-coast expansion. And after the world and cold wars ended, America was permanently—let's face it; sorry, Putin—the leading global power. Economically, as we saw in Cheat Sheet 7, America is still the number one economy in the world.

There's always work to do, but I sort of think you got your happy ending, America.

TALKING POINTS

- Twenty-seven states get their names from Indian languages, and of the crops now being grown on America's farms, more than half were already being grown on this land before the Native Americans were colonized.

- During World War II, the United States used the uniqueness of the Navajo language spoken by some Native Americans from the Southwest. As a substitute for the encryption of US marine radio messages, it proved quicker and easier for Navajos to speak to each other in their native tongue to convey high-security messages. Unlike with machine codes, the Japanese never broke the Navajo.

- America has got a lot to thank second-son syndrome for. The sea-dog leaders of English colonial expeditions were often second sons (their elder brothers got the property at home, so they had to go off and do something)—including Sir Francis Drake and Sir Walter Raleigh.

- Washington, DC, became the nation's capital in 1800. It had previously been located in New York and Philadelphia.

- The lyrics to "The Star-Spangled Banner" were written by an American in 1814 after the Brits, who by then had burned Washington, were beaten in Baltimore. The one-and-a-half-octave impossible-to-sing tune is actually British, composed by John Stafford Smith for a London men's club, the Anacreontic Society. So it was originally "The Anacreontic Song." In 1931 President Herbert Hoover signed a congressional resolution making it the national anthem.

RED FLAGS

- Out and about with Eurotrash types? Don't mention that it was a German cartographer, Martin Waldseemüller, who labeled America *America* in 1507—a tribute to the Italian cartographer and explorer Amerigo Vespucci. You'll never hear the end of it.

- If you see two immigrants meet, they will within five minutes be speaking in a code you do not understand. It will involve H1s, EB1s, and O1s. Best leave them to it—you simply don't want to know, and if you're an American citizen, through no fault of your own, you may put your foot in it.

- Until 1965 the immigration system was particularly odious toward Africans, Latin Americans, and Asians. Ironic, since Asians arrived in America first.

- "The British are coming!" Nobody shouted that when you think they did. It would have confused people, as at the time many Americans thought they were British.

- Pocahontas was real; she was no fairy tale. She was the daughter of Chief Powhatan and wife of Jamestown settler John Rolfe.

- Dealing with teenage girls in the midst of a full-on obsession with the latest teen idol? You can think but not say that you now have the explanation of the "witchcraft" events of Salem in 1692 and 1693.

WISE WORDS

Europe was created by history. America was created by philosophy.

—Margaret Thatcher

SOCIAL SURVIVAL STRATEGY

Argument: "For centuries Europeans would arrive somewhere and disrupt ways of life to the detriment of those already in residence. Some would argue that Uncle Sam subsequently took up where those predecessors left off."

Foreign policy debate that you'll end up engaging in will typically break down to this: Is America being imperialist or just saving the world (yet again)? There's no right answer, which you can point out after you've instigated the dialogue.

Crisp Fact: "Henry Hudson sailed up the New York river that would later bear his name on September 11, 1609."

This fact always provokes somber food for thought; use it when you need to halt a cantankerous conversation.

Pivot: "The tune to 'The Star-Spangled Banner' was composed by a Brit, John Stafford Smith, for a London men's club. Are you a member of any clubs, or do you think such institutions are as antiquated as the Brits?"

People you never expect can suddenly reveal they're members of clubs, whether they're golf or artistic. Ask them to take you for a drink there; clubs always provide an opportunity for intriguing people watching.

CHEAT SHEET 13—GRID
OF AMERICAN PRESIDENTS

NO.	NAME/PARTY/TERM	QUALIFICATION(S)	QUIRK(S)	NOTABLE FEAT(S)/FIASCO(S)
1	George Washington Independent 1789–1797	Commander in chief of the Continental Army.	His first inaugural address was 183 words; his second, the shortest ever, was 135.	Only president to be unanimously elected by the Electoral College. Started tradition of foreign policy largely being a presidential concern.
2	John Adams Federalist 1797–1801	Veep. Had helped negotiate the official end to the American Revolutionary War with the 1783 Treaty of Paris.	First president to live in the White House. Started smoking when he was eight.	Thomas Jefferson prevented him from getting a second term.
3	Thomas Jefferson Democratic-Republican 1801–1809	Veep. Author of Declaration of Independence.	Started the custom of shaking hands with the president; before him, people bowed. Wrote beautifully, but dreadful public speaker. Would not have excelled in the TV era.	Acquired the Louisiana Territory from Napoleon in 1803.

(cont.)

NO.	NAME/PARTY/TERM	QUALIFICATION(S)	QUIRK(S)	NOTABLE FEAT(S)/FIASCO(S)
4	James Madison Democratic-Republican 1809–1817	Secretary of state. Coauthor of Federalist Papers, so influential in getting Constitution ratified.	Small, old, and wrinkly but his cheerfully curvaceous wife Dolley was the toast of Washington.	Controversial War of 1812 happened on his watch.
5	James Monroe Democratic-Republican 1817–1825	Secretary of state. Helped negotiate the Louisiana Purchase.	Last president to wear a wig. Well, you know what I mean. Monroe Doctrine named after him. Basically it's the idea that Europe shouldn't meddle with the Americas anymore.	He acquired Florida (not sure Al Gore would agree that was a good thing). Missouri Compromise, which some claim helped delay the Civil War, occurred under his watch. Missouri, a slave state, wanted admission to the Union, but that would upset the balance of slave and free states. Compromise involved both Missouri (slave) and Maine (free) being admitted.
6	John Quincy Adams Democratic-Republican 1825–1829	Secretary of state.	First president who was son of a former president. Had a penchant for nude bathing. Journalist Anne Royall once sat on his clothes while he was in the Potomac and wouldn't move until he answered her questions.	Served only one term, then went on to the House of Representatives. Highly vocal against slavery. Later collapsed on floor of the House and died two days later.

NO.	NAME/PARTY/TERM	QUALIFICATION(S)	QUIRK(S)	NOTABLE FEAT(S)/FIASCO(S)
7	Andrew Jackson Democrat 1829–1837	Senator (Tennessee). Major general in War of 1812, defeating the British at New Orleans.	As a young man was a brawler and killed a man in a duel for insulting his wife. First president to be born in a log cabin—and to see indoor bathrooms in the White House.	Supporter of states' rights, the extension of slavery into the western territories, and forced relocation of Native American tribes living east of the Mississippi.
8	Martin Van Buren Democrat 1837–1841	Veep.	Impeccably dressed red-haired short man was the first president to be born a United States citizen and not a British subject.	He hit a bust in the boom/bust cycle in 1837. His continuation of Jackson's deflationary policies extended the depression, the worst in America's history at the time.
9	William Henry Harrison Whig 1841	Minister to Colombia. Fought Native Americans.	Supposedly a big cider drinker.	Died of pneumonia after a month in office, the shortest tenure of any president.
10	John Tyler Whig, then Independent 1841–1845	Veep.	Nicknamed "his accidency" after becoming first veep to take over the presidency not by winning an election.	1845 annexation of Texas.

(cont.)

NO.	NAME/PARTY/TERM	QUALIFICATION(S)	QUIRK(S)	NOTABLE FEAT(S)/FIASCO(S)
11	James K. Polk Democrat 1845–1849	Governor (Tennessee).	First president to be a dark horse (not expected to win), to have "Hail to the Chief" played when he entered a room (rumor was he was short so needed the help with his entrance), and to have his photo taken while in office.	Under him, for the first time America's territory extended across the continent, growing by more than a third.
12	Zachary Taylor Whig 1849–1850	US Army major general from the 1st Infantry Regiment. Served in the army for four decades.	His wife promised God she wouldn't make public appearances, so their daughter Betty took that role.	Second president to die on the job.
13	Millard Filmore Whig 1850–1853	Veep.	Helped fight the blaze when the Library of Congress burned in 1851.	President when California became a state in 1850.
14	Franklin Pierce Democrat 1853–1857	Senator (New Hampshire).	Gave his 3,319-word inaugural address without notes.	Signed the 1854 Kansas-Nebraska Act, which repealed the Missouri Compromise and reopened the slavery question in the West. Antislavery northerners were furious, and this helped lead to the appearance of the new Republican Party.

NO.	NAME/PARTY/TERM	QUALIFICATION(S)	QUIRK(S)	NOTABLE FEAT(S)/FIASCO(S)
15	James Buchanan Democrat 1857–1861	Minister to the United Kingdom.	Only president to never marry.	Miserable time in office, trying to govern during the Secession Crisis, with the country splitting apart.
16	Abraham Lincoln Republican 1861–1865	Representative (Illinois).	Lincoln was interested in psychic phenomena and held séances with his wife in the White House. It's speculated that this was partly to do with the death of their son in the White House in 1862. Take that, Mrs. Reagan's astrologer.	Lincoln's 1863 Emancipation Proclamation (during the Civil War) freed all slaves in the "rebel" states and paved the way for the abolition of slavery. Confederate (rebel) sympathizer and actor John Wilkes Booth assassinated him on April 14, 1865, at Ford's Theatre in Washington.
17	Andrew Johnson Democrat 1865–1869	Veep. Only southern senator during the Civil War to be loyal to the Union.	Hosted the first White House Easter egg roll.	First president to be impeached. However, he was not removed from office.
18	Ulysses S. Grant Republican 1869–1877	Commanding general of the US Army.	Liked a cucumber soaked in vinegar for breakfast.	The transcontinental railroad was completed during his tenure. Grant himself was honest, but his administration was consistently beset by scandals (see Cheat Sheet 20).

(cont.)

NO.	NAME/PARTY/TERM	QUALIFICATION(S)	QUIRK(S)	NOTABLE FEAT(S)/FIASCO(S)
19	Rutherford B. Hayes Republican 1877–1881	Governor (Ohio).	Hayes talked to Alexander Graham Bell on the first White House phone. Their telephone number was 1.	Won tough, tight presidential election against Samuel J. Tilden (185 to 184 electoral votes). Many saw his withdrawal of troops from Reconstruction states as betraying the African-Americans who lived there.
20	James Garfield Republican 1881	Representative (Ohio).	Garfield had a dog named Veto.	Sworn in as president in March 1881, shot by a disgruntled constituent in July that year, dying eleven weeks later on September 19.
21	Chester Arthur Republican 1881–1885	Veep.	Arthur could play the banjo.	Advocated civil service reform. Signed the Pendleton Civil Service Reform Act in 1883; government jobs depended on ability.
22	Grover Cleveland Democrat 1885–1889	Governor (New York).	Only president ever to serve two nonconsecutive terms.	Only Democrat to win the presidency between Lincoln and Taft—1860 to 1912. He successfully managed the scandal surrounding the existence of a love child, which hit during his presidential campaign, by going for the honest hands-up approach. The only president to be married physically in the White House (not to the mom of the love child).
23	Benjamin Harrison Republican 1889–1893	Senator (Indiana).	Harrison's grandfather was the ninth president. But unlike Gramps, Benjamin had electric light—they were installed in the White House during his tenure.	He did a Bush II: He lost the popular vote and carried the Electoral College. Proposed Hawaii should be annexed.

NO.	NAME/PARTY/TERM	QUALIFICATION(S)	QUIRK(S)	NOTABLE FEAT(S)/FIASCO(S)
24	Grover Cleveland Democrat 1893–1897	Also president No. 22.	Cleveland answered the White House phone himself.	In total he vetoed more than 300 bills. Got stuck with the 1893 panic and depression. He called his autobiography *Presidential Problems*.
25	William McKinley Republican 1897–1901	Governor (Ohio).	First president to have his inauguration filmed.	Went to war with Spain in 1898 over Cuban independence; the US ended the war possessing Guam, the Philippines, and Puerto Rico. Won reelection in 1900 only to be assassinated by an anarchist in 1901.
26	Theodore Roosevelt Republican 1901–1909	Veep.	Roosevelt officially labeled his presidential home the White House. Before then people had called it a variety of names, including the President's Palace.	Got presidency after McKinley assassination, then won election. Won a Nobel Peace Prize for helping negotiate end of the Russo-Japanese War and aggressively enabled construction on the Panama Canal.
27	William Howard Taft Republican 1909–1913	Secretary of war.	Taft had his own cow at the White House because he was such a big milk fan.	Taft's talents lay in areas other than politics. After his presidency, Warren Harding appointed him SCOTUS's chief justice. Taft is the only person to have led both of America's executive and judicial branches.

(cont.)

NO.	NAME/PARTY/TERM	QUALIFICATION(S)	QUIRK(S)	NOTABLE FEAT(S)/FIASCO(S)
28	Woodrow Wilson Democrat 1913–1921	Governor (New Jersey).	Won the fight to have the first Jewish person appointed to SCOTUS, Louis Brandeis.	Attempted to keep America out of the world war, which began in 1914, but eventually entered it in 1917; the Germans signed the Armistice in November 1918. Wilson was the second president to win the Nobel Peace Prize, in 1920.
29	Warren Harding Republican 1921–1923	Senator (Ohio).	Despite the fact that his mother wanted to call him Winfield, every Sunday he either visited her with a bouquet of flowers or had them delivered.	There was somewhat of a Ulysses S. Grant situation going on. Harding wasn't naughty, but a number in his administration were. Died on the job, so Coolidge got it.
30	Calvin Coolidge Republican 1923–1929	Veep.	The first president to make a public radio address.	Cleaned up the Harding messes and presided over the Roaring Twenties. Some of his more laissez-faire policies didn't exactly help prevent the Great Depression.
31	Herbert Hoover Republican 1929–1933	Secretary of commerce.	First president to have a phone on his desk.	Talk about timing. He entered office just as the US economy plummeted. While he was eating seven-course meals, the poor were starving.
32	Franklin D. Roosevelt Democrat 1933–1945	Governor (New York). Related by blood or marriage to eleven presidents, including Theodore (fifth cousin).	Only American president to be elected four times. He was married to the legend that was Eleanor Roosevelt. First president to appoint a	Stated in his inaugural address that "the only thing we have to fear is fear itself." Spoke to the people through his radio broadcasts, which he called fireside chats.

NO.	NAME/PARTY/TERM	QUALIFICATION(S)	QUIRK(S)	NOTABLE FEAT(S)/FIASCO(S)
32 (cont.)		One could thus argue that Jeb Bush and Hillary Clinton were merely carrying on a long American tradition.	woman to his cabinet, Frances Perkins.	His New Deal programs of relief, recovery, and reform changed American lives forever.
				Guided the US from isolationism to fighting the Nazis and their allies in World War II.
				Helped plan for what became the United Nations, hoping it would settle international issues.
33	Harry S. Truman Democrat 1945–1953	Veep.	He had the legendary *The Buck Stops Here* sign on his desk.	Ordered the use of the atomic bomb against Japan.
				The Marshall Plan, named after his secretary of state, facilitated Europe's rebuilding.
				In essence, he began the cold war with what came to be called the Truman Doctrine: America would assist democratic countries threatened by authoritarian forces—basically an attempt to contain the spread of communism. The Korean War began in 1950.
				In 1948 he ended racial segregation in the civil service and armed forces.

(cont.)

NO.	NAME/PARTY/TERM	QUALIFICATION(S)	QUIRK(S)	NOTABLE FEAT(S)/FIASCO(S)
34	Dwight D. Eisenhower Republican 1953–1961	Supreme Allied Commander Europe.	First and only sitting president to be baptized in office.	Ended the Korean War. Authorized all sorts of CIA anticommunist operations. Created the Interstate Highway System. Sent troops into Little Rock, Arkansas, in 1957 to ensure compliance with SCOTUS's desegregation decision on schools in 1954.
35	John F. Kennedy Democrat 1961–1963	Senator (Massachusetts).	The first boy scout to become president, JFK was the first US president to be born in the twentieth century, the youngest man elected president, and the youngest to die, when he was assassinated on November 22, 1963.	JFK's inaugural address included the immortal injunction: "Ask not what your country can do for you—ask what you can do for your country." Cuban Missile Crisis was on his watch.
36	Lyndon B. Johnson Democrat 1963–1969	Veep.	Johnson installed a Fresca soda fountain in a room adjacent to the Oval Office.	Impressive Great Society domestic roster of reforms, including Medicare. He signed the Civil Rights Act into law and also appointed the first African-American to SCOTUS. BUT he sent in ground combat troops to Vietnam in 1965, whereupon America got stuck.

NO.	NAME/PARTY/TERM	QUALIFICATION(S)	QUIRK(S)	NOTABLE FEAT(S)/FIASCO(S)
37	Richard Nixon Republican 1969–1974	Veep.	President when man landed on the moon.	Only president to ever resign from office—did so over Watergate.
				Got US troops out of Vietnam, ended the draft, launched détente, and strengthened diplomatic links with the USSR and China. *But he was the only president to ever resign from office.*
38	Gerald Ford Republican 1974–1977	Veep.	Was a male model who even made the front cover of Cosmo (in his Navy uniform) in 1942.	Ford was America's only unelected president—he wasn't voted in as president OR vice-president. Nixon appointed him veep when Vice-President Agnew resigned (tax evasion).
39	James Carter Democrat 1977–1981	Governor (Georgia).	Infamous speed-reader.	The Argo president. Iran hostage crisis occurred on his watch. As did the 1979 energy crisis.
40	Ronald Reagan Republican 1981–1989	Governor (California).	Comic and jelly bean fan.	The Great Communicator. The Reagan Revolution was all about conservatism and free markets. Peace through strength in foreign policy.
				His 1984 win was a landslide—carried forty-nine states, winning 525 out of 538 electoral votes.
41	George H. W. Bush Republican 1989–1993	Veep, and before that director of central intelligence (DCI). Extremely qualified.	Dislikes broccoli.	Sent troops into Panama and Iraq—and presided over a recession.
				His campaign promise, "Read my lips: no new taxes," penned by later infamous *Wall Street Journal* columnist Peggy Noonan, came back to haunt him.

(cont.)

NO.	NAME/PARTY/TERM	QUALIFICATION(S)	QUIRK(S)	NOTABLE FEAT(S)/FIASCO(S)
42	William J. Clinton Democrat 1993–2001	Governor (Arkansas).	Sent just two e-mails as president.	Budget surplus, low unemployment, peace—and first female US secretary of state, Madeleine Albright. Second US president to be impeached by the House of Representatives (relating to his lying about his relationship with an intern); Senate found him not guilty.
43	George W. Bush Republican 2001–2009	Governor (Texas).	In 2001, Bush II gave first ever speech in Spanish by a US president.	Narrowly defeated (to the extent the Supreme Court weighed in about the Florida result) Al Gore to be transformed after 9/11 into a wartime president.
44	Barack Obama Democrat 2009–2016	Senator (Illinois).	First two-term president to say the presidential oath four times. Supreme Court justice made an error at inauguration No. 1, so Obama took it again the following day. For No. 2, he had to take it the previous day. The Constitution requires the president be sworn in at noon on January 20, but in 2013 it fell on a Sunday, when inaugurations can't happen.	First African-American president. Won a Nobel Peace Prize in 2009. Obama, echoing worldwide public opinion, admitted that he was "surprised." Looks like, thanks to an unlikely ally in conservative (George W. Bush–appointed) Chief Justice John Roberts, Obama's signature achievement will be Obamacare aka the Affordable Care Act.

SOCIAL SURVIVAL STRATEGY

Argument: "Well, of course it was George Washington who started the tradition of foreign policy largely being a presidential concern."
Someone, somewhere, will be complaining about the president's overreach in foreign policy. Use this statement to point out that it is not a new phenomenon, before reflecting that your view on the current occupant of the White House will likely depend on whether you voted for the current occupant or not.

Crisp Fact: "Bill Clinton sent just two e-mails as president."
The way the world operates has changed beyond recognition in so many ways. This should defuse a combustible political discussion, as you can then start reminiscing about landlines.

Pivot: "Gerald Ford (a Republican) was a male model who even made the front cover of *Cosmo*. Perhaps we can blame him for the slippery slope that has led to President X's lightweight publicity choices?"
Presidents (and presidential candidates) submit to increasingly more ridiculous stunts to try and appeal to young voters (the word currently on everyone's lips is *millennials*); they rarely work but are always amusing. This will spark a jovial musing about some of them.

CHEAT SHEET 14—AMERICAN IMPERIALISM

BACKGROUND BRIEFING

Empire is hardly a new phenomenon. Remember the Romans? And of course the Brits had one where the sun never set, before the world wars put the final nail in that particular coffin. The story of history has been one empire ending and another appearing to fill the void.

Whether you label America an empire or prefer to refer to it as the only superpower, albeit one that under the Obama administration increasingly looked inward until ISIS and President Putin had other ideas, history students of the future will perceive the United States as the latest in a long line of empires. They'll write essays pronouncing how ironic it was that America fought against an imperial power and then became one. The past suggests that the age of American empire will end, probably replaced by one to its west—which would make it Asia. We are unlikely to live to see it.

America has always had a touch of the imperialist about it, the urge for expansion. This was first exemplified by its move westward, with Manifest Destiny and all that—consider the treatment of Native American Indians. There was the 1846 Mexican-American War. Subsequently America has been all about influencing other countries via its economic power, its culture—from missionaries to Hollywood—and on occasions by its military clout.

Britain's justification of empire was habitually painted as benevolence. America has often denied empire, but claimed exceptionalism, that it is protecting its extraordinary values. America's values are remarkable, but they are not for everyone, and exceptionalism has predictably higher approval ratings within the US borders than everywhere else. Yes, Americans do have an unease about occupying other countries, but they have done so and there has been much support of surrogates over the years. Small wonder that so many foreigners view America as imperialistic.

Before 1890, America's holdings were basically next-door states and Alaska. By the close of World War I, it had all got a bit foreign. In the 1890s American Samoa and Hawaii were annexed. The 1898 Spanish-American War, aka the "splendid little war," came about because America wanted the Spanish to stop being so oppressive in Cuba. This kerfuffle led to America's winning Guam, the Philippines, and Puerto Rico, while Cuba became "independent"—i.e., America was keeping its puppeteer-like eye on the puppet it had installed.

It should be pointed out that there was a bit of navel-gazing going on in that some American critics pointed out that America was coming over all imperialist. However, that didn't stop President Theodore Roosevelt continuing in the same vein, adding the Roosevelt Corollary to the Monroe Doctrine. Teddy announced in 1904's State of the Union that basically the American sphere of influence included the whole western hemisphere. His motto was "Speak softly and carry a big stick."

Roosevelt didn't actually speak all that softly. He was quite vociferous over the construction of the Panama Canal. Under his successor President William H. Taft, Arizona became a state, completing mainland USA. On President Woodrow Wilson's watch, America bought the Virgin Islands off Denmark in 1917 to counter the threat from the German navy.

For the record books—and if you come across an ungrateful foreigner at a party—American exceptionalism has been needed by the world; it was the game changer in both world wars.

We cover World War I, which kicked off in Europe in 1914, in Cheat Sheet 16. Initially, America's isolationism was the name of the game. President Wilson declared neutrality; America would even trade with both sides. Britain had other ideas. The UK still ruled the waves and its navy imposed a blockade, so America's trade with England and France tripled . . . and its trade with Germany was reduced by 90 percent. The Germans thus engaged in submarine warfare with the Americans, and in 1915 sank the RMS *Lusitania*, a British passenger ship heading from New York to Liverpool that just happened to be carrying four million rounds of ammunition. (Charles Frohman, the American theater producer who put on J. M. "Peter Pan" Barrie's works and is featured in the film and stage musical *Finding Neverland*, was among those who perished on the *Lusitania*.)

The Germans also sent the Zimmermann Telegram, which along with the *Lusitania* helped sway American public opinion toward war. In early 1917 Germany promised Mexico, via coded message, portions of American land (including Texas) in return for Mexico's joining the war against the United States. The Zimmermann Telegram was intercepted and interpreted by the Brits, who showed it to the US. We were coming over all James Bond even back then.

The United States officially entered the Great War in April 1917 with supplies and eventually, after they were trained, troops. Allied victory came in 1918, and the 1919 Treaty of Versailles decided postwar borders from the Middle East to Europe and established an international peace organization called the League of Nations. Incidentally, even though President Woodrow Wilson had been a key player in the organization's formation, America refused to join, as Senate Republicans thought it a supranational government that would limit America's independence in deciding its own policies. You will recognize this as the very same argument that they deploy about the UN and various bits of international law today.

The conditions imposed on Germany were so harsh they caused instability and allowed the rise of Hitler. We reach World War II, also focused on in Cheat Sheet 16. Britain and France declared war after the Nazis invaded Poland in 1939. America turned up when Germany's pal Japan bombed Pearl Harbor in 1941. The Germans surrendered on May 8, 1945—which we know as VE (Victory in Europe) Day, just after President Roosevelt had died of a brain hemorrhage, leaving Harry Truman to finish it all off. Thanks to the Manhattan Project, America now had the bomb. In August Truman dropped it on Hiroshima and then Nagasaki. The Japanese surrendered. Approximately 45 to 60 million people died during World War II, including around 6 million Jews in the Holocaust—and Pandora's box had been opened.

The Soviet Union may have been America's wartime ally, but America was not about to sit about while an alternative version of totalitarianism spread westward. Winston Churchill, as usual, put it best when in 1946 he noted that an "iron curtain has descended across the continent." The cold war began, which we also cover in Cheat Sheet 16. It really is quite the read (or something).

Not to put too fine a point on a description of the cold war, its concept can essentially be understood by the song lyrics "Anything you can do, / I can do better." etc. By August 1949 the Soviets had tested their first nuclear weapon. So instead of total mutual annihilation, there were arms races, space races, and communism's "containment" via proxy wars in Korea from 1950 to 1953 and then... Vietnam.

KEY TERM: MCCARTHYISM

Paranoia about the rise of communism, named after Senator Joseph McCarthy, who ferreted out communists in 1950s with all the accuracy they sussed out witches in Salem in 1692.

Backing up for a second, JFK was elected in 1960. He may have been in office for only two years and ten months, but he managed to accelerate the space race and the American role in Vietnam, plus he oversaw the Bay of Pigs fiasco and the Cuban Missile Crisis. The energy of youth—he was the youngest person ever elected president, after all.

KEY TERMS: BAY OF PIGS AND CUBAN MISSILE CRISIS

- In 1959 Castro overthrew Cuba's America-backed, repressive, corrupt dictator-type president (sound familiar?). Cue the CIA and State Department trying to remove the too-friendly-with-communism Castro, culminating in April 1961 with an invasion by 1,400 CIA-trained Cuban exiles at Cuba's Bay of Pigs. They were outnumbered and surrendered, although the espionage and sabotage campaigns continued with Operation Mongoose.

- The Cuban Missile Crisis took place in October 1962. The USSR was trying to install nuclear-armed missiles in Cuba. Since Cuba is around a hundred miles from the USA, the idea went down like a lead balloon in Washington. The Americans blockaded Cuba and a game of chicken transpired. Disaster was averted when Nikita Khrushchev removed the missiles and Kennedy agreed not to invade Cuba—and clandestinely said he'd take American missiles out of Turkey.

To the quagmire of Vietnam. The seeds of Vietnam were sown in the Truman administration, which committed to South Vietnam that America would protect it from communist advances. Eisenhower sent CIA operatives and military advisors, while JFK sent troops. It was his successor Lyndon Jonson who sent the troops into full combat in 1965—and Richard Nixon who ordered their withdrawal in 1973. America failed with this one. In 1975 communist forces took Saigon, and in 1976 the country was unified as the Socialist Republic of Vietnam. More than 3 million people, including more than 55,000 Americans, died and billions of dollars were spent. This was perhaps the moment America should have learned the lesson forever that being a superpower doesn't mean you have superpowers.

Now Nixon may have got in trouble for his stage management of the domestic side of things. But he—along with his man Henry Kissinger—was a bit of an operator when it came to foreign policy. China and the Soviet Union were intrinsically suspicious of each other, and Nixon, known for his anticommunism early in his career (so no one was about to accuse him of being procommunist), played on that. Nixon's triangular diplomacy—he even trotted off to both China and the USSR in 1972—attained détente, a relaxation in the tension between the other two countries and America.

The 1970s were not a pretty sight, and we're not talking about the shaggy hair. There were the OPEC shenanigans with oil, looked at in Cheat Sheet 17, that caused high energy prices. Worth noting, however, this high point. President Carter was not just the Iran-hostage-crisis/*Argo* president, but he also did sort a deal between Egypt and Israel in the form of the Camp David Accords, which we also delve into in Cheat Sheet 17.

Détente pretty much died with the 1979 Soviet occupation of Afghanistan, swiftly followed by the arrival of President evil-empire-rhetoric Reagan. The Reagan Doctrine was all about supporting "Freedom Fighters" for anyone opposing Communism.

Including . . . the mujahideen rebels fighting against the Soviets in Afghanistan. Note that *mujahideen* is the plural of *mujahid*, which means in Arabic someone engaged in jihad, which you may also know by the term *jihadist*. There is much debate about the consequences of this: Did America essentially create Islamic terrorism? What happened to those arms and those rebels when America later waged its own Afghan war? If you ever meet specialists on the subject, sit them down and ask them questions. You know enough to know that you don't know enough about this, and it would take an entire book to answer them. This is a Cheat Sheet.

So, back to this era, where state-sponsored terrorism was a real problem. A suicide bomber killed 241 US service personnel in Lebanon in 1983. Governments including those in Syria, Libya, and Iran (yes, them) were believed to be training terrorists.

Mikhail Gorbachev got power in 1985, tensions reduced thanks to his glasnost (openness) and perestroika (reform), and by 1991 the Soviet Union had collapsed and the Berlin Wall fell.

All's well that ends well. Well, not exactly . . .

WHY IT MATTERS TODAY

America had won! The world's only superpower. But the rules changed.

WISE WORDS

Christ, I miss the cold war.

—M, James Bond's head of MI6 in
Casino Royale, 2006

There is a big difference between pre– and post–cold war foreign policy. During the cold war, America was trying to affect nations' external behavior. It didn't really matter what they were doing internally, as long as they were allies and not procommunist. Intervention potentially led to superpower confrontation.

Post cold war? Foreign policy is about affecting what is going on internally in nations.

But here's the thing. It is very tricky to have an impact on what is going on inside a nation, to reconstruct politics and culture in foreign lands, where your priorities and beliefs are not necessarily theirs. The people who populate these places are not objects, but subjects. Mere money and rhetoric won't cut it. Examples: Bosnia, Afghanistan, Libya, Iraq, Egypt, Syria, Ukraine . . .

Initially the 1991 Gulf War in Iraq seemed quite the success. It was no Vietnam. Saddam Hussein's Iraq had invaded Kuwait, which had a large amount of oil that needed rescuing, while neighboring Saudi Arabia had a large amount of oil that needed protecting. Sorry, did I slip with my typing there? Nation-states needed rescuing and protecting. The big change now was that Russia wasn't standing in America's way or anything. And that CNN broadcast all of Bush I's war was a major television event.

But the Gulf War didn't stop conflict and resentment brewing in the region. We leave historian-psychologists to talk about the father-son Iraq complex—Bush II of course had his Iraq moment in 2003.

President Clinton had to deal with the end of cold war fallout in Yugoslavia, which caused centuries' worth of hatred between competing ethnic groups to bubble up. Peacekeeping troops were dispatched to Bosnia to stop ethnic cleansing. As civilians starved in Somalia, American troops were sent to provide food in the war-ravaged region, as they were to reinstate Haiti's democratically elected president. Clinton also ordered the bombing of supposed terrorist bases in Sudan and Afghanistan.

That's worth a repeat, because I certainly had forgotten about it. Well, I was at school, all I was interested in coming out of America was *Beverly Hills 90210*. Yes, Clinton I bombed Afghanistan.

Say what you will and you do about President George W. Bush, but his presidency became defined by an unimaginable, horrific event: 9/11. Three thousand people were killed when nineteen Al-Qaeda militants hijacked four planes and crashed into the World Trade Center, a field in Western Pennsylvania, and the Pentagon. They were allegedly acting in retaliation for America's support of Israel, its involvement in the Gulf War, and its continued military presence in the Middle East. Bush II announced the "War on Terror" on September 20, swiftly followed by intervention in Afghanistan. Unfortunately the Brits couldn't find a solution in Afghanistan, the Soviets couldn't find a solution in Afghanistan—and the definition of insanity is? Doing the same thing over and over again and expecting different results.

The debate will rage for centuries to come about America's reaction to 9/11 and what it has done to civil liberties. The Patriot Act expanded intelligence services and law enforcement's investigative and surveillance powers. The Department of Homeland Security was founded to manage federal counterterrorism. So came the controversies over the alleged human rights abuses to detainees at Guantánamo Bay, aka Gitmo, and the 2003 invasion of Iraq for possessing "weapons of mass destruction." Bush II called the "intelligence failure" in Iraq his biggest presidential regret. For Iraq's WMD stockpiles didn't exist, however much some have tried to rewrite evidence on the issue.

Obama was elected to end wars, not start them. Which he managed to do in Iraq by 2011. (We look at what happened next—ISIS et al.—in Cheat Sheet 17.) What perhaps was surprising, especially to his most fervent fans, was how very similar he was in some ways to his predecessors. More troops initially ended up in Afghanistan. He didn't close Gitmo. He did get Bin Laden. And his National Security Agency brought us a new concept of global surveillance.

For those who have seen me on air, this is where I drone on.

About drones. It's my thing, skip it if I'm boring you, but it's my book and I'll rant if I want to.

Armed drones are remote-controlled pilotless aerial vehicles that are able to hit targets of interest, including killing individuals. The US army purchased its first spy drone in 1959, and the first strike by an armed drone took place in Pakistan in 2004, under then-president Bush II. Under Obama they became America's go-to tool of choice in both its conventional and its shadow wars.

I believe history will judge President Obama harshly on his short-termism on the drone issue. Along with the arguments about the way his intelligence agencies have been collecting data on us all, Obama's use of drones has been about as far away from his first presidential campaign slogan of hope and change and his Nobel Peace Prize as you can get. Perhaps the reason this is so disappointing is that President Obama is a constitutional lawyer whose actions are likely to land our descendants in a world that looks like a James Cameron *Terminator* movie. Obama's attempts to address drone protocol in his second term were too little, too late.

Domestically it is estimated that by 2020, up to 30,000 drones will be peering down on US soil snooping on US citizens.

Internationally? The precedent set by the Obama administration is a disaster. It went ahead and regularly utilized drone attacks when where they stand in law was murky at best. They've assassinated people, including Americans. There's the question of who pulled the trigger. Under international conventions, civilians cannot engage in war, but CIA members, behind the controls of some of those drone strikes, are civilians. America unilaterally decided that it could send drones over borders to kill its enemies. Into countries it had not declared war on. Unsurprisingly, the world is now involved in a new arms race. What happens when everyone else starts using drones the way the United States has already done in Yemen, Pakistan,

Somalia, and elsewhere? When the Chinese start taking out perceived threats to their state in other states? When governments of other countries assassinate escaped dissidents and other enemies in a country not their own? If Uncle Sam protests, which it will inevitably do, America will be looking mighty hypocritical. A collective international decision was needed about the rules of engagement of killing by remote control before America started doing it. The US has set a dangerous precedent—for itself.

Added to which, the use of drones is often counterproductive. In some countries, drones have been the only face of American foreign policy for years. Drones don't treat terrorism's symptoms. They more often than not worsen them, inevitably sometimes killing the wrong targets, radicalizing local populations, and thus causing more terrorism. And they have security flaws—the Nevada US base from which some are remotely flown has not proven immune to computer viruses.

A science fiction scenario is becoming real. Experts believe that unmanned aircraft will eventually take over most tasks currently undertaken by manned systems. That drones will one day be the size of insects and birds and that swarms may be used to overwhelm modern defense systems. Obama's riding roughshod over international law has put America in danger in the future.

It's a balance. America famously has a somewhat apathetic view of international law. The argument often goes that it is incompatible with the US constitution. Guantánamo was such a scandal inside America because it flouted American law. America has not signed on to the International Criminal Court, which was founded in 2002 to "bring to justice the perpetrators of the worst crimes known to humankind—war crimes, crimes against humanity, and genocide." The counterargument is that if America led the way in a global standard of justice, some of the nations who have a more dubious approach to it, such as Saudi Arabia and China, might be forced into a bit of a rethink.

Enough. America did rescue the world twice, after all. And after a phase of neoisolationism, the rise of ISIS and Russia's hard-line posturing has reminded much of the world how much it needs America the Beautiful.

TALKING POINTS

Classic lines to make you seem wise:
- Foreign policy? All politics are local.

- What happens when an exceptional country behaves in an ungovernable way?

- Foreign policy is often determined by unanticipated events.

- America considering intervention in foreign lands? These will see you through—they have done me on air enough times:

   *Can America afford to be the world's policeman either financially or personally? An estimated twenty-two veterens take their own lives every day. Surely it is excessive that America accounts for around half of the total global defense spending? Perhaps America should be aiming to be global police chief instead? A Fox News host refused to ever have me return to a show I did most weekends after I employed that line on him.

   *Statecraft is not moral empathy. You have to balance the humanitarian urge to intervene with what happens next.

   *There is a limit to what the US can do—we're in a no-win situation: America can harm with the best of intentions and it is extremely difficult to get good outcomes inside other countries. Example? Afghanistan, Somalia, Iraq, Syria . . .

   *Post the Iraq catastrophe, Americans know that, as a superpower, when you take sides in a civil war, the outcome is your responsibility to shoulder.

   *What about the law of diminishing returns?

* As Churchill said, "to jaw-jaw is always better than to war-war."

- The French called the American soldiers pitching up in France in 1918 "doughboys," as they were immature. It cost millions of dollars to treat the around 15 percent who contracted VD from Parisian prostitutes.

- During World War I, the German army dropped leaflets to try to convince African-American troops that if the Germans won, society would be less racist.

- In April 1917, when America finally got into World War I, the United States military had only enough bullets for two days of fighting. Oh, how things change . . .

- In 1961, the USSR built the Berlin Wall, which divided East Berlin from West Berlin. JFK pitched up to West Berlin in 1963 to show solidarity and ended his speech with *"Ich bin ein Berliner,"* which translates to "I am a jelly doughnut." Maybe.

- Russia acting up again? Quote Churchill (again): "Russia is a riddle wrapped in a mystery inside an enigma." For an added bonus, mention that *fun* is not a word that exists in the Russian language.

RED FLAGS

- Foreign, and with an American talking about Uncle Sam? He or she is probably referring to the United States, not to his or her uncle Sam. The nickname apparently appeared in the vernacular during the War of 1812 and was drawn from the Troy, New York, meat-packer Samuel "Uncle Sam" Wilson.

- Don't get these mixed up: A hawk is someone who advocates an aggressive foreign policy, while a dove believes in a conciliatory and peaceful one. Just to confuse matters, it's perfectly possible to have a Republican dove and a Democratic hawk.

- Don't start going on about how much America gives in foreign aid, as you'll probably bump into someone who will wipe the floor with your argument.

  * It doesn't, compared to other countries in percentage terms (somewhere around 0.2 percent in national income versus, say, the UK, which is 0.5 percent).

  * The foreign aid bill is in the tens of billions, while Iraq and Afghanistan cost in the trillions. It's a drop in the ocean compared to what the taxpayer contributes to defense spending (just under 20 percent of your federal taxes go to it).

  * Arguably foreign aid has a much better—cheaper—outcome for America than invasion.

  * Israel gets more than $3 billion a year in foreign aid from America, about $77 per Israeli. Those in the poorest nations get around $3. Go down a route discussing this and it's highly likely things will get very ugly very quickly.

- The 1970s TV show *M*A*S*H* was set in a Korean War innovation, the Mobile Army Surgical Hospital. It's not about Vietnam.

- Trying to keep the peace with a gun lover? Possibly not wise to get on your high horse and claim America is better at dealing with foreign threats than home ones, using US gun death versus terrorist death statistics. Or to point out that more Americans have died from guns in the United States since 1970 than they have in all the wars in Uncle Sam's two-hundred-plus-year history.

- With a French person? Don't bring up "freedom fries." Such relabeling happened in 2003 because the French opposed the Iraq War (quite). Sort of ruined the more distinguished history of renaming dishes here. During World War I, frankfurters and hamburgers were called hot dogs and liberty meat, respectively.

- The military is comprised of 0.5 percent of the US population, the lowest rate since World War II, and is mostly made up of men and women from rural and southern states. Careful of the phrase: "Thank you for your service." Does it really mean "thank you for doing something I don't want to do and I certainly don't want my kids doing"?

WISE WORDS

No foreign policy—no matter how ingenious—has any chance of success if it is born in the minds of a few and carried in the hearts of none.

—Henry A. Kissinger

SOCIAL SURVIVAL STRATEGY

Argument: "History suggests that the age of American empire will end, probably replaced by one to its west—which would make it Asia. We are unlikely to live to see it."
This can elevate a dispute about America's so-called demise to a higher and thus less offensive level. Empire seems to be going forever westward—we kick off with ancient Egypt, then ancient Greece, then the Europeans (especially those Victorian Brits), followed by the Americans.

Crisp Fact: "During World War I, the German army dropped leaflets in an attempt to convince African-American troops that if they won, society would be less racist."
In every war, propagandists look for a weakness in the enemy's society that they can exploit and thus divide. If you're on the topic and you want to make jaws drop, this deed will do it.

Pivot: "Domestically it is estimated that by 2020, up to 30,000 drones will be peering down on US soil snooping on US citizens.

Would you own one, or do you consider them a menace to society—and planes?"

To many, the FAA is going to be working overtime on this one. But you can soon get out of any sort of tricky terrain by moving toward travel in the here and now and inquiring if the person you're talking to has any tips about not being assigned a middle seat on an airplane.

CHEAT SHEET 15—GRID OF KINGS AND QUEENS OF ENGLAND FROM 1066

NO.	NAME/HOUSE/ AREAS OF UK RULED/REIGN	QUALIFICATION(S)	QUIRK(S)	NOTABLE FEAT(S)/FIASCO(S)
1	William I Normandy England 1066–1087	Aka William the Conqueror. Managed to do what Hitler couldn't over 800 years later and invade England. Defeated King Harold II, the last Anglo-Saxon king of England, at the Battle of Hastings. According to legend Harold died courtesy of an arrow through his eye.	Until the Middletons, William I's was the last family with real working-class antecedents to be associated with the royal family. His mother, a washerwoman of Falaise in Normandy, gave birth to him illegitimately in 1028.	Commissioned the Domesday survey, which collected thorough records of property and land. It resulted in the two-volume Domesday Book of 1086, which still exists today. William I completed the establishment of feudalism and kept the barons under control.
2	William II Normandy England 1087–1100	Third son of William the Conqueror. Nicknamed Rufus, as he was strong, ruddy, and opinionated.	Died on a hunting trip in the New Forest—he was shot by an arrow. May have been assassination. Rumored that Walter Tirel did it on the orders of William's little brother Henry, who promptly seized the throne.	Spent most of his time trying to capture Normandy from his older brother Robert (William I split the inheritance up). Had a lot of skirmishes with Malcolm of Scotland, who in the end was killed/defeated at the Battle of Alnwick.

(cont.)

NO.	NAME/HOUSE/ AREAS OF UK RULED/REIGN	QUALIFICATION(S)	QUIRK(S)	NOTABLE FEAT(S)/FIASCO(S)
3	Henry I Normandy England 1100–1135	William II's little brother. (Elder bro Robert was a threat hanging over him too). Nicknamed Beauclerc, as he was a bit of a scholar. Probably first Norman king fluent in English.	By marrying Mathilda of Scotland, he established peaceful relations with the country. Allegedly had around twenty illegitimate children. In 1120, his legitimate sons William (his heir) and Richard drowned in the White Ship, which sank in the English Channel. Henry died in Normandy after apparently eating a "surfeit of lampreys" (an eel-like fish).	Terribly good bureaucrat—lots of centralizing of administration going on. His Pipe Roll of 1130 was the first exchequer account to survive. Finally managed to get Normandy off Robert at the Battle of Tinchebrai in 1106 in France. Robert spent the remaining twenty-eight years of his life as his brother's prisoner.
4	Stephen Blois England 1135–1154	Slight drama here. Henry had a legitimate daughter, Matilda, but the barons were not into the female ruler concept. Stephen, a grandson of William the Conqueror, was elected king in 1135.	Extremely handsome and charming, supposedly.	Unimpressed at being bypassed, Matilda landed in England in 1139. Cue civil war— Matilda was even briefly declared queen but was eventually defeated at the Battle of Faringdon in 1145. Her eldest son Henry invaded England in 1149 and 1153. Stephen wanted his son Eustace to be heir, but he died in 1153, so Henry was named it.

NO.	NAME/HOUSE/ AREAS OF UK RULED/REIGN	QUALIFICATION(S)	QUIRK(S)	NOTABLE FEAT(S)/FIASCO(S)
5	Henry II Plantagenet (Angevin) England 1154–1189	Son of Henry I's daughter Matilda and Geoffrey Plantagenet, aka Geoffrey V, Count of Anjou. First of fourteen Plantagenet kings. Within that line there were four distinct houses: Angevin, Plantagenet, Lancaster, and York.	His sons rebelled. Against him. Most markedly in 1173–74. Henry actually died while at war with his son Richard.	Began his reign probably the most powerful European monarch. His empire stretched from the Scottish border to the Pyrenees. As a result he spent only thirteen years of his reign in England; the remaining twenty-one were on the continent. Thus he established a more efficient government/justice system. His mate Thomas à Becket (HIM) became archbishop of Canterbury in 1162. But instead of helping curb church privileges, as obviously the king would have preferred, Becket defended them. In 1170, four knights of the king's household murdered Becket. The pope was furious with Henry.
6	Richard I Plantagenet (Angevin) England 1189–1199	You know this one. He was Richard I the Lionheart or Coeur de Lion, Henry II's son.	Richard defined the term crusader. Spent just ten months of a ten-year reign in England thanks to his participation in the Crusades. Obsessed with the Holy Lands. Spoke only French. Killed by a crossbow bolt in a minor siege at Châlus-Chabrol in 1199. No heir.	Appointed William Longchamp to be chancellor of England while he was globetrotting, but Richard's brother John overthrew him. Richard turned up after at one point being captured on his travels and was recrowned in 1194.

(cont.)

NO.	NAME/HOUSE/ AREAS OF UK RULED/REIGN	QUALIFICATION(S)	QUIRK(S)	NOTABLE FEAT(S)/FIASCO(S)
7	John Plantagenet (Angevin) England 1199–1216	Richard's brother John. Nicknamed Lackland, probably because he was lacking land, as he was the youngest of Henry II's five sons.	He's the Bad King John in the Robin Hood legend. Died with England in civil war.	History has not been kind to John. Henry II's vast lands were reduced to a fragment. He fell out with the pope and was into high taxation and ruthless policies, as he was embroiled in constant war in France. As a result John was forced to sign—drumroll; this is the big one, impacts the USA; the Fifth Amendment is a direct descendant of it—the Magna Carta in 1215. It set LIMITS on the king's powers—the king was subject to the law, not above it. It restated the rights of the barons and the church. The Magna Carta subsequently became the basis of the liberties of the English people, a significant definition of aspects of English law.
8	Henry III Plantagenet England 1216–1272	King John's son. Crowned at age nine, so England ruled by regents. Got power himself in 1227 on the basis he accepted the Magna Carta.	Extravagant, everyone hated his tax demands, but he did donate a lot to charity—including to the rebuilding of Westminster Abbey (Diana's funeral, the marriage venue of Kate and Wills), which began in 1245.	Annoyed the barons with foreign schemes and favorites. Ended up being imprisoned thanks to the Second Barons' War of 1264 led by Simon de Montfort. Henry escaped and finally got the better of de Montfort at the Battle of Evesham in 1265. Royal authority was restored.

NO.	NAME/HOUSE/ AREAS OF UK RULED/REIGN	QUALIFICATION(S)	QUIRK(S)	NOTABLE FEAT(S)/FIASCO(S)
9	Edward I Plantagenet England and Wales 1272–1307	Son of Henry III. On a crusade when he inherited the throne. Nicknamed Longshanks.	Loved building castles. Behind Caernarfon Castle, Beaumaris Castle, Harlech Castle, and Conwy Castle. During the fourteenth and fifteenth centuries, the Exchequer paid to keep the candles burning around his dead (entombed) body.	Edward I wanted to create a British empire (dominated by England, naturally). He conquered Wales and named his eldest son the Prince of Wales—a tradition which continues until this day. The "Great Cause" of Scotland proved trickier. Cue Sir William Wallace and Robert the Bruce fighting off Edward's pretensions. Oh, and Parliament began to develop its modern form with the Model Parliament of 1295.
10	Edward II Plantagenet England and Wales 1307–1327	Son of Edward I. He was created the first Prince of Wales in 1301.	Edward II was deposed by his wife Isabella (Philip IV of France's daughter) and her amour Roger Mortimer. Edward II gave up his crown to Edward III. Edward II was later murdered at Berkeley Castle.	Into favorites, most famously Piers Gaveston and Hugh le Despenser. Edward II was inept. Cue the barons getting very irritated. He also was defeated by Scot Robert the Bruce in 1314 at Bannockburn, which did nothing for his popularity.

(cont.)

NO.	NAME/HOUSE/ AREAS OF UK RULED/REIGN	QUALIFICATION(S)	QUIRK(S)	NOTABLE FEAT(S)/FIASCO(S)
11	Edward III Plantagenet England and Wales 1327–1377	Although king in title from 1327 (when he was fourteen), he took power from his mother and her lover Roger Mortimer in 1330. She spent the rest of her life imprisoned.	Created the Duchy of Cornwall so the heir to the throne had an independent income. This is where Prince Charles gets his cash from today (you can even buy Duchy of Cornwall biscuits). Edward III also founded the Order of the Garter in 1348. This still exists and is normally what the royals are wearing when you see them in particularly flouncy garb in the *Mail Online*'s sidebar of shame.	Managed to start the Hundred Years' War between England and France. Also had the unfortunate timing to have to deal with the Black Death plague outbreaks of 1348–49, 1361–62, and 1369. This caused massive social issues and deflation. Dad to both the Black Prince, the infamously brilliant military man, and John of Gaunt, who from now on in keeps cropping up.
12	Richard II Plantagenet England and Wales 1377–1399	The Black Prince, Edward III's eldest son, died in 1376, and his son, the king's grandson, ten-year-old Richard II, succeeded. Initially Richard's uncles John of Gaunt and Thomas of Gloucester ruled.	Extremely cultured, Richard II was one of the greatest royal patrons of the arts. Patron to Chaucer. Transformed the Norman Westminster Hall.	Authoritarian and argued with Parliament. Then had to face the Peasants' Revolt in 1381 (the 1380 Poll Tax was deeply unpopular). Managed to get a twenty-eight-year truce in the Hundred Years' War. His cousin Henry of Bolingbroke (son of John of Gaunt and Blanche of Lancaster) led a revolt against him in 1399. Richard was captured, deposed, and then murdered in Pontefract Castle. Henry did have him buried in Westminster Abbey, though.

NO.	NAME/HOUSE/ AREAS OF UK RULED/REIGN	QUALIFICATION(S)	QUIRK(S)	NOTABLE FEAT(S)/FIASCO(S)
13	Henry IV Plantagenet (Lancaster) England and Wales 1399–1413	Stole the throne off his cousin Richard II after Richard deprived Henry of his inheritance when his dad John of Gaunt died.	Beleaguered by illness from 1405 onward, his son Henry played a bigger role in government, even opposing his dad at times.	Unsurprisingly, considering how he got the throne, his reign was full of rebellion and instability. There was also an outbreak of plague in 1400.
14	Henry V Plantagenet (Lancaster) England and Wales 1413–1422	Son of Henry IV.	Educated and into liturgical music. He even gave pensions to the well-known composers of his time.	British people still talk about Henry V's notorious win in the Hundred Years' War at the 1415 Battle of Agincourt, especially if you're traveling to France. I'm not joking. Six thousand French-men were killed and fewer than four hundred English soldiers were, despite the fact that the English force was inferior. Shakespeare later immortalized the encounter, giving Henry V the line: "Once more unto the breach, dear friends, once more." Henry V managed to die of dysentery early despite doing rather well with France, even being recognized as heir to the French throne.

(cont.)

NO.	NAME/HOUSE/ AREAS OF UK RULED/REIGN	QUALIFICATION(S)	QUIRK(S)	NOTABLE FEAT(S)/FIASCO(S)
15	Henry VI Plantagenet (Lancaster) England and Wales 1422–1461	Son of Henry V, he ended up with the throne when he was less than a year old. Also got the French crown when his grandfather Charles VI of France died, but the lands proved tricky to hold on to, what with Joan of Arc and all. In England, his uncles Cardinal Beaufort and the Duke of Gloucester ran things, although they didn't get on.	Loved education. Founded Eton College (where Wills and Harry went to school) and King's College, Cambridge (they weren't clever enough to go there).	1453 marked the end of the Hundred Years' War, so his reign wasn't all bad. Scrap that, it was a disaster. Henry had a very domineering wife, Margaret of Anjou, which didn't help with the Yorkist (symbol: the white rose) and Lancastrian (symbol: the red rose) factions. Civil war, the War of the Roses, broke out. It was Henry (Lancaster) versus Richard, Duke of York, and had its roots in the sons of Edward III and whether succession could pass through girls. Richard was killed in 1460, but his son Edward continued the fight. Henry was deposed in 1461, captured in 1465, restored in 1470, and imprisoned and put to death in 1471.
16	Edward IV Plantagenet (York) England and Wales 1461–1483	Son of Richard, Duke of York. Lost the throne briefly back to Henry VI.	Ever watch the Starz series *The White Queen*? He's THAT Edward, the Max Irons one. Fell in love with Elizabeth Woodville. Had three sons, including the Princes in the Tower, and seven daughters, including Elizabeth (impor- tant later). Oh, and four illegitimate children.	Actually managed to restore some order. Big falling out with his pal the Earl of Warwick, who ended up switching sides in the War of the Roses. Made peace with France in cunning fashion. Made friends with the merchant community and made loads of money off of wool. The War of the Roses did rumble on, though, until the start of the sixteenth century.

NO.	NAME/HOUSE/ AREAS OF UK RULED/REIGN	QUALIFICATION(S)	QUIRK(S)	NOTABLE FEAT(S)/FIASCO(S)
17	Edward V Plantagenet (York) England and Wales 1483	Edward IV's son by Elizabeth Woodville. Got the throne at age twelve. Since he was a minor, his uncle Richard, Duke of Gloucester, was made Protector.	Elizabeth, his mother, had three daughters before she finally gave birth to Edward in Westminster Abbey (it was while dad Edward IV was briefly out of power). NB: She already had two sons by her first husband Sir John Grey (he died before she ended up with Edward IV).	Richard, Duke of Gloucester, didn't do much protecting. Edward V and his little brother Richard were declared illegitimate, were taken to the Tower of London, and were never seen again. Hence the Princes in the Tower.
18	Richard III Plantagenet (York) England and Wales 1483–1485	Stole the throne off Edward V, whom he was supposed to be protecting.	First laws written entirely in English passed in his reign. In September 2012 his bones were found in a car park—seems Shakespeare had it right, and he did have curvature of the spine.	Richard III actually wasn't the worst ruler England's ever had, but the Princes in the Tower thing did nothing for his popularity. Henry Tudor (a descendant of John of Gaunt, one of Edward III's younger sons) claimed the throne when Richard took it. Henry defeated Richard's army in 1485 at the Battle of Bosworth Field. Richard was the last English king to die in battle, and this was the final big altercation of the War of the Roses.

(cont.)

NO.	NAME/HOUSE/ AREAS OF UK RULED/REIGN	QUALIFICATION(S)	QUIRK(S)	NOTABLE FEAT(S)/FIASCO(S)
19	Henry VII Tudor England, Wales, and Ireland 1485–1509	In a GENIUS move, one you should talk about whenever mentioning English history, in 1486 Henry VII married Elizabeth of York, Edward IV's daughter, thus uniting the Houses of York and Lancaster. So started the Tudor dynasty, which lasted until Elizabeth I's death in 1603. The Tudor rose emblem is the combined red (Lancaster) and white (York) rose.	Henry VII had to deal with revolts, so he formed a personal bodyguard, the Yeomen of the Guard. They still protect the queen and are the oldest military corps in existence.	Good at administration. Shrewd with money and left a full treasury. Married his children off to other royals to help maintain peace. One daughter, Margaret, married James IV of Scottish (the man who unified the English and Scottish crowns in 1603; James VI of Scotland, aka James I of England, was descended from her).
20	Henry VIII Tudor England, Wales, and Ireland 1509–1547	Was Henry VII's second son and was not supposed to be king. Then his elder brother Arthur died in 1502 and Henry married Arthur's wife, Catherine of Aragon, daughter of King Ferdinand and Queen Isabella of Spain.	You know this. Checkered love life. Divorced (Catherine of Aragon), beheaded (Anne Boleyn), died (Jane Seymour, the big love who died giving him his longed-for son), divorced (Anne of Cleves), beheaded (Catherine Howard), survived (Catherine Parr). The wives gave him three legitimate children that lived beyond infancy—	Strong, ruthless; buy a specialist book to read about his foreign policy. As a young man he was athletic and highly intelligent. Wrote books, played musical instruments, and was a composer. Given the title Defender of the Faith by the pope in 1521 for writing a bestseller attacking Martin Luther and supporting the Roman Catholic church. Cardinal Wolsey, an Ipswich butcher's son, became lord chancellor in 1515 and built Hampton Court Palace, which was much grander than anything the king owned at the time. Wolsey, however, failed to get

NO.	NAME/HOUSE/ AREAS OF UK RULED/REIGN	QUALIFICATION(S)	QUIRK(S)	NOTABLE FEAT(S)/FIASCO(S)
20 (cont.)			Mary, Elizabeth, and the sickly Edward. Both princesses at one stage or another were declared illegitimate.	Henry a divorce from his first wife, so he was replaced with Thomas More. Then came the break with Catholic Rome and the English Protestant Reformation, and through Thomas Cromwell came the Dissolution of the Monasteries (Henry appropriated the church's assets). See/read Hilary Mantel's *Wolf Hall*.
21	Edward VI Tudor England, Wales, and Ireland 1547–1553	Son of Henry VIII and his third wife Jane Seymour. Became king at age nine. As a result, the Duke of Somerset and then the Earl of Warwick (later created Duke of Northumberland) ran the show.	Northumberland married off his son Lord Guilford Dudley to Lady Jane Grey, a great-niece of Henry VIII. Edward, contrary to the succession sorted by Henry VIII, made Jane his heir and died.	Intellectual, fluent in Greek and Latin, but physically a bit of a weakling. Edward was educated by those who believed in Protestantism rather than Catholicism and introduced the *Book of Common Prayer* in 1549. Latin services were replaced with English ones and various Roman Catholic practices including statues and stained glass were eradicated. Cue rebellions in Cornwall and Devon.
*	Lady Jane Grey	Sixteen years old, she was a pawn in the game of her father-in-law, the Duke of Northumberland.	Reigned for nine days and later executed with her husband, the Duke of Northumberland's son.	The country wasn't having this. They rallied to Catholic Mary, the daughter of Henry VIII and Catherine of Aragon.

(cont.)

NO.	NAME/HOUSE/ AREAS OF UK RULED/REIGN	QUALIFICATION(S)	QUIRK(S)	NOTABLE FEAT(S)/FIASCO(S)
22	Mary I Tudor England, Wales, and Ireland 1553–1558	Daughter of Henry VIII and Catherine of Aragon. Nicknamed "Bloody Mary," as she persecuted Protestants. Penchant for burning them.	First queen regnant—i.e., reigning in her own right, rather than being a queen via marriage to a king.	Somewhat limited in getting Catholicism fully back, partly because loads of aristocrats had benefited from the dissolution of the monasteries. Aged thirty-seven on her accession, she married Philip II of Spain in 1554. Craved an heir to consolidate her religious reforms and ensure her half sister Elizabeth would be out of the running. The nuptials were unpopular with the public and the marriage was childless.
23	Elizabeth I Tudor England, Wales, and Ireland 1558–1603	Daughter of Henry VIII and Anne Boleyn. Rock star. Reigned for forty-five years. Aka Gloriana, Good Queen Bess, and the Virgin Queen.	Well-educated, bright, fluent in six languages. Used her feminine wiles as a political weapon (taking after her mother?). Endless rulers of European states tried to woo her. Fable has it her true love was her homegrown favorite Robert Dudley, first Earl of Leicester. Died a legend in her own lifetime. The date of her accession was a national holiday for two hundred years.	Established a secure Church of England. The doctrines set in the 39 Articles of 1563 were a compromise between Roman Catholicism and Protestantism. Elizabeth was a pragmatist, refused to "make windows into men's souls . . . there is only one Jesus Christ and all the rest is a dispute over trifles" and just asked for outward uniformity. Skilled at choosing her ministers. Made at least twenty-three regional visits, "progresses," so the nation could fall in love with her. Dealt with plots by Mary Queen of Scots and had a big victory in 1588 over the Spanish Armada—a fleet of ships attempting invasion. This was the era of Shakespeare, Francis Drake, and Walter Raleigh. The first American colony was founded and named Virginia after Elizabeth the Virgin Queen.

NO.	NAME/HOUSE/ AREAS OF UK RULED/REIGN	QUALIFICATION(S)	QUIRK(S)	NOTABLE FEAT(S)/FIASCO(S)
24	James I Stuart England, Wales, Scotland, and Ireland 1603–1625	Son of Mary Queen of Scots (a woman who had caused Elizabeth all sorts of drama) and descended from Henry VII's daughter Margaret. Had already been King James VI of Scotland for thirty-six years (he became king as a baby) when he got the English throne. Thus for the first time the English and Scottish thrones were combined and a single monarch now reigned both realms.	The UK still celebrates the fact (with fireworks and bonfires) that James I wasn't killed on November 5, 1605, with Guy Fawkes's Gunpowder Plot, which was an attempt by Catholics to blow up the Houses of Parliament. Very fond of the Duke of Buckingham. Arts patron who still had Shakespeare about. Employed the architect Inigo Jones to build the current Banqueting House in Whitehall.	Able theologian (Presbyterian and Calvinist type), which was useful as religious debate was far from over. The new translation of the Bible that he ordered became known as the Authorized King James's Version of the Bible. Jamestown founded in Virginia. Mixed relations with Parliament during his reign.

(cont.)

NO.	NAME/HOUSE/ AREAS OF UK RULED/REIGN	QUALIFICATION(S)	QUIRK(S)	NOTABLE FEAT(S)/FIASCO(S)
25	Charles I Stuart England, Wales, Scotland, and Ireland 1625–1649	Son of James I and Anne of Denmark. Became heir after the death of his older brother Prince Henry. Oh, what might have been.	Kept up with his dad's fondness for the (same) Duke of Buckingham. Buckingham was so irritating he was actually impeached by Parliament in 1628 and later murdered by a nutcase. Charles I was an arts patron and invited both Peter Paul Rubens and Anthony van Dyck to England. Bought pictures by Titian and Raphael. This sort of expenditure wasn't cheap and didn't help his money situation, which got dire. He then tried to raise money without going via Parliament. Bad move. Really bad move. Seriously unpopular move.	Historians will never stop arguing about Charles. All you need to know: Charles was not a successful ruler. Deeply self-righteous, he was an Anglican, so he loved church ritual and rubbed Puritans up the wrong way. Really wasn't helped by the fact he was married to a Catholic, Henrietta Maria of France. Fell out with Parliament and the country ended up in civil wars essentially about monarchy and Parliament's authority. Royalists sided with Charles; Roundheads supported Parliament (led by some very competent generals, including one Oliver Cromwell). Charles I was beheaded on a scaffold outside the Banqueting House in Whitehall, London, on January 30, 1649. Asked for warm clothing so people didn't mistake his shivering in the cold weather for fear. Death became him—it martyred Charles in the eyes of many.

NO.	NAME/HOUSE/ AREAS OF UK RULED/REIGN	QUALIFICATION(S)	QUIRK(S)	NOTABLE FEAT(S)/FIASCO(S)
*	Commonwealth, 1649–1653 Oliver Cromwell, Lord Protector 1653–1658 Richard Cromwell, Lord Protector 1658–1659	England was a republic. This period is referred to as the Interregnum ("between reigns"). Charles I's son, Charles, was forced into exile.	There were various political experiments as those in charge tried to define a constitution without a monarchy. They were no founding fathers. At one point Cromwell was actually offered the throne.	Cromwell—yes, Cromwell—fell out with Parliament. In 1653 he dissolved it—yes, dissolved it—and became Lord Protector. At one point there was basically military rule. Cromwell died in 1658 and his son Richard took over (I'm not joking about any of this—some republic). General Monk, leader of the army, invited Charles I's son Charles back to become king. And there ended the Brits' brush with a monarch-free zone. Scarred forever.
26	Charles II Stuart England, Wales, Scotland, and Ireland 1660–1685	Restoration of the crown. Charles II was Charles I's son. Had spent a lot of time in French exile, although he had attempted to invade England in 1651. Legend has it he escaped by hiding in an oak tree.	Married his niece in 1677. She didn't produce heirs, although his multiple mistresses, including Lady Castlemaine and Nell Gwyn, did. Became a Catholic on his deathbed.	Into sharing power and political and religious tolerance. Lots of pardons and confirmations of land purchases and "liberty of tender consciences" in religious matters, although those who signed his dad's death warrant were punished. He had Cromwell's body exhumed from Westminster Abbey and decapitated. Early years of reign were mired by a dreadful

(cont.)

NO.	NAME/HOUSE/ AREAS OF UK RULED/REIGN	QUALIFICATION(S)	QUIRK(S)	NOTABLE FEAT(S)/FIASCO(S)
26 (cont.)				plague, plus in 1666 there was the Great Fire of London, which obliterated St. Paul's and many other buildings. Charles was a patron of Christopher Wren, who designed and rebuilt St. Paul's (marriage venue of Charles and Diana).
27	James II Stuart England, Wales, Scotland, and Ireland 1685–1688	Charles II's brother. Although James converted to Catholicism in 1669, he still got the throne.	James II's first wife was scandalously a commoner, Anne Hyde, whom he married in 1660. Only two of their seven children survived infancy, Mary (later Queen Mary II) and Anne (later Queen Anne). The girls were raised Protestants. On Hyde's death James married a Catholic, who in June 1688 gave birth to a son, James Stuart, later known as the "Old Pretender."	Charles had left the monarchy in good shape, with a revenue of around £2 million and standing armies of nearly 20,000 men. However, there was an innate suspicion of Catholics, who of course James was fond of. Cue James's rapidly alienating Parliament and his subjects. The birth of James II's son proved a tipping point: James's daughter Mary's husband, the Protestant William of Orange, was invited by disgruntled parliamentarians to invade and restore Protestantism and democracy. In what was called the Glorious Revolution (basically for the lack of blood being shed), James fled and died in exile.

NO.	NAME/HOUSE/ AREAS OF UK RULED/REIGN	QUALIFICATION(S)	QUIRK(S)	NOTABLE FEAT(S)/FIASCO(S)
28	William III of Orange and Mary II (jointly) 1689–1694 William III (alone) 1694–1702 England, Wales, Scotland, and Ireland	William's mother Mary was the eldest daughter of Charles I. William married James II's daughter Mary in 1677. They were JOINT monarchs. Mary died in 1694, leaving William to rule alone. None of their children survived.	William was several inches shorter and twelve years older than Mary. In 1694, the Bank of England was founded to sort expenditure. William died after complications from a riding accident. Exiled Stuarts believed that his horse had stumbled on a molehill and toasted "the gentleman in black velvet."	Americans, this is your moment to pay attention. As discussed in Cheat Sheet 18, it's important to your Constitution and to the Brits' evolution of constitutional monarchy. William and Mary accepted the Bill of Rights (1689), which limited the sovereign's power and reaffirmed Parliament's. The 1701 Act of Settlement further restricted the Crown's powers, excluded Catholics from the throne, and secured the succession.
29	Anne I Stuart Great Britain and Ireland 1702–1714	Mary II's sister. Protestant younger daughter of James II and his first wife. In 1683 married Prince George of Denmark. Of her sixteen to eighteen pregnancies, only one child survived, William, Duke of Gloucester, but he died of smallpox in 1700.	Big-time BFF in Sarah Churchill, wife of the infamous military man the Duke of Marlborough. However, Anne and Sarah had a big tiff, and in 1710 Sarah was dismissed from court.	Anne's reign saw the rise of party politics. The Tories (pro the religious status quo and a strong monarchy) contested for power with the Whigs (pro a limited monarchy and often supported by religious dissenters). After much acrimonious debate between the English and Scots (the Scots were naturally sympathetic to the male Stuart cause), with the 1707 Acts of Union, the Scottish and English Parliaments agreed to unite.

(cont.)

NO.	NAME/HOUSE/ AREAS OF UK RULED/REIGN	QUALIFICATION(S)	QUIRK(S)	NOTABLE FEAT(S)/FIASCO(S)
29 (cont.)			Supposedly a bit of a lush, she was nicknamed Brandy Nan.	One British Parliament would sit at Westminster and the two countries would share coinage and a flag (although the separate ones do still exist). However the Scots would retain their own church and legal and educational systems. Hence the Lockerbie bomber drama—remember?
30	George I Hanover Great Britain and Ireland 1714–1727	Tenuous. Fifty-second in line to the throne, but according to the Act of Settlement, the nearest Protestant. As a result, George I had to keep dealing with "Jacobites" threatening the throne. His mother was the grand-daughter of James I, while his dad was the first elector of Hanover.	Spoke limited English. The two mistresses he shipped to England with him were nicknamed Elephant and Castle after the area in London, as one was fat and the other thin and tall. Imprisoned his wife (she eloped with a Swedish count) in 1694, where she remained until her death thirty years later. He and his son George deeply disliked each other—he wasn't terribly impressed about his mother's treatment.	Against all odds, the Hanoverian period was pretty stable. Yes, there was the South Sea Bubble crisis of 1720 (not good for royal or government investments), but there was Walpole. Robert Walpole, aka the first prime minister, had the longest-running administration in British history (1721–1742). George's political options were limited because the Jacobites had such a point.

NO.	NAME/HOUSE/ AREAS OF UK RULED/REIGN	QUALIFICATION(S)	QUIRK(S)	NOTABLE FEAT(S)/FIASCO(S)
31	George II Hanover Great Britain and Ireland 1727–1760	Son of George I. Married well, to the clever and attractive Caroline of Brandenburg-Ansbach. Nine children.	Last British sovereign to fight alongside his soldiers. Occurred in 1743 in Germany, at the Battle of Dettingen, against France. Oh, and in 1752 the Brits started using the Georgian Calendar—January 1 instead of March 25 marked the first day of the year.	The Jacobite cause rumbled on and many Tories (a political party) were pro it. Its threat was finally over after the Young Pretender, Charles Edward Stuart, was defeated at the Battle of Culloden in April 1746. But the development of a constitutional monarchy had moved inexorably forward. The foundations of the Industrial Revolution were laid and British dominance overseas increased. Upshot? Rise in George's popularity.
32	George III Hanover Great Britain and Ireland 1760–1820	George II's grandson. His dad, George II's eldest son Frederick, had died in 1751. George met his wife, Charlotte of Mecklenburg-Strelitz, on his wedding day. They were happy. He wasn't a mistress man and they had fifteen children and were married for almost sixty years. So furious was he with the loose morals of his	First Hanoverian king born in England with English as his first language. The longest-reigning KING (not, of course, queen) in British history: almost sixty years. Purchased Buckingham House in 1762 for the queen, now known as Buckingham Palace. Cultured, collected books, and founded the Royal	There is more to George III than losing America and going "mad." He was a constitutional monarch—unpopular American policies can't all be pinned on him, don't you know; Parliament had something to do with it. Remember the big picture: the French Revolution of 1789. King Louis XVI was guillotined in 1793. Britain at war with France. Dealing with Napoleon. Had two very able ministers in the form of Lord North (1770–1782) and Pitt the Younger (1783–1801).

(cont.)

NO.	NAME/HOUSE/ AREAS OF UK RULED/REIGN	QUALIFICATION(S)	QUIRK(S)	NOTABLE FEAT(S)/FIASCO(S)
32 (cont.)		relatives that in 1772 he had the Royal Marriage Act brought in—members of the royal family now had to get the sovereign's permission to marry.	Academy of Arts (you can still go and see its exhibitions). First king to study science. Loved agriculture and farming and nicknamed Farmer George.	Conscientious, which sometimes annoyed his ministers, as he read all his government papers and had an interest. Also note this: Between 1787 and 1833, the UK outlawed the slave trade and abolished slavery throughout the colonies. The Brits initially led the slave system, then led the struggle to stop it.
33	George IV Hanover Great Britain and Ireland 1820–1830	George III's son. Had already been regent since 1811 as his dad was ill. Had secretly and illegally married the Catholic Mrs. Fitzherbert. In 1795 he was officially married to Princess Caroline of Brunswick. The union was unhappy and he kept trying to ditch her. They had one daughter.	Loved food and drinking and art and pageantry and all sorts of ceremonial bits of monarchy were developed. Rebuilt Buckingham Palace and Windsor Castle. This was the Regency Period, when John Nash and others were building classic architecture you see in London and Bath and so forth.	He was in debt, which put him in a weak political position with his cabinet of ministers. Forced to agree to Catholic emancipation in 1829, which reduced religious discrimination.

NO.	NAME/HOUSE/ AREAS OF UK RULED/REIGN	QUALIFICATION(S)	QUIRK(S)	NOTABLE FEAT(S)/FIASCO(S)
34	William IV Hanover Great Britain and Ireland 1830–1837	George IV's only legitimate daughter, Princess Charlotte, died giving birth to a stillborn child. So George IV's brother, George III's third son William, got the throne. William had no surviving legitimate children.	Sent off to the Royal Navy at thirteen (he was the third son, he was expendable—he didn't become heir apparent until he was sixty-two). Created Duke of Clarence in 1791, he moved in with his mistress, an actress, who bred. The family was known as the Fitzclarences. His official marriage took place in 1818 to Princess Adelaide of Saxe-Meiningen, but their children didn't make it out of infancy. His London residence was Clarence House. Yes, where Prince Charles lives now. It was built for him by John Nash.	William IV's reign was dominated by the Reform crisis. The Reform Act was passed in 1832, sorting out some of the worst electoral system abuses including "rotten boroughs" (the argument goes that that's what the GOP's gerrymandered seats are today). It also widened the electorate (not to women, obviously), but it meant the middle classes had more of an investment in the political system. Now, I think this is heroic. William managed to die a month after his heir and niece Victoria came of age, so there wasn't another regency. Oh, and FYI, the empire was still expanding.

(cont.)

NO.	NAME/HOUSE/ AREAS OF UK RULED/REIGN	QUALIFICATION(S)	QUIRK(S)	NOTABLE FEAT(S)/FIASCO(S)
35	Victoria I Hanover Great Britain and Ireland 1837–1901	Here we go . . . Victoria was the only daughter of Edward, Duke of Kent, George III's fourth son. Edward died shortly after she was born. Because her three uncles ahead of her in the succession died with no legitimate heirs, she got the gig. Becoming queen at eighteen, she reigned for almost sixty-four years. Had an overbearing mother who kept her away from her naughty uncles and had a very sheltered upbringing.	Married Prince Albert of Saxe-Coburg and Gotha in February 1840. They loved each other and had nine children. Most of them were married off to other royal families in Europe. Consequence? She was the "grandmother of Europe," with something like forty-two grandchildren on the continent. Her granddaughter was married to the last tsar of Russia. Victoria was Britain's longest-running Buckingham Palace Attraction (aka reigning monarch) until Queen Elizabeth beat her in 2015.	Oh, you know, the sun never set on her empire. And it didn't. Literally. Given title of empress of India in 1876. Massive industrial expansion during her reign; she was the first monarch to use trains. Victoria was all about taking a constitutional role and leaving actual rule to Parliament. More people were enfranchised. Albert died in 1861 and she never recovered, going into deep mourning. Seven attempts were made to assassinate her between 1840 and 1882, and the courage she displayed endeared her to her people (which was needed, as they weren't too impressed when she disappeared from public life after Albert's death). Opposed women getting the vote but was prone to helping the poor.

NO.	NAME/HOUSE/ AREAS OF UK RULED/REIGN	QUALIFICATION(S)	QUIRK(S)	NOTABLE FEAT(S)/FIASCO(S)
36	Edward VII Saxe-Coburg-Gotha 1901–1910	Eldest son of Victoria and Albert. Saxe-Coburg-Gotha comes from his father, and he was the only British monarch of that house. Had been heir apparent for longer than anyone else in British history; Prince Charles is a case of history repeating itself.	Known as the "uncle of Europe" because he was related to nearly every Continental sovereign.	Social. Relatively happy marriage but still lots of mistresses. His disapproving mother wouldn't let him act as her deputy until 1898. Fluent in French and German and contributed to the Anglo-French Entente Cordiale signed in 1904 and also the Triple Entente between Britain, Russia, and France. They would both later prove pivotal in regards to World War I—see Cheat Sheet 16.
37	George V Windsor Great Britain and Ireland (from 1922 Northern Ireland) 1910–1936	Second son of Edward VII (his elder brother Albert had died of pneumonia in 1892). Saxe-Coburg-Gotha was far too German sounding what with the Great War and all, so George V replaced it with Windsor (after the castle) in 1917. His granddaughter Elizabeth by his second son Bertie called him Grandpa	Joined the navy at age twelve, where he stayed until his eldest brother died. Pulled the Henry VIII maneuver. He married his dead brother's girl, in this case Princess Victoria Mary of Teck (Queen Mary). Despite this, they made a success of it, he never took a mistress, and they had six	George V's reign began with a constitutional crisis over the House of Lords. Then came World War I in 1914 (the king made over 450 visits to troops and over 300 visits to hospitals visiting wounded servicemen). Pressed for humane treatment of German prisoners of war and conscientious objectors. Unhappy times for royals elsewhere: His cousin was killed in the Russian Revolution, and in 1922 George V sent a ship to rescue the one-year-old Prince Philip (our queen's husband) and the Greek royal family. With the

(cont.)

NO.	NAME/HOUSE/ AREAS OF UK RULED/REIGN	QUALIFICATION(S)	QUIRK(S)	NOTABLE FEAT(S)/FIASCO(S)
37 (cont.)		England. He called her Lilibet.	children. Stamp collector. Started the Christmas broadcast (on radio!) in 1932. The British monarch has continued the tradition to this day.	rise of socialism and the general strike, there was a risk that the British royal family would be the next to be flattened by the revolution bandwagon, but actually, by 1935, the king celebrated his Silver Jubilee and there was lots of rejoicing going on.
38	Edward VIII Windsor Great Britain and Northern Ireland 1936	Eldest son of King George V. Never crowned; his reign lasted only 325 days. He abdicated to marry one Wallis Simpson. After-ward, Edward was created Duke of Windsor.	First monarch to be a qualified pilot. Met Hitler in 1937 and perceived to be rather too sympathetic in that direction. The British government sent him to be governor of the Bahamas during World War II, as there were worries the Germans would use him as a pawn.	Was actually a popular Prince of Wales. Visited around Britain and beyond, cared for the underprivileged. And oh, you know the rest. He fell in love with a married American woman. Mrs. Simpson got a divorce from her second husband in 1936, Edward wanted to marry her. She wasn't viewed as acceptable by the establishment, so he chose love over the crown. When he abdicated, he agreed that any children he might have were excluded from succession to the throne. In the end that proved unnecessary, as he and Wallis didn't breed (I'll leave you to go into your own Internet spiral on that one). We'd have still ended up with Queen Elizabeth . . .

NO.	NAME/HOUSE/ AREAS OF UK RULED/REIGN	QUALIFICATION(S)	QUIRK(S)	NOTABLE FEAT(S)/FIASCO(S)
39	George VI Windsor Great Britain and Northern Ireland 1936–1952	Edward VIII's brother. His first name was Albert, Bertie, but he went with his last middle name of George for the title. Little Prince George, William and Kate's son, could change his name to one of his others in the unlikely event that he wanted to. George VI was greatly helped by his wife, who on his death became the Queen Mother—Lady Elizabeth Bowes-Lyon. They had two daughters—Elizabeth and Margaret.	This is the *King's Speech* monarch. Suffered a speech impediment but was brave, had fought in World War I—and was the first member of the royal family to learn to fly. First British monarch to enter the United States.	Got Britain through World War II along with Churchill. Remained based at Buckingham Palace throughout, even though it was hit by bombs nine times in the blitz. George VI and Queen Elizabeth were very hands-on—visiting areas of bomb damage especially in London's East End. Went to visit troops whenever possible, including 1939 in France to inspect the British Expeditionary Force, and to North Africa in 1943 after the victory of El Alamein. Made the Normandy beaches ten days after D Day. Buckingham Palace was the focal point for celebrations on VE Day, May 8, 1945. Post–World War II the British empire began to be replaced by the commonwealth. The strain of World War II took its toll on the king, who died in 1952. Churchill wrote on the government's wreath card at his funeral "For Valour."

(cont.)

NO.	NAME/HOUSE/ AREAS OF UK RULED/REIGN	QUALIFICATION(S)	QUIRK(S)	NOTABLE FEAT(S)/FIASCO(S)
40	Elizabeth II Windsor Great Britain and Northern Ireland 1952–	George VI's eldest daughter. Was in Kenya when she succeeded to the crown at age twenty-five. She married Prince Philip, Duke of Edinburgh, on November 20, 1947.	On her twenty-first birthday she dedicated her life to the service of the commonwealth. "I declare before you all that my whole life, whether it be long or short, shall be devoted to your service and the service of our great imperial family to which we all belong." Between that and her coronation oath, it is absolutely clear that she will not be abdicating, although she is giving more responsibility to Charles and William.	Elizabeth II's reign has withstood massive social, political, economic, and technological change. The rise and fall of the Berlin Wall, man walking on the moon, the Concorde, mass communication, the press, the World Wide Web, and Diana. The queen is the embodiment of national unity, identity, and pride. Through the commonwealth she is figurehead to two billion people, a third of the world. Her approval rating hovers at around 90 percent. So when Sean Hannity asked me what was the point of the royals, my response was "Is Obama a unifying figure?" He asked, "Is this a trick question?" No. We Brits choose monarchy, as politicizing the process seems a more divisive force when we Brits want a unifying one as our head of state. Monarchy will survive if it masters the trick of adapting

NO.	NAME/HOUSE/ AREAS OF UK RULED/REIGN	QUALIFICATION(S)	QUIRK(S)	NOTABLE FEAT(S)/FIASCO(S)
40 (cont.)				over time. The birth of Prince George marks the first era since Victoria's reign that a monarch has met a great grandchild born in direct succession to the crown. Prince Charles, the queen's son, Prince William, and Prince George secure and symbolize the future of the royal family, "the Firm," probably into the twenty-second century. Antiquated? Yes. But stable? Absolutely. There is something very comforting knowing who will be reigning—but not ruling—over me when I die.

SOCIAL SURVIVAL STRATEGY

Argument: "The British monarchy will survive if it continues to adapt over time."
It may be antiquated, but there's a reason monarchy exists, so it's an opportunity for you to show off your intellect here the next time a minor royal is involved in some naked transgression. There's a fine line for monarchy: It's there to represent stability, but it also needs to be seen as in touch. Elizabeth II has had a few wobbles, but has preserved it. The question is, will the more meddling Charles manage to pass it down to William (who would never insult his dad by taking his crown over him)? Charles has been urging his mother to create a more "slimmed-down" monarchy (thus shutting out minor members who cause embarrassment), so it's in with a chance of surviving.

Crisp Fact: "The Brits did experiment with republicanism in the seventeenth century. They ended up offering the leader the throne."
If you are going to remove the existing system, have a plan acceptable to the majority to replace it; otherwise it won't work. You can cite this example when talking about anything from health care to TV networks.

Pivot: "Whatever you think of the monarchy, Colin Firth's performance in The King's Speech was extraordinary, as is Helen Mirren's whenever she's played the queen—she's won an Oscar and a Tony for it. Seen any good films or theater lately?"
Everyone you want to continue talking to will have watched a movie or been to the theater recently, even if it wasn't any good—it's called being a well-rounded human being. You have permission to stop talking to them if they've done neither.

CHEAT SHEET 16—WORLD WAR I, WORLD WAR II, AND THE COLD WAR

I remember it well. Sort of.

No, I'm not THAT old (as far as World War I and II goes, at least). It was the summer term of my first year at Cambridge. The university is made up of colleges, and I belonged to Girton. My director of studies at Girton had arranged for my weekly supervisions in modern European history to be conducted by a renowned professor at Trinity College. At least I think it was Trinity—I spent most of that term drinking or feeling the aftereffects of Pimm's. And note THAT THE ENGLISH DO NOT ATTACH A CUP TO THE TERM. Hopefully a jug is, though—one glass of Pimm's never being enough. Anyway, in the college I had to traipse to once a week to be challenged on my latest essay and be set a new one, there were "quads" and impressive architecture and point being, I do remember my jaw dropping when the aforementioned professor, one of the world's finest minds (in modern European history at least), gave me a week to cover Hitler and Stalin.

I did it. I recall I even got a good grade on my essay. But that may have been the Pimm's.

So now, possibly in a futile attempt to prove I'm still as mentally if not physically capable as I was at age nineteen, I'm going to cover World War I, World War II, and the cold war *in a single Cheat Sheet*.

Stay with me, people. Modern foreign relations depend on this one. And I'm sure Sarah Palin's team are wondering where I was when she ran for veep.

MINI REPORT 1. WORLD WAR I

The best ever description (indeed, helpful tutorial on World War I, aka the Great War) comes from back when Hugh Laurie hadn't even contemplated using an American accent at work. It was in the classic British comedy series *Blackadder Goes Forth* that the *House* actor costarred in. The character of Baldrick, never the fizziest drink in the fridge, believed the war started when "Archie Duke shot an ostrich because he was hungry."

For the generation before 1914, imperial European powers had managed to export their wars, thus avoiding ones with each other. Interlocking alliances, supposed to keep the peace, burgeoned. Trouble kicked off in June 1914, when a Serbian nationalist in Sarajevo, Bosnia, assassinated Archduke Franz Ferdinand, the heir apparent to the Austro-Hungarian Empire. Ferdinand's death sparked the simmering tensions that had been going on for years in Europe, particularly in the Balkan region (an area of Southeast Europe). Austria-Hungary, which was allied with Germany, blamed the Serbian government, which was backed by Russia, who was allied with France. Threats mounted and on July 28, Austria-Hungary declared war on Serbia. By mid-August World War I had started.

Scholars are locked into an eternal discussion about why the war escalated as it did. Some suggest that Germany wanted a war and that it and Austria-Hungary had been busy laying the foundations of the struggle for some time. Others point the finger at pre-1914 military planners, including those in Russia, insisting that once their mobilization plans were in motion, there was no room for diplomacy. Whatever the roots of the war, the scale of the bloodbath was unprecedented.

NOTEWORTHY NUGGETS: EVENTUAL SIDES OF THE MAIN PLAYERS IN WORLD WAR ONE

Pause and take this in. Look where Italy and Japan are.

Allied (Entente) Powers	Central Powers
Serbia	Austria-Hungary
British Empire	Germany
France	Ottoman Empire
Russia	Bulgaria
Italy	
Japan	
Belgium	
America (eventually, and then not a formal member, an "Associated Power"—Woodrow Wilson preserving US free hand)	

An unfortunate by-product of the Industrial Revolution's technological advances was modern weaponry, first fully seen during what was known then as the Great War: chemical weapons, tanks, machine guns, and even airplanes. The majority of the war was conducted via trench warfare. To advance from their trenches, troops had to cross no-man's-land, with frequently fatal consequences.

Thus World War I was very much a war of attrition—all about wearing down the other side. It was believed that the one with the most men would win.

Victory calculations were based on national birthrates. Hideous. Also note the secondary social effect. Women had fewer men to marry, so they needed to work. But when the men who were alive came back from the war, they wanted jobs. See Cheat Sheet 25 on feminism for perhaps obviously corresponding but no less interesting dates.

There were two fronts you are always hearing about. The Western Front, the primary theater of the war. Essentially, Germany invaded France through Belgium and then everyone was in a perpetual deadlock, a stalemate. This was the setting of the infamous Battle of the Somme in 1916, which saw a British military record that still stands. On the first day of the Allied attack, the British lost 58,000 troops—a third killed, the others injured. The Eastern Front involved Russia versus Germany (and the rest).

NOTEWORTHY NUGGETS: BIOLOGICAL AND CHEMICAL WARFARE

- Germany first used chemical weapons on a mass scale in April 1915 in Belgium.

- Around 2 percent of the war's casualties and less than 1 percent of the war's deaths came from their use, but it led to universal revulsion.

- Poison in warfare, going back to the Greeks, had caused disgust. In 1675, France and the Holy Roman Empire agreed not to use poisoned bullets. It's thought that Britain was the first country to use smallpox on its adversaries, allegedly doing so during the American Revolutionary War.

- The Geneva Protocol in 1925 banned the use, but not the possession, of biological and chemical weapons.

- The protocol is one of the few almost universally accepted treaties, and chemical warfare has rarely been used since World War I. Note that Syria is a signatory to the protocol.

- No Western army used gas on the battlefield in World War II. Hitler would not order it against combatants—he had been gassed himself in World War I. However, the Nazis did use it against noncombatant Jews and others.
- Tear gas is banned in war ... but is used in peace, as protesters in Berkeley and Ferguson in 2014 can attest.
- President Nixon officially halted the US offensive biological weapons program in November 1969 (a result of public outrage over questionable chemical use in Vietnam). The USA, UK, and USSR all signed up to the Biological Weapons Convention in 1972, outlawing their development and production.

There were forays elsewhere. These included British-led forces against the Turks in Egypt and Mesopotamia. The Italians and Austrians had a go at one another in Northern Italy. There was also the naval element, the Brits in ruling wave mode versus Germany's U-boats (submarines). The aquatic fight, as we saw in Cheat Sheet 14, in no small part helped usher America into game-changing mode and entering the war.

The Central Powers weren't all the Russians were dealing with. Internally, there was the rise of Lenin and co. In March 1917 the tsar's government fell, and with the October revolution came the armistice between Russia and the Central Powers (they agreed to stop fighting).

Meanwhile, the Americans arrived on the scene. They declared war in April 1917, and although it took a while, they eventually got lots of troops to turn up. Armistice between the Allied and the Central Powers came into effect on the eleventh hour of the eleventh day of the eleventh month—at 11 AM, November 11, 1918. Hence remembrance days around the world are marked then. The poppy, a symbol that so many wear in tribute at this time of year, comes from the Great War poem "In Flanders Fields." Bloodred poppies still grew, despite some of the worst fighting, in the battlefields of Flanders, in Belgium.

With an estimated more than 9 million military deaths, the Great War decimated a generation of men. A further 20 million were wounded. Millions of civilians were killed. Thought to cost around $260 billion (BIG money then), the Great War was supposed to be the war to end all wars.

By the conflict's close, four imperial powers were no longer—the German, Austro-Hungarian, Ottoman, and Russian empires. Maps were redrawn big-time—look at Cheat Sheet 17 for the formation of the Middle East as we know it today. Central Europe was now composed of lots of smaller states.

Formal peace came with the Treaty of Versailles, signed on June 28, 1919. Germany was punished by loss of territory, reparations, and war guilt (the war was officially blamed solely on Germany and her allies). The Germans were also denied entrance into the League of Nations, the organization established after the war to maintain world peace. The very same organization that the Russians and Americans refused to join. This is a case study in how to set up a peace organization for failure. The United Nations, the post–World War II peace organization, is thus an attempt to learn from history. Something to remember when Russia and China, as permanent members of the UN Security Council, block American desires.

Unfortunately World War I's legacy was laying the foundations for World War II. Germany was humiliated by the terms of the peace treaty, and that contributed to the rise of the conquest-driven Hitler and Nazism. But that is not its only legacy. It is perfectly possible that without it there would have been no Soviet Union, and as a result, no Communist China (for which Soviet support was initially key). Think about it: without World War I, no Hitler, Stalin, or Mao, and as a result no World War II, no Holocaust, no Korean or Vietnam War. Not to mention so much of the trouble in the Middle East can be traced back to what happened at the end of the Great War. Staggering.

Enough conjecture. You've not got the luxury of time, or I of space. The certain result of the War to End All Wars was the worst war this planet has ever seen. Read on.

MINI REPORT 2. WORLD WAR II

World War II lasted for six years, from September 1939 to September 1945. Truly global, it killed an estimated 45 to 60 million people, including around 6 million Jews murdered as a result of the Nazis' "Final Solution."

The power struggle of the Great War was not resolved by it. Added to which, in the areas destabilized by World War I, it proved all too easy for totalitarianism—communism and fascism—to rise. The states around Germany were divided and weak. Meanwhile, Germany itself had been left socially, politically, and economically unstable, ripe for exploitation by Adolf Hitler and his National Socialist German Workers' Party, aka the Nazi Party. Hitler, who became German chancellor in 1933, ranted and raved and stirred up German discontent about the perceived injustices of the Treaty of Versailles. He spewed anti-Semitic rhetoric and harped on about how Germany's defeat was self-inflicted. Overturning and avenging Versailles was one of his most successful ideological weapons. The Germans militarized. As did the Italians, under fascist dictator Benito Mussolini.

It was not actually Germany that performed the era's first act of European aggression. The Italian army invaded Ethiopia in 1935. Despite Ethiopian pleas, the weak League of Nations did nothing about it.

NOTEWORTHY NUGGETS:
EVENTUAL SIDES OF THE MAIN PLAYERS
IN WORLD WAR II

Note where China is. Also who the Axis Powers were. And remember the word *Axis,* and never, ever confuse it with *Allied.*

Allied Powers	Axis Powers
Brits and co.	Germany
(It's complicated,	Italy
but basically think	Japan
of the Empire.)	Hungary
Soviet Union*	Romania
USA	Bulgaria
China	
France	
Poland	
Greece	
Netherlands	

* They sort of switched sides during, but this is where the Russians ended up.

Natural pals, in 1936 Mussolini and Hitler made it official with the Rome-Berlin Axis, labeled as such because they thought the world revolved around them. Months later, in a direct breach of the Treaty of Versailles, Hitler marched troops into the Rhineland of Germany. With the support of Hitler and Mussolini, the fascist General Franco attempted to overthrow Spain's government, which in turn was receiving aid from the USSR.

Outside of Europe, in 1937, an altercation between Japanese and Chinese troops broke out at the Marco Polo Bridge near Beijing. The Japanese used it as an excuse to invade China, which fought back.

Back to Hitler. In 1938 the führer marched his troops into Austria and annexed the nation. He was now eyeing the Sudetenland, an area of Czechoslovakia populated by a few million Germans.

America, Britain, and France were basically sitting it out at this point. Their populations were war-weary. Nobody wanted a repeat of World War I. Call me controversial (and some will), your author doesn't think this is quite as pathetic as it has often been made out to be. How would we feel going to war if a whole generation of men had just been annihilated? Concessions to avoid another bloodbath would seem somewhat appealing. History has the great benefit of hindsight.

You've probably guessed where I'm going with this. It's what certain hosts on Fox News are always going on about when President Obama "leads from behind." In September 1938 German, Italian, French, and British leaders, the latter represented by one Prime Minister Neville Chamberlain, met in Munich to try and calm the circumstances. Hitler and Mussolini agreed not to get aggressive elsewhere if they could hold on to the Sudetenland and Ethiopia respectively.

Chamberlain at this point made what was to become one of the most unfortunate statements of all time. He declared that with this appeasement he had achieved "peace in our time."

The situation got increasingly dire. Six months later German troops were in the rest of Czechoslovakia. In August 1939, Stalin and Hitler signed a nonaggression pact. By September, Hitler was marching his military into Poland (Germany had lost territory there thanks to . . . the Treaty of Versailles).

All hell broke loose. The Brits and French had guaranteed Poland military support if it underwent German military attack. Finally the Brits and the French declared war on Germany. And so began World War II.

The Soviets invaded Poland from the east. It stood no chance and fell. The Germans and Russians divided it. Germany stepped the war up a notch in April 1940 by occupying Denmark and invading Norway. The Netherlands and Belgium followed.

KEY TERM: BLITZKRIEG

- Means lightning war.
- It's how the Germans got Poland, Netherlands, Belgium, and so forth and so forth.

German forces reached Paris by June 1940. There was an armistice. Now, this is important for when you read war novels and get a bit hazy about what's going on. France was divided into two zones. The Germans occupied one in the north and northwest, which covered three-fifths of the country. A French one, installed at Vichy, administered the two-fifths in the south. Which Mussolini promptly started attacking.

Now it's time for my tiny island nation's big moment. After Germany occupied France, Britain—and its empire—was ALL ALONE against the Germans. Until the Soviet Union's side-switching in 1941. Just saying.

The Brits did have an advantage, which with these massive odds against it was vital. It was surrounded by water. That didn't stop Hitler trying to invade it with Operation Sea Lion in the summer of 1940. Cue the Battle of Britain and the inspiration of a thousand films. This is the name given to the air battle between the Royal Air Force (RAF) and the Luftwaffe, the German air force. Beginning in July 1940 and ending that September, the battle was a close-run thing. The Brits prevailed and Germany abandoned immediate invasion plans. Interestingly, you can still see the bomb damage if you walk around London today. Go to almost any street and you'll have a line of old (as in Victorian or older) houses and an awful 1950s monstrosity in the middle. That was a German bomb. Tit for tat: The Brits annihilated parts of Berlin.

KEY TERM: LEND-LEASE

- The Brits needed resources and so Congress passed the Lend-Lease Act in early 1941.

- Roosevelt's argument was that if a neighbor's house was on fire, you didn't sell him a hose to put it out. You lent it to him and he returned it when the fire was extinguished.

- Thanks to the act, $50 billion of aid went to the Allies.

- Hitler did not see this as neutrality—he ordered American ships be attacked.

A bit of water didn't put Hitler off his stride that much, he just focused his energies elsewhere. His troops marched through Yugoslavia and Greece, aka the Balkans, in April 1941. Hitler was in position. To invade the Soviet Union. That's right. His "comrade" Stalin.

As we touched on in the introduction, the Germans' Operation Barbarossa, ordered in June 1941, took Stalin and co. by surprise, and initially Hitler's troops managed to get within tens of miles of Moscow. The war in the East got as brutal as the Russian weather and included the infamous street-by-street battle in Stalingrad from 1942 to 1943.

We're in danger of being too Eurocentric. This was, after all, a world war. The Brits (and their commonwealth forces) were fighting the Germans and Italians in North Africa and in the Atlantic. The Japanese had set their sights on a huge empire spanning East Asia. But they had one large obstacle. Uncle Sam.

We have reached December of 1941. You know this one. Don't tell me you didn't see *Pearl Harbor,* that rather underrated Josh Hartnett and Ben Affleck film (and doesn't Kate Beckinsale look younger now than she did when making it?). America's turn to be blindsided. The Japanese, trying to neutralize America's Pacific power, attacked Pearl Harbor on December 7. As we all know, this act didn't exactly have the intended consequences. The deaths of more than two thousand American military personnel and the destruction of twenty naval vessels and almost two hundred airplanes killed off American isolationist sentiment and galvanized American support for war. The next day Congress declared war on Japan. Japanese allies Germany and Italy subsequently declared war on America. Congress reciprocated. America was in a two-ocean war.

NOTEWORTHY NUGGETS: THE WARTIME US ECONOMY

- The mass mobilization of the US economy for the war effort vanquished not just the Axis powers, but the Great Depression.

- There was full employment. Both African-Americans—many migrating from the rural South to the industrial North—and women were sourced for work, setting the stage for civil rights and feminism.

- The increase in GDP was dramatic. For the first time the American standard of living was higher than the pre-Depression era.

- Tax rates were raised—up to 90 percent for some—to generate revenue and keep a lid on inflation.

Game-change time. Germany was concentrated on first. By 1943 the Brits and Americans had beaten the Germans and Italians in North Africa. The Allies then invaded Italy, and by July 1943 Mussolini's government had fallen. The fight was dogged and dirty in the East, but Stalin eventually prevailed. In November 1943 came that rather classic photo op: FDR, Churchill, and Stalin met at the Tehran Conference. Yes. You read that right. Tehran. I can just feel your excitement about the Middle East Cheat Sheet coming up.

D Day (not to be confused with Dunkirk, which was when the British Expeditionary Force got evacuated out of France in May 1940) occurred on June 6, 1944. Allied forces invaded Nazi-occupied France, eventually pushing through to Berlin from the west while the Soviet-led Allied armies converged from the east. Hitler took his own life on April 30, 1945, eighteen days after Roosevelt's untimely death. The Germans surrendered on May 8, 1945, hereafter known as VE (Victory in Europe) Day.

It was at this stage that Germany got divided, and the remainder of Europe split into Western and Soviet spheres of influence.

Meanwhile the war in the Pacific was still raging, and the US was island-hopping to get to the Japanese mainland. Roosevelt's death left the decision to drop the bomb to Truman. He did so in August 1945 on Hiroshima and Nagasaki. The Japanese surrendered. Justification for its use? Prolonging the war would have cost more lives in war-weary nations, both Japanese and American. The Japanese were prone to kamikaze raids (suicide attacks), and an invasion would supposedly have led to a million casualties.

KEY TERM: THE MANHATTAN PROJECT

- There was a very real fear that German scientists would figure out how to harness nuclear fission to produce an atomic bomb.

- Enrico Fermi and Albert Einstein, scientists who had fled Italy and Germany respectively, told the US government that they needed an atomic research program.

- The US government launched a program, the Manhattan Project. It was so top secret that Truman—the vice-president— knew of it only when he BECAME president. Roosevelt and Churchill were determined to keep not only the Germans and Japanese in the dark, but also the Russians.

  * Los Alamos, New Mexico, housed the main assembly plant.

  * A Soviet spy, Klaus Fuchs, penetrated the scientists' inner circle.

  * The first bomb was tested in July 1945. By August they were in use over Japan.

World War II was history's most destructive war. The precise number of people who lost their lives is unknown, but the atrocities were like nothing seen before. The Allies suffered 85 percent of the deaths, mostly Soviet and Chinese; the Axis powers 15 percent. It is thought 27 million Soviets perished, helping shape a defensive Soviet mind-set, the legacy of which can be seen during the cold war and arguably through to today. More than 400,000 Americans died.

It was a civilian war. Forty million civilians died, double the number of military. The Holocaust killed around 12 million. The Nazis murdered those they believed unworthy of life, including Jews, ethnic Europeans, homosexuals, and the disabled. The Japanese also believed they were racially superior and were notoriously cruel. It is thought 7.5 million civilians died in China under Japanese occupation. At the infamous Nanking Massacre, several hundred thousand Chinese civilians were slaughtered, many being raped and buried alive. The Japanese prisoner-of-war camps had a death rate seven times higher than those of the Germans and the Italians.

The Soviets had gulags, their labor camps. Although the other allies didn't have official systems in place, there was their fair share of torture, murder, and rape. Reports were received by the American Joint Chiefs of US forces raping many Italian, French, and Japanese women. Civil liberties were compromised, as we note in Cheat Sheet 19, when Japanese Americans and German Americans were placed in camps.

The legacies of World War II included massive social changes, including the rise of feminism and America's civil rights movement. There were huge ramifications in Europe financially, as we saw in Subject Two, math and economics, but also with decolonization and therefore the emergence of the third world. There was the creation of Israel, which we cover in the next Cheat Sheet. Then there were the major technological breakthroughs, including the bomb and space programs.

And of course the spread of communism.

> ## WISE WORDS
>
> The world must know what happened, and never forget.
>
> —General Dwight D. Eisenhower,
> supreme commander, Allied
> Expeditionary Force, European
> Theater of Operations, while visiting
> Nazi death camps, 1945

MINI REPORT 3. THE COLD WAR

Times had changed. America didn't turn up late in the day for the cold war: It was one of the two main protagonists. Whatever internal debate raged, America's public game face was: Isolationism is over.

George Orwell is typically credited for coining the term *cold war,* after America had deployed the first nuclear bombs. By 1949 the Soviets exploded their first atomic bomb in a test. H. G. Wells and others had foreseen that one day there would be two peers threatened with mutual annihilation who never meet in war directly but instead conduct proxy wars. So it proved. Nuclear weapons have not been used since 1945, and the only country that has deployed them is America. However, between 1947 and 1991 we had the cold war, which was littered with skirmishes between client states. Throw around the phrase "fault lines of the cold war" here. People will nod and look terribly impressed.

The West had always been against the idea of communism. As the saying goes, politics makes strange bedfellows, but war makes even stranger bedfellows. The Brits, Americans, and Russians got into bed with one another only because they really had no choice. It took until 1933 for the US to recognize the USSR after the Bolsheviks took charge in 1917. As far as Stalin went, he was furious that the Brits and Americans had taken their time in massing a French front during World War II. The wait had kept immense pressure on the Eastern Front, leading to millions of deaths. The Soviet leader wasn't too impressed either that the Soviet version of Lend-Lease ended during the war.

In the aftermath of World War II, the earth's most populous nation, China, ended up communist, becoming the sleeping giant that was the People's Republic of China. Half of Europe was under Soviet influence behind the Iron Curtain, while much of the remainder lost its grip on its colonies. As the British and French empires succumbed to independence movements, a new third world emerged. With the decolonization of Africa and Asia, every new state found itself wooed by the superpowers. Indeed, the third world became the major battleground of the cold war as the United States and the Soviet Union struggled to bring new nations into their respective orbits, squaring off against each other care of proxy armies. The Israel independence in 1948 had massive ramifications in the Middle East, which we cover more extensively in Cheat Sheet 17.

KEY TERM: THE THIRD WORLD

- A cold war term. Initially NATO-type countries were first world, the Communist bloc was second world, and the third world was for countries that weren't aligned with either of them.

- Use of the term *third world,* however, did not stick to this strict definition. We now often use it as a blanket term to refer to developing, poorer countries.

There are three organizations you should be aware of if discussing the cold war or partaking in a spy thriller. There was the North Atlantic Treaty Organization (NATO) and the Warsaw Pact, which were the military alliances of the US and the USSR respectively. There was also the UN, an international peace organization that the US managed to sign up to this time.

NOTEWORTHY NUGGETS: THE UN

- The United Nations was an attempt to keep the peace where the League of Nations had failed to do.

- The executive branch, the Security Council, is made up of fifteen seats and must authorize the use of force, deployment of peacekeeping troops, etc. There are five permanent members, the Great Powers: France, Britain, China, Russia (then the USSR), and the US. Well, they were all great in 1945; the first two don't exactly punch above their weight anymore. The ten remaining seats go to countries the General Assembly elects to two-year terms. If any of the big five objects about pretty much anything, action is prohibited. Action is prohibited quite a bit.

- The main body is the General Assembly—every member nation has a seat.

- The Secretariat manages the daily logistic-type things of the UN.

- Oh, and there's an International Court of Justice, which rules on arguments between governments, which is the only major bit of the UN not in New York—it's in the Hague in the Netherlands. This is not to be confused with the later-established International Criminal Court, also in the Hague, which has the ability to try individuals, which the International Court of Justice does not.

As soon as World War II ended, the US and USSR immediately entered into competition—to get hold of the best German scientists, who had also been working on the nuclear side of things and been busy developing a rocket program so that they could fire missiles at the Brits. This contributed to the development of intercontinental ballistic missiles capable of carrying nuclear warheads and the space race.

The cold war provided the impetus for humanity to get beyond the confines of earth. The Russians got there first with Sputnik, the first satellite to go into orbit in 1957. The survivalists you see on modern-day reality shows have NOTHING on how people were acting back then. A very real fear of nuclear holocaust reached into the fabric of everyday life. The cold war made an indelible mark on popular culture. This was the age of James Bond, of the propaganda broadcasts of Radio Free Europe/Liberty.

Congress's and Eisenhower's response to Sputnik was to invent the National Aeronautics and Space Administration, NASA, and find some cash for science. From 1961 to 1964, NASA's budget was increased almost 500 percent. Americans won the space race in 1969 when Apollo 11 landed astronauts on the moon.

The Americans and Soviets were also locked in a deadly arms race.

KEY TERMS: THE HUNGARIAN REVOLUTION AND PRAGUE SPRING

- The Hungarian Revolution took place in 1956. An uprising against the Soviet-backed government, it ended with Soviet tanks rolling into Budapest to regain control.

- The Prague Spring was an era of political liberalization in Czechoslovakia in 1968. In response, the Soviet Army, along with the majority of the Warsaw Pact allies, invaded.

- The external impact of these acts was that the number of those who had supported communism in the West diminished. The cold war became less about ideological clashes, more about geopolitical ones.

Other important notes. With all the financial drama surrounding the euro we've been through in the past few years, you may have been asking WHY? Why did Europeans want to be so close that they shared a currency? The roots of the European Union can be traced back to the 1950s, as Western Europe began policies that moved it closer together militarily, economically, and politically. It was next door to the Soviet sphere of influence, after all. Also please observe that Stalin died in 1953, and after some maneuvering Khrushchev was in charge.

KEY TERMS: THE DOCTRINES

Most of these have cropped up elsewhere, but they're worth a summary now. The Cold War ones are all in the same vein.

Monroe Doctrine (president 1817–1825): Europe shouldn't meddle with the Americas anymore.

Truman Doctrine (president 1945–1953): America would assist democratic countries threatened by authoritarian forces—in essence attempt to contain the spread of communism.

Eisenhower Doctrine (president 1953–1961): Came from a speech to Congress re the Middle East in 1957, after the Suez crisis. Offered America's economic and military assistance to countries being threatened by armed aggression. Communism singled out.

Reagan Doctrine (president 1981–1989): All about supporting "freedom fighters"—that is to say, anyone opposing communism.

We've previously talked in other Cheat Sheets of the financial phenom that was the Marshall Plan, of containment and triangular diplomacy and détente. There were moments, as you can see in the box below, when the cold war heated up

NOTEWORTHY NUGGETS:
NINE TENSEST MOMENTS OF THE COLD WAR

1. The Berlin Blockade (1948–49)

A legacy of World War II was that Berlin was effectively divided into two: West (democratic) and East (communist). Now, here's the thing—Berlin was COMPLETELY surrounded by East Germany. I'd forgotten that until I wrote this book. During the Berlin blockade, Stalin stopped supplies arriving via ground to West Berlin, so the US, Britain, and co. started the Berlin airlift to fly them in. Apart from during the blockade, it was possible to travel through East Germany from West Berlin via certain trains or roads—but this involved paperwork and checks.

2. The Korean War (1950–53)

First military action of the cold war. The Soviet-backed North Korean People's Army invaded the pro-Western South. The American government was concerned it was the first step in a plan for communist world takeover, so it intervened. Result? Stalemate in 1953.

3. The Suez Crisis (1956)

The 120-mile Suez Canal in Egypt links the Red Sea to the Mediterranean. It opened in 1869 and had a massive impact on world trade. For years it was a neutral zone under British control, hence the big defense of it by the Brits during World War I against the Ottoman Empire and their subsequent lingering interest.

In 1948, the US recognized Israel, which upset the Arab nations and drove them toward the Soviets' arms. When Egyptian President Gamal Abdel Nasser started cozying up to the USSR, the US refused to honor its promise to help him construct the Aswan Dam on the Nile River. So Nasser nationalized Suez and the Israeli (their troops were having sporadic battles with Egyptian ones on their shared border), French (thought Nasser was supporting rebels in the French colony of Algeria), and British armies invaded Egypt. This nearly brought the Soviet Union directly into the conflict, not just via proxy. President Eisenhower and the Americans effectively coerced the British, French, and Israelis into some restraint. Ultimately the British, French, and Israeli governments withdrew their troops. Suez permanently weakened Britain and France on the international scene. And the UN proved useful, as it took charge of the area.

4. The Berlin Crisis (1961)

Last big incident of the cold war re Berlin. West Berlin had become a loophole thanks to its location—thousands of East Germans used it to flee to the West. This caused much fury on the Soviet side, the culmination being the building of a wall that totally encircled West Berlin on August 14, 1961. Worth noting that despite being completely surrounded by Soviet-controlled territory, West Berlin had the most inhabitants of any cold war German city.

5. The Cuban Missile Crisis (1962)

Kennedy's biggest foreign policy success and failure both involved Cuba. There was the Bay of Pigs fiasco—CIA-trained Cuban exiles failing to incite an uprising and bring down Castro—and the Cuban Missile Crisis, the closest the USSR and USA got to direct confrontation. The standoff brought the world to the brink of destruction, but ultimately both Kennedy and Khrushchev accepted that if blood was spilled, it would be almost impossible to stop the situation from spiraling out of control. Kennedy was helped in no small part by the insight into Khrushchev given to him by the CIA and British SIS (the proper term for MI6) agent Colonel Oleg Penkovsky, deputy head of the foreign section of the GRU (the Soviets didn't just have the KGB, don't you know). Some historians have gone as far to label Penkovsky as the spy who saved the world from nuclear war. His HUMINT, human intelligence, helped, but IMINT, imagery intelligence, from the new satellite technology and aerial photography played its part as well. Each verified the other. The best intelligence is always confirmed from different sources, both human and technological.

6. Vietnam (1955–75)

The communist threat now appeared to be coming from the unstable postcolonial third world. The Vietnam War was a result of the collapse of the French colonial regime and a power struggle between the US-backed nationalist Ngo Dinh Diem in the south and the communist nationalist Ho Chi Minh in the north. Initially many Americans believed that it was in their national interest to defend South Vietnam from communism. If they didn't, other revolutions might be more likely to occur against free governments elsewhere. But as the human and financial costs spiraled and the impact of the draft made itself felt (NB: if you went to college, it was deferred, so if you were rich, you were less likely to fight—quite), so the peace movement grew. The *New York Times* published excerpts from the Pentagon Papers in 1971, a top-secret overview of US government involvement in Vietnam. These showed that the Johnson administration had been deceiving the American public and many statements made about Vietnam had been a lie. The credibility gap led to more cynicism, and popular support diminished still further. Ultimately it proved impossible to win a protracted war without it. As covered in Cheat Sheet 14, Vietnam was ultimately a loss to America.

7. The Yom Kippur War (1973)

This threatened direct conflict between the USSR and the USA for the first time since the Cuban Missile Crisis. American forces hit Stage 3 alert (scary stuff—Stage 5 was when nuclear weapons were launched).

Egypt and Syria, using Soviet weapons, launched a surprise attack on Israel. Israel fought back with the help of the Americans, and the Egyptians found themselves surrounded by the Israelis in the Sinai Desert. The Soviets threatened to rescue the Egyptians themselves. Kissinger flew into action with shuttle diplomacy, which is what it sounds like. He flew in and out of different countries being diplomatic. Eventually a peace accord was reached.

8. The Soviet War in Afghanistan (1979–89)

When all's said and done, the Soviets' Vietnam. The USSR invaded Afghanistan in 1979, with Soviet premier Leonid Brezhnev claiming to dubious Americans that Afghani leaders had asked for military assistance. The Americans were concerned about Soviet expansion in the Middle East, so the Carter administration ordered a grain (and athlete—Americans didn't turn up to the 1980 Moscow Olympics) boycott. The regime propped up by the Soviets was opposed by the mujahideen, which by 1982 controlled 75 percent of Afghanistan. Somehow the mujahideen fighters ended up in possession of American surface-to-air missiles . . .

Mikhail Gorbachev took Russia out of the Afghanistan fiasco when he realized what many Russian leaders had been too scared to admit in public—that Russia could not win the war, plus the cost of maintaining such a vast force in Afghanistan was crippling Russia's already weak economy.

9. Korean Air Lines Flight 007 and Able Archer (1983)

Alluded to in the history introduction and occurred during the height of President Ronald Reagan's "evil empire" rhetoric against the Soviets. The Russians were so convinced that America was about to launch a nuclear first strike that they launched the intelligence operation RYAN, to give them due warning.
The upshot of RYAN was that the Soviets got increasingly hysterical about the Americans, misinterpreting everything they did as suspicious. As a result, the Russians shot down an off-course South Korean airliner, KAL007, in September 1983. In October, the Americans invaded Grenada. Cue absolute Soviet panic in November with NATO's training exercise Able Archer—the Soviets misinterpreted it as a potential first strike. The Brits had a double agent, Oleg Gordievsky, who revealed the Soviet mind-set and sent over to the White House a fifty-page paper entitled "Soviet Perceptions of Nuclear Warfare." Unusually, Reagan read all of it. Tensions cooled.

President Reagan of course burst on the international scene talking the talk and walking the walk in the 1980s. He was Mr. Swashbuckler when it came to fighting communism in Central America. And then there was his Strategic Defense Initiative, popularly known as Star Wars. Although the plan—something to do with shooting down missiles using lasers in space—was never fully developed or deployed, it put the fear into the Soviet Union, which was in the midst of economic stagnation.

As the US turned up the economic, military, and diplomatic heat, the stage was set for one Soviet President Mikhail Gorbachev. The new leader of the USSR implemented his reforms of reorganization, perestroika, and openness, glasnost. Prime Minister Margaret Thatcher identified him as a man she could do business with, and by 1987 Gorbachev and Reagan agreed in principle to an Intermediate-Range Nuclear Forces Treaty, which for the first time eliminated an entire class of existing nuclear weapons. That was also the year that the American president stood at the Brandenburg Gate in Berlin and urged, "Mr. Gorbachev, tear down this wall."

The resulting climate enabled the rise of independence movements in Eastern Europe. In the summer of 1989, Poland became the first noncommunist government in the Eastern Bloc. A wave of peaceful revolutions among the USSR's satellite states ensued (apart from Romania, and also note that Yugoslavia rapidly ended up in violent civil war). Gorbachev, by choosing not to use force to quell the popular uprisings in Eastern Europe, essentially allowed the Soviet Union to disintegrate. In November 1989, the Berlin Wall, the most visible symbol of the cold war, was destroyed.

Soviet conservative hard-liners did not go down without a fight. In a coup in August 1991, Gorbachev was placed under house arrest. Boris Yeltsin demanded the arrest of the hard-liners—and the public sided with him. Though Gorbachev was freed, his stature was not what it was. In late 1991 the USSR itself was formally dissolved and Boris Yeltsin became the first president of the Russian Federation. There was more to him than a penchant for vodka, don't you know.

Who won the cold war? Well, the United States became the sole superpower. Some Republicans claimed credit for America's "win."

Democrats were quick to point out that containment was a bipartisan policy invented by the Democratic president Truman. John McCain's favorite talking point is that Russia is now a "gas station masquerading as a country."

The safest argument to deploy here is that nobody won the cold war. The Swahili have a proverb: When two elephants fight, it's the grass that gets trampled. Although the US and the USSR never squared off directly against each other, the contest cost billions of dollars and millions of lives. The cold war also proved that America might be a superpower, but it doesn't have superpowers.

The conclusion of the cold war: uncertainty.

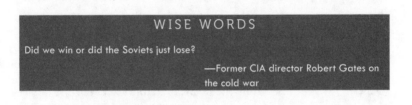

WISE WORDS

Did we win or did the Soviets just lose?

—Former CIA director Robert Gates on the cold war

SOCIAL SURVIVAL STRATEGY

Argument: "America was the obvious game changer (if late in the day in their arrival) in the world wars; nobody won the cold war."
If in doubt, deploy this safe strategy of stating the obvious: There can be no doubt that twice America was the (incredibly late) knight in shining armor to the world. Post the cold war, there has been nothing but confusion.

Crisp Fact: "During World War I, victory calculations were based on national birthrates."
Thanks to technology, World War I warfare reached a new level of brutality. If you're with a group that could do with a dose of humility, throw in this humbling detail.

Pivot: "Extraordinary to think how Berlin was entirely surrounded by East Germany during the cold war. Have you been? I found it/ hear that it's fascinating."

This will provoke a solid destination discussion. Berlin is one of the most fascinating places to visit in the world—it's living, breathing history. Everyone you speak to has a story. My German publisher for *The Single Girl's Guide* grew up behind the wall in East Berlin; with a family blacklisted by the Stasi, he had little hope to dream of future prospects until the wall came down. Now he owns a publishing company. Berliners' sense of guilt for their history, for the Holocaust, is palpable. And Berlin is where the politicians and artists live—the bankers are in Frankfurt—so it is made up of an extraordinarily eclectic mix of people.

CHEAT SHEET 17—MIDDLE EASTERN HISTORY

I've got an admission to make with this Cheat Sheet. I'm writing it last. For some reason, I thought awards season conversation would be less of a challenge. However, I'm trying not to beat myself up too badly over this. After all, I'm not the first and I will not be the last to be in a quandary when it comes to the Middle East.

Your key reference point almost every time something in the region makes the news or comes up in conversation is this: The Saudis are Sunni Muslims and the Iranians are Shia Muslims. The likely end game of all the current unrest in the Middle East is that you will have a Sunni sphere of influence controlled by Saudi Arabia and a Shia sphere of influence run by the Iranians. How much blood will have to be shed and how long that will take, nobody knows.

This is a history Cheat Sheet, and in it we will discover that there are two Western countries that you can safely criticize for the present problems in the Middle East. First of all, blame the British. Everyone can actually agree on that. Following on from this, I'm afraid you're going to need to admit that the United States has in recent times created power vacuums in the region (removal of Saddam Hussein on false intelligence being the prime example), which

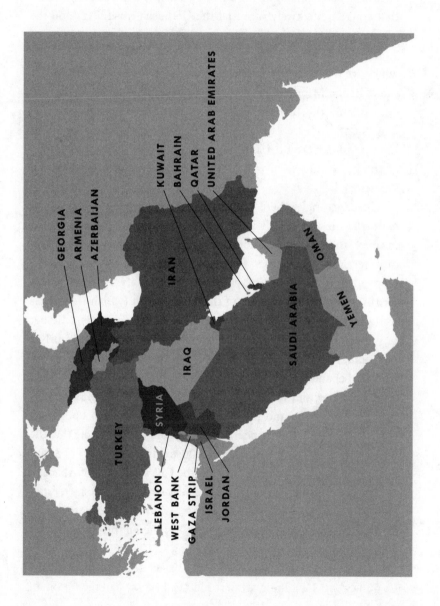

has contributed to/caused the current chaos. You might also venture that you're not entirely sure that the US hasn't misunderstood the Sunni and Shia relationship.

We will begin by examining the overall history of the region, where we will note that we need to think beyond borders because those in the Middle East do. That is because they are false borders (blame the British). However, since these borders are still consistently referred to, especially in Western discussion about the region, we are utilizing them and will then zero in on some of the hotter hot spots of the Middle East, including Israel and Palestine.

Unsurprisingly, there are no hard-and-fast rules about which countries are specifically in the Middle East. And of course at the moment they are not all countries. There is no state of Palestine, only territories (the Gaza Strip and portions of the West Bank) controlled by the Palestinian National Authority. At time of this writing, the CIA's definition of the Middle East (which we may as well use, since whatever they are doing clearly impacts us, whether or not you believe their intelligence is always intelligent) comprises Armenia, Azerbaijan, Bahrain, Georgia, Iran, Iraq, Israel, Jordan, Kuwait, Lebanon, Oman, Qatar, Saudi Arabia, Syria, Turkey, United Arab Emirates, and Yemen. Under this umbrella, the CIA separately lists the Gaza Strip and the West Bank, but since this is a history chapter, I have put them under the banner of Palestine. Note that the CIA places Afghanistan, India, and Pakistan in the category of South Asia. Egypt and Libya are located in the CIA's category of Africa.

Let's start at the very beginning, a very good place to start, especially in the case of the Middle East, where civilization began. There were the ancient empires including the Egyptians (c. 3000–1000 BC), the Assyrians and Babylonians (c. 1000–500 BC), the Persians (c. 550–330 BC), the Greeks (c. 330–60 BC), and the Romans (c. 60 BC—AD 140). From around 1300 to 1918 we had the Ottoman empire, the focal point of which was Istanbul, which of course is in modern-day Turkey. It was the biggest political entity in western Asia; the Ottoman empire's territory encompassed much of what we know now of as the Middle East. Meanwhile, for some of that period, the area of modern Iran was dominated by the Safavid dynasty (1501–c. 1722).

But it wasn't just about empire. Around AD 600, Islam began in Mecca, in western Saudi Arabia. There was also the tribal factor; many of the Arab peoples of the Arabian Peninsula were organized into tribal groups.

Arguably the real problems began with the Europeans. Sigh. I'm not talking about the Crusades of the Middle Ages/Medieval period involving Richard the Lionheart, et al. I'm talking the later phenom of colonialism. Which to most intents and purposes in this area means, yes, the Brits.

It was actually an American naval officer named Alfred Thayer Mahan who in 1902 first coined the geopolitical term *Middle East*. It might have previously made an appearance in the British India Office in the nineteenth century, but it was Mahan who was most influential in getting it into the vernacular. Prior to it, the label *Near East* had been bandied about. You might ask near to whom, but if you think about it, you'll know the depressing answer. Near to those dreadful Europeans. Far was, of course, in the direction of China.

The height of the Europeans' interference came after World War I when the Ottoman empire (which had sided with Germany and co.) was broken up and given over to the Brits and French as a result of the League of Nations. Tribal sensitivity in the division of the lands? Not so much. With scant regard to the local population, political boundaries were drawn. We are still paying the price for these partitions today, for the post–World War I boundaries made no sense on religious or ethnic grounds.

NOTEWORTHY NUGGET: LAWRENCE OF ARABIA

- Not just a 1962 film starring Peter O'Toole.

- Based on the real-life T. E. Lawrence, an illegitimately born British army officer.

- In 1916 during World War I, with the employment of Lawrence's diplomacy, bags of gold, and promises of Arab independence, the Brits encouraged an Arab uprising against the Turks (who had sided with the Germans in World War I). Although the Arabs received some territory as a result of the deal, they weren't best pleased when Western powers, particularly the Brits, later drew borders and created nations with scant regard for the local inhabitants.

- Further fury came with the 1917 Balfour Declaration. In a letter to Baron Rothschild, the UK's foreign secretary, Arthur Balfour, expressed that the British government was in favor of establishing a national home for the Jewish people in Palestine.

Some Middle Eastern states received their independence from Britain and France in the 1920s and 1930s. Others had to wait for post–World War II. I'm mentioning France here, because it wasn't just the Brits, but safe to say my countrymen, as the dominant power in the region, really were the worst culprits. When Hitler put paid to the Brits' true leading player status, the Middle East subsequently became a cold war battleground, with the Americans and Soviets up to their own shenanigans.

The backdrop of all this was that some countries in the region had struck the trump card of oil. Whenever you look at a Middle East state's international dealings, you must initially establish whether it is one of those that have copious quantities of black gold, such as Saudi Arabia, Qatar, Kuwait, and UAE, or one that doesn't, such as Yemen and Jordan. The first Gulf War came about because by invading Kuwait in 1990, Saddam Hussein had control of a fifth of the world's oil supplies and was on the doorstep of Saudi Arabia. That was a threat to the US at the time, as over the past fifty years America has needed the region because of the strategic commodity of oil. Over the next fifty years, with America becoming an exporter of oil and the economic factor off the table, it will be interesting to see how the focus of US foreign policy shifts—and how Asia's does. Because moving forward, Asia will become increasingly concerned with Middle East stability, as it needs the area's oil.

NOTEWORTHY NUGGETS: OIL AND OPEC

- OPEC (Organization of the Petroleum Exporting Countries) is a cartel of oil producers. The majority of them are based in the Middle East. Original members include Saudi Arabia, Iran, Iraq, and Kuwait.

- Arab oil exporters, in protest at America's support for Israel in the Yom Kippur War, put an embargo on shipments to the West on October 17, 1973.

- Long term, you could argue the embargo was a loss for OPEC. Along with the overthrow of the shah in Iran in 1979, it led to the first auto mileage standards in America, and it meant that the US and co. had a serious incentive to exploit oil elsewhere. And they did (Alaska, etc.).

In terms of history, the Middle East's peoples thus tend to have a longer link to their ethnicity and religion than to their nationality. Arabs constitute the major ethnic group in all of the Middle East states except Iran (Persian), Israel (Jewish), and Turkey (Turkic). The Kurds are a significant ethnic group, especially in Iraq, Syria, Iran, and Turkey. The Middle East is also the emotional and geographic center of Islam, Christianity, and Judaism.

The majority of those in the Middle East apart from those in Israel practice Islam. As we discussed under the subject of religion, there are a number of sects of Islam. Most people in the Middle East are Sunni. However, Shiite or Shia Islam is the majority religion in Iran, Iraq, and Bahrain. There is also significant Shiite presence in Lebanon, Kuwait, and Yemen. Historically, Sunni Muslim rulers have persecuted Shiites. In terms of language, Arabic is the most common, the second being Persian (aka Farsi), which is mostly in Iran. Red flag: Do not confuse Arabic and Persian/Farsi. They are completely different languages. Also note that neither of them are Urdu, which about 100 million people speak and is the official language of Pakistan. Urdu is also spoken in many areas of the Middle East, India, Nepal, and Bangladesh.

What about terrorism? Because that's what unfortunately tends to crop up when the region of the Middle East is discussed. Modern Islamic terrorism can be traced to the Wahhabi movement, an Arabian fundamentalist movement that started to find a wide following in the nineteenth century and inspired various fundamentalist movements during the twentieth century. It should be observed that they took note of and learned from what European terrorist organizations such as the Armenian Revolutionary Federation and the Irish Republican Army were doing. And also this: The United States saw and backed fundamentalist groups in the Middle East as a way to stop Soviet expansion. The Soviet invasion of Afghanistan has been described as the global trigger of Islamic terrorism.

KEY TERM: MUSLIM BROTHERHOOD

- The Muslim Brotherhood was founded in 1928. Strictly conservative and based in Egypt, it is devoted to establishing a nation based on Islamic principles. It became a radical underground force in Egypt and other Sunni countries and has performed terrorist acts.

- After the 2011 Egyptian revolution, the Muslim Brotherhood initially had much success and its candidate, Mohamed Morsi, won the presidential election in the summer of 2012. However, he was overthrown within a year.

- Note that fundamentalists willing to employ terrorism and violence in pursuit of political power tend to fail. You can cite the Muslim Brotherhood in Egypt, the Al-Qaeda core being dismantled and forced to go underground, and that Hamas is confined mostly to Gaza.

America has discovered in the post-9/11 world with forays into Iraq and Afghanistan that it can harm with the best intentions. It is very tricky to shape positive outcomes inside other countries. Remaking societies is just too hard. After the Arab Spring, taking out Muammar Gaddafi in Libya, America is now faced with the fact that in regards to the stability of the Middle East, the US has more to fear from weak governments than from strong ones. The rise of militias and terrorist groups is threatening American national security. The word on everyone's lips is ISIS, the origins of which we looked at in Cheat Sheet 11 on page 97.

KEY TERM: THE ARAB SPRING

A wave of antigovernment protests that kicked off in December 2010 in Tunisia and spread across the Middle East in early 2011. The term has its roots in the 1989 unrest in Eastern Europe, which led to the downfall of most of the communist regimes in the bloc. It's not been as clear-cut in the Middle East. The rich monarchies in the Persian Gulf held on, Syria and Libya ended up in civil war— and Tunisia, Egypt, and Yemen got an ambiguous period of transition.

Although we are going to take a look now at specific nations within the Middle East, with all this, I once again stress that it is necessary to keep in mind it's not as simple as a matter of borders. And I couldn't resist including the strangest strategy I've ever seen by a government website covering international relations. The CIA, when describing other nations, compares their land size to areas in America. Sensitivity chip? Not so much.

PHRASES TO DEPLOY WHEN TALKING ABOUT THE MIDDLE EAST

I've commentated live on air on the Middle East. The revolutionary wave of the Arab Spring, which began in late 2010, when talking heads had even less idea than usual about what was going on in the region, coincided with my political punditry taking hold. I've used every single one of the below lines. And when in doubt? Let me hear you say it: Just blame the British.

- "The Middle East is a graveyard for ethical foreign policies."
- "Technology means we can no longer have a hypocritical foreign policy."
- "The region was defined by European colonial powers a hundred years ago and defended by Arab autocrats ever since."
- "What about the law of diminishing returns?"
- "America should be the global police chief rather than the sole policeman."
- "All politics are local." (It can be easy to fall into the trap of viewing the Middle East from our perspective. To understand it, it has to be considered from theirs.)

IRAN

The land of Iran has played host to some of the world's oldest civilizations. Previously known as Persia, in 1935 the Iranian government requested that the international community instead use the moniker of Iran, which is the country's name in Persian and has been in use since the Sassanian period (AD 224–651). Geographically, the country is of immense geopolitical importance. It sits at the crossroads of Central Asia, Western Asia, and South Asia and is the only country to border both the Caspian Sea and the Indian Ocean. Iran also borders the north coast of the Strait of Hormuz, through which around a fifth of the world's petroleum passes. Just in case you were wondering why we don't invade and instead in 2015 spent a lengthy amount of time around a negotiating table, it has about three times the population of Iraq and a far more potent military.

Historically, Iran is one of the most fascinating countries in the world, so go study it. But vital information you must get into your brain immediately is what occurred during the cold war era. By the Americans (and the Brits), Iran was perceived as a safeguard against Soviet expansion and a place of stability in the oil-rich Persian Gulf. During World War II, the "constitutional" and pro-British monarch Shah Mohammad Reza Pahlavi came to power. However in 1951, under the democratically elected Prime Minister Mohammad Mossadegh, Iran's oil holdings were nationalized, which certainly didn't work for the British, who had made more money out of Iran's oil than Iran ever had, or for America. What if Mossadegh properly palled up with the Soviets? Cue a CIA-backed coup that removed Mossadegh in 1953. The "friendly" (to the Brits and Americans) shah, who had briefly fled into exile, was reinstalled to lead.

That's right. America took Iran's new democracy. And smothered it. With a monarchy. There's a reason that some Iranians have labeled Uncle Sam the "Great Satan." The US backed the shah with cash and in 1957 even aided in the setting up of Iran's intelligence agency, which was subsequently brutally repressive. The monarchy ended up being autocratic, corrupt, and cruel. In 1979 the Ayatollah Ruhollah Khomeini returned from exile and seized power, while the overthrown shah escaped and died in 1980. Homework at this point: See *Argo*. We have the Iran hostage crisis. Referred to in Persian as the "Conquest of the American Spy Den," it lasted for 444 days, from November 1979 through January 1981 (just after Reagan delivered his inaugural address—it probably cost Jimmy Carter a second term). After the deposed shah had been allowed into the US for medical treatment, Iranian students stormed the US embassy in Iran and took more than sixty hostages, supposedly believing that the CIA would put him back on the throne. The invasion outraged America as it violated every law going, both moral and religious. It was a turning point in the history of both the Middle East and America, and to this day has resulted in some Americans still believing that Iranians are irrational, hateful terrorists.

America's dubious dealings in the matter of Iran went on. In 1980, with American help—yes, American help—Saddam Hussein invaded Iran and we ended up with the eight-year Iran-Iraq war, which cost up to 1.5 million people their lives. In addition to this, there were various skirmishes going on by proxy. Iran wasn't taking this lying down and became embroiled in Lebanon's civil war, supporting the Shiite militant group Hezbollah, which was responsible for the 1983 bombings of the Beirut US embassy and barracks in which 241 American service personnel lost their lives. In July 1988, America mistakenly shot down an Iranian passenger jet, killing 290 people. And who could forget the Iran-Contra affair—where Reagan's White House was selling arms to Iran to bankroll a covert Central America war.

In more recent times, in an attempt to stop Iran from getting a nuclear weapon, the international community has levied incredibly tough sanctions on the country (seriously upsetting the mega wealthy—where are they supposed to get their caviar now?). One can argue that they worked. The "moderate" Hassan Rouhani was elected president in August 2013 and negotiations commenced. Please note that there's nothing in international law that outlaws uranium enrichment. Many countries have nuclear power. Various countries are on the threshold: They have the ability to produce nuclear weapons but choose not to do so, which is a perfectly legal ambition. Something some senators and other Fox News pundits seem to forget. The Iranians have also been helping the Iraqis fight ISIS. Yes, Iran, Iraq, and America now share a common enemy.

There's another important factor to remember when discussing Iran in the here and now. It is not just comprised of the older religious leaders and hard-liners that we sometimes see on TV spouting anti-American and anti-Israeli rhetoric. More than 70 percent or Iranians are under thirty-five years old. They do have the Internet (state censors may have blocked Facebook, but it's still pretty easy to access), and many of them would like a country with a future. These are the Iranians President Obama was hoping to empower in the ten years following his 2015 deal.

Main language: Persian, aka Farsi.

Main religion: Shia Islam. It is home to the world's largest Shia population.

CIA compares it in terms of size to: Slightly smaller than Alaska.

Capital: Tehran.

Political system: Complex; combines democracy with modern Islamic theocracy. Universal suffrage over the age of eighteen. A president and parliament are elected by the people, but the unelected supreme leader controls a network of institutions.

IRAQ

Formerly known as Mesopotamia, which means "land between the rivers." Beginning around 4000 BC, Mesopotamia is also known as the cradle of civilization, from where such trifles as writing pretty much originated. The area ended up as part of the Ottoman empire, and in its post–World War I division, Iraq was put under British authority as the British Mandate of Mesopotamia, at which a point a monarchy was established. The kingdom gained its independence in 1932; the monarchy was overthrown and a republic created in 1958. The country subsequently saw a succession of dictators, ending with Saddam Hussein, who took office in 1979.

Hussein was thus the dictator in charge for the Iran-Iraq War (1980–88) and the 1990 invasion of Kuwait . . . and the man removed by the US-led invasion in 2003. American presence eventually ended in 2011. Economically, the oil-rich country is ripe for exploitation—cue jostling by many a foreigner at that point. As outlined in Cheat Sheet 11, the government and military is now predominantly Shia; previously the minority Sunni had essentially ruled Iraq for centuries. (Saddam Hussein was a Sunni Muslim.) ISIS is mostly Sunni, its rise a symptom of a larger issue between Sunnis and Shiites.

Main language: Arabic and Kurdish.

Main religion: Shia Islam (c. 40 percent Sunni)—note the Shia predominance is something it shares with Iran and that the numbers are fluctuating owing to the number of refugees in the region.

CIA compares it in terms of size to: slightly more than twice the size of Idaho.

Capital: Baghdad.

Political system: Pre-2003, basically a dictatorship. Transitional period to a democracy followed after occupation by US-led forces (which were supposedly asked to leave, so they did, in 2011, although that is becoming increasingly controversial after ISIS's emergence). Universal suffrage over the age of eighteen. Still unstable as proven by the rise of ISIS. It will be tricky to get rid of ISIS when old Middle Eastern nation-states are collapsing and power vacuums are occurring; containment is the likely best-case scenario. This is not something the US can solve, but only support; ISIS is a regional problem and regional ownership of the issue is key in limiting its expansion. The good news, as noted on page 216, is that fundamentalists willing to employ terrorism and violence in pursuit of political power usually fail.

LEBANON

Positioned at the crossroads of the Arabian hinterland and the Mediterranean Basin, Lebanon and its maritime culture is perfectly placed to be a regional center for finance and trade. And also for instability—it does border Syria and Israel, after all.

There was civilization in Lebanon before historical records began. The Phoenicians were based there c. 1550–539 BC. Later it became part of the Roman empire and subsequently one of the foremost homes for Christianity. Eventually the area ended up as part of the Ottoman empire. Post–World War I, France (finally, not just those terrible Brits) got the mandate over the northern part of the former Ottoman empire province of Syria. In 1920 the French demarcated the region of Lebanon; the area received independence in 1943. Now, for good financial and cultural reasons, Lebanon was known as the Switzerland of the (Middle) East and Beirut as the Paris of the Middle East. But it has been notoriously politically unstable: There was a civil war from 1975 to 1990; its next-door neighbor Syria's military occupied Lebanon from 1976 to 2005. Also Israel and the Lebanon-based Shiite Hezbollah militia continued attacking each other, which even resulted in a short war in 2006. Red flag: Please don't confuse Hezbollah with Hamas, which we talk about in the Palestinian section.

Main language: Arabic.

Main religion: Muslims—including Shia, Sunni, Druze, Ismailite, Alawite, and Nusayri—make up around 60 percent of the population. Christians—including Maronite Catholic, Greek

Orthodox, Melkite Catholic, Armenian Orthodox, Syrian Catholic, Armenian Catholic, Syrian Orthodox, Roman Catholic, Chaldean, Assyrian, Coptic, and most of the remainder Protestant.

Capital: Beirut.

CIA compares it in terms of size to: c. 0.7 times the size of Connecticut.

Political system: Parliamentary democratic republic that operates under the backdrop of confessionalism, which proportionally allocates power among a number of religious communities. Suffrage is compulsory for males over twenty-one. Women with elementary education are allowed to vote.

QATAR

Before: used to be an impoverished backwater of a British protectorate. Now: major world player punching above its weight thanks to its oil and natural gas revenues. Qatar has been ruled by the absolute monarchy of the Al Thani family since the mid-1800s; independence was gained from the UK in 1971. Qatar's citizens don't pay taxes. It is the world's wealthiest country per capita and has been using its riches to buy global clout. The news station Al Jazeera is based in Doha (and before you go off on the TV station's being evil—it's terribly colonialist to demand everyone get Western-centric news, no?). The Qataris are diversifying and investing in everything they can—from London real estate to art, for when the oil and gas is no more. They will be front and center of the news over the next decade. Notable for trying to bridge the gap between Muslim and non-Muslim countries, Qatar was supposed, pre-FIFA scandal, to be the first Arab country to host the FIFA World Cup, which they won the bid for in 2022. Qatar has not seen the unrest of its neighbors during the Arab Spring—indeed, it spent billions supporting revolts. Over 90 percent of its citizens are in government-funded jobs and it is a relatively moderate Islamic state. Women can drive, while non-Muslims can purchase alcohol. You know someone who knows someone who has moved to Qatar or is at least trying to get on its gravy train.

Main language: Arabic.

Main religion: Sunni Islam.

Capital: Doha.

CIA compares it in terms of size to: slightly smaller than Connecticut.

Political system: Absolute monarchy heading into the realms of constitutional. Slightly.

SAUDI ARABIA

Birthplace of Islam. Mecca and Medina, the religion's two holiest shrines, are based there. The king's official title is actually the Custodian of the Two Holy Mosques.

After a campaign lasting several decades to unify most of the Arabian Peninsula, the modern Saudi state was founded in 1932 by Ibn Saud; in 1938 the country struck oil. Oh, did it strike oil—today the country is one of the world's main producers of oil and gas. One of Ibn Saud's male descendants still rules. After some protests during the Arab Spring, the government announced a number of benefits to Saudi citizens. It has the money for such large-scale "bribery." The largest country in the world without a river (and quite possibly a movie theater—seriously, no cinemas in the kingdom), Saudi Arabia is also the only nation with both a Persian Gulf and a coast on the Red Sea. If I start going off on their treatment of women I won't stop, so in the interest of brevity I'll move on.

Main language: Arabic.

Main religion: Sunni Islam.

CIA compares it in terms of size to: slightly more than one-fifth the size of the US.

Political system: Absolute monarchy bending a little toward limited political involvement in government for those outside the ruling royal family.

SYRIA

Several ancient empires and kingdoms were based in parts of what we now know as Syria, and its capital, Damascus, is one of the oldest continuously inhabited cities in the world. Post–World War I, it was the French who got the mandate over the northern portion of the former Ottoman empire province of Syria; hence it has been so noisy in recent years about what is to become of the nation. Syria was granted independence in 1946. Instability followed. In 1958 Syria joined with Egypt to become the United Arab Republic, but the two separated in 1961, with Syria reestablishing itself as the Syrian Arab Republic. In 1967 Syria lost the Golan Heights to Israel in the Arab-Israeli war. Fast-forward to 1970. Hafez al-Assad, a member of the minority Alawite sect and the socialist Ba'ath Party, orchestrated a bloodless coup. Stability followed. His son, Bashar al-Assad, who was actually supposed to be an eye surgeon until his brother died, became president in 2000 when his father passed away. Allied with Iran, Hezbollah, and the Russians, who have their one and only Mediterranean naval base in the country. The Arab Spring made its presence felt in Syria and the country fell into civil war, allowing ISIS to establish a significant presence. Odd fact? I was at school with Bashar's wife. We weren't brought up to marry dictators and not answer back. She's a *Lifetime* movie waiting to happen.

Main language: Arabic.

Main religion: Sunnis make up the majority, but Syria is diverse. The Alawites, which the Assads follow, have their historical heartlands in Syria. Alawites follow the Shiite version of Islam but with some variations.

Capital: Damascus.

CIA compares it in terms of size to: slightly larger than North Dakota.

Political system: fallen apart.

JORDAN

Post–World War I, the Brits demarcated a semiautonomous region of Transjordan from Palestine. The country gained its independence in 1946, when the area was subsequently called the Hashemite Kingdom of Jordan. Note its strategic location at the head of the Gulf of Aqaba and as the Arab country that has the longest border with Israel (they share control of the Dead Sea) and the occupied West Bank. In 1967 Jordan lost the West Bank to Israel; in 1988 King Hussein permanently relinquished its claims to it.

Main language: Arabic (official).

Main religion: Sunni Islam.

Capital: Amman, not to be confused with Oman, which is a country.

CIA compares it in terms of size to: slightly smaller than Indiana.

Political System: A constitutional monarchy, although the king exercises considerable power, which has proven especially controversial since the Arab Spring. Suffrage is universal over the age of eighteen, but well, the king has a lot of power.

YEMEN

Yemen is situated at the southern entrance of the Red Sea, a strategically important position in regards to trade and communication routes since ancient times. In the nineteenth century the Brits basically seized "control" of what became South Yemen; in 1918, North Yemen became independent from the Ottoman empire. In 1967 the Brits withdrew—and it took until 1990, and much instability, for North and South to officially unite. Civil war occurred in 1994, and in 2008 the southern secessionist movement strengthened once more. Whenever discussing Yemen, keep in mind that it borders Saudi Arabia and that this is a constant factor in all foreign policy.

The Arab Spring brought the downfall of President Ali Abdullah Saleh (later to openly ally with Houthis) and the rise of President Abd Rabbuh Mansur Hadi (Sunni) in 2011–2012. However, deep divisions remained in the economically challenged country, with the Hadi-led government in dispute with Islamist militants and Houthi rebels. Note the Houthi are Shia and allied to Iran; the Sunni Saudi Arabia fears a Houthi takeover, as they want free passage through the southern entrance of the Red Sea . . .

Main language: Arabic.

Main religion: estimated 65 percent Sunni, 35 percent Shia.

Capital: Sana'a, but in February 2015 it came under rebel control, so was provisionally relocated to Aden on the southern coast.

CIA compares it in terms of size to: almost four times the size of Alabama; slightly larger than twice the size of Wyoming.

Political System: uncertain after a coup d'état in 2014–2015. The Houthis were all about dissolving parliament and installing a council, while deposed President Abd Rabbuh Mansur Hadi was declaring he was still in office.

PALESTINE AND ISRAEL

It is apparent in debates about Palestine and Israel that I eavesdrop on (I've learned, especially in America, that biting my tongue is the safest path—Europeans often have a somewhat different perspective on the region than Yanks) that what is often lacking is a basic grasp of historical events in the area. Make sure you are cognizant of these facts before entering into an argument.

Palestine is the birthplace of both Judaism and Christianity and sits between Arabia, Syria, and Egypt. It is at a key crossroads geographically, politically, and emotionally.

Before 1948, Palestine referred to the area between the Jordan River and the Mediterranean. Throughout history, the region fell under the control of many empires, including the Egyptian, Assyrian, Roman, and Byzantine, and thus experienced associated boundary changes. From the early sixteenth century through 1917, Palestine was part of the Ottoman empire.

As noted earlier, during World War I, there was the Balfour Declaration. In 1917 the British government acknowledged that they were in favor of establishing a national home for the Jewish people in Palestine. Post–World War I, the Brits got the mandate for Palestine, which lasted through World War II.

Palestine's eastern half became the emirate of Transjordan; the western half was administered directly by the Brits.

This arrangement ended post–World War II. In the aftermath of the Holocaust, in 1947 the United Nations proposed a plan to partition Palestine, dividing it into an Arab state and a Jewish one, with the Jerusalem-Bethlehem area administered by the United Nations. Note that the West Bank was part of the territory that the UN proposed be Arab.

The Partition Plan was accepted by Jewish, but not by Arab, leaders. This resulted in the first Arab-Israeli War in 1948, which the Arabs labeled "the catastrophe." Now take a look at this timeline of key events.

1949: The outcome of the war was that Egypt got the Gaza Strip and Transjordan the West Bank and East Jerusalem, while Israel got some land that under the Partition Plan had been designated Arab.

1967: The Six-Day War ended in a decisive loss for the Muslim side. Israel won power over:

- The Golan Heights from Syria.

- The West Bank and East Jerusalem from Jordan.

- The Sinai Peninsula and the Gaza Strip from Egypt.

1972: Palestinian terrorists murdered eleven Israeli athletes, coaches, and judges at the Munich Olympics, aiming to force the release of two hundred Arabs in Israeli prisons.

1973: The Yom Kippur War. Israel fights Syria, Jordan, and Egypt. As we noted in Cheat Sheet 16, thanks to the cold war, the US (pro-Israel) and USSR (pro-Arab) got involved. The Arab side had early success in the conflict, which helped them psychologically after 1967. Israel fought back but there was a realization they might not always win. Paved the way for negotiations.

1974: The Palestine Liberation Organization (PLO) was formed.

1978: Camp David Accords: Jimmy Carter's high point. The Egyptians and Israelis negotiated and signed agreements at Camp David that set out a framework for peace between them. This led to Israel signing a 1979 peace treaty with Egypt, the first between Israel and any of its Arab neighbors. There is no longer a prospect of a united Arab military front.

1988: Jordan cedes its claim to the West Bank.

1993: Oslo Accords—the PLO, led by Yasser Arafat, and Israeli officials, led by Yitzhak Rabin, agreed on a framework for peace.

Arafat in the process recognized Israel's right to exist. This was Bill Clinton's "handshake" moment—when he got the two to shake hands. The Palestinian Authority was established to govern the West Bank and Gaza Strip. Rabin was later assassinated in 1995 by an Israeli Zionist terrorist who was against the peace initiative. That's right, an Israeli Zionist terrorist.

1994: Israel-Jordan peace treaty, formally ending the state of war between them.

1994–1999: A series of agreements in which Israel transfers security and civilian responsibility for many Palestinian-populated areas of the West Bank as well as the Gaza Strip.

1990s: Fall of communism—significant number of Russian Jews emigrate to Israel, thus bolstering ties with a leading oil supplier and power broker.

Mid-2000: Negotiations to sort out the permanent status of the West Bank and Gaza Strip stall after an intifada (Arab uprising—in this case Palestinians against Israeli occupation) outbreak. Known as the Second Intifada—the first was from 1987 to, many would argue, the Oslo Accords).

2003: The UN, Russia, the EU, and the US present a road map for a peace settlement by 2005, for two states: a democratic Palestine and Israel.

2004: Palestinian leader Yasser Arafat dies; Mahmoud Abbas elected. Both were members of Fatah, a Palestinian political party and the largest faction in the PLO. Israel and the PA agree to move forward with peace process.

2005: Israel dismantles its military facilities and withdraws all its soldiers and settlers from the Gaza Strip. Some of its military is redeployed from the West Bank, but Israel still controls maritime and airspace access, etc. Still settlement activity

(Jewish civilian communities on lands occupied by Israel in 1967) in the West Bank and East Jerusalem.

2006: Hamas (an offshoot of the Muslim Brotherhood, a Palestinian Sunni Islamist movement with a military wing—there's a debate about how linked they are) wins the elections and control of the PA government. Cue internal factions fighting within the PA between Hamas and Fatah. Note that Hamas is basically a terrorist organization that nobody likes, including Arab governments in the Middle East.

2007: For the first time the "two-state solution" is established as foundation for future negotiations between Israel and the PA at the Annapolis Conference.

2008: Israel invades Gaza to stop Hamas and others from launching rockets.

2010: Direct discussions between Israel and the PA, but they fail to go anywhere, unable to resolve the issue of settlements.

2012: After months of increasing rocket attacks, Israel starts a week-long military campaign against Gaza-based armed groups.

2013: More talks.

2014: Three Jewish teenagers are kidnapped and murdered in the West Bank; Israel arrests multiple Hamas members. Militants increase rocket fire from Gaza; Israel launches military campaign. Egypt brokers a cease-fire.

2015: To everybody's surprise, quite possibly most of all his own, Prime Minister Benjamin Netanyahu is reelected in Israel. During his campaign, he declared that if in power he would never establish a Palestinian state. Bibi's subsequently tried to walk that one back.

As of time of writing, there is no state of Palestine, only two territories, the West Bank and the Gaza Strip. Legally they remain occupied by Israel, regardless of agreements made between the Israeli
and Palestinian authorities. Both populations are predominantly
Palestinian Arab and Sunni Muslim. Half a million Israelis live
across the "green line," the 1967 border.

Israel is the world's only Jewish state: More than 75 percent of its
population is Jewish; the majority of the remainder are mostly Arab.
A democracy, with universal suffrage at eighteen, it uses the system
of proportional representation, so extremes do get a voice. Its capital is controversially Jerusalem; its financial center—and the location of the US embassy—is Tel Aviv. Israel, Republican invitations
to Bibi Netanyahu to speak in Congress and bypassing the White
House in 2015 notwithstanding, is a bipartisan issue in America.
There is unilateral support for the country and Israel needs its
closest friend, not just because of its isolated position in the Middle
East. Anti-Semitism has existed in one form or another for a thousand years in Europe. There has recently been a rise once again in
anti-Semitism in the region, although it should be noted that multiple European leaders and those in the media have spoken out
against it, and millions in Europe are horrified by it.

The million-dollar question? Is a two-state solution possible?
There is a very real fear that a fundamentalist Palestine rather than
a nation with a secular government could take hold. Should a true
mixed state be the aim?

God promised Abraham a son, but his wife was very old, so he
had a son with a servant, named Ishmael. Then his wife had a son,
Isaac. Muslims trace their lineage to Ishmael, the Jews to Isaac.
Christians worship the same God as the Jews, but the Jews do not
believe that Jesus Christ was the promised Messiah. Oh, but what
might have been, Abraham.

SOCIAL SURVIVAL STRATEGY

Argument: "The post–World War I boundaries made no sense on religious or ethnic grounds."
This is a safe point to make and means you can blame the British, who will willingly admit fault.

Crisp Fact: Feeling brave? "Abraham should have kept it in his pants: God promised Abraham a son, but his wife was very old, so he had a son with a servant, Ishmael. Then his wife had a son, Isaac. Muslims trace their lineage to Ishmael, the Jews to Isaac. Oh, but what might have been, Abraham."
Employ this one only if you're utterly sure that nobody within hearing will be offended by it; the right company will find it fascinating.

Pivot: "Qatar won the bid to be the first Arab country to host the FIFA World Cup in 2022. Are you a soccer [*football* if you're speaking to anyone who isn't North American] fan?"
Most people can muster an opinion on soccer, even if it's "I don't get it." It should swing the chat onto safer territory.

SUBJECT FIVE—POLITICS

POLITICS SUMMARY

The key theme to keep in mind when discussing anything related to this subject is that, as the former British Labour Party Prime Minister Harold Wilson said, "A week is a long time in politics." If you sprinkle the phrase around, you will find people will nod sagely before offering their own anecdote or changing the conversation for you. Think about dropping into the mix that the word *filibuster* comes from a Dutch word meaning pirate—everyone has something to contribute about pirates, even if it's just how Johnny Depp looks in eye makeup. And if you really can't stand one more second of election chat, just mutter, "Wake me up on November [insert the day after the presidential/midterm election]" and switch the dialogue to anything else. Anyone worth talking to will be relieved.

America is exceptional. In most democracies, people stand for election. In the US they keep running, unless they are a second-term president, in which case they are labeled a lame duck and might as well be *Peter Pan*'s crocodile the way their clock is ticking out their presidency so loud. The foundation of America is also so intrinsically linked to democracy (if you take Britain, we evolved—you Americans arrived) that an understanding of the political system is essential to understanding the fabric of American life. It is well-nigh impossible to have a conversation of significant length with anyone semi-intelligent in America without someone making semi-intelligent remarks about unintelligent politicians and politics. The next few Cheat Sheets will provide you with some smart observations. Well, at least as clever as anything that appears on cable news, as I've used most of them. Which actually may not be a selling point.

I digress. We begin at the beginning. The American Constitution. If you're American, you'll have been taught all about this, but we remind you of the parts that would be helpful to have nearer the front of your brain. Despite being a document of unparalleled brilliance with astonishing execution (just look at the way Egypt struggled to come up with a constitution that people stuck to), for some reason, this subject rarely makes the basic school curriculum in foreign parts. Especially Britain. Speaking of limeys, there is a way to blame the Second Amendment gun drama on them. Quite. We have it here.

This will be followed up with a look at American law. Apart from unraveling some noteworthy legalese, we will focus on the headline bits of federal law enabling you to further compliment—or more likely criticize—Congress, POTUS, and SCOTUS. As a latecomer to your Constitution, I'm rather fond—indeed, protective—of it, so I clearly go off on a bit of a rant about the Foreign Intelligence Surveillance Court (FISC), which was established by Congress in the Foreign Intelligence Surveillance Act (FISA) of 1978. Disclaimer: This is not a lawbook and you can/will need to hire an actual lawyer if you have any actual brushes with the law.

We then turn to political scandals. Which are hilarious when they don't actually have an impact on you or your life or your time. If it's the latter, they do become a little sad even if they involve a Weiner. In Cheat Sheet 20 we give a bit of historical context on scandals and then focus on some case studies of American politicians' naughtiness, from which we derive some top behavioral tips for anyone contemplating a run for office. Setting the scene right now, we would be remiss not to give a honorable mention to a few international classics. Dominique Strauss-Kahn, International Monetary Fund head and supposedly future French president, allegedly assaulted a maid in a New York City hotel room, and was later removed and arrested from an Air France flight at JFK (fitting, perhaps, bearing in mind Kennedy's predilections). Charges were later dropped. Possibly the most amusing thing British Prime Minister David Cameron ever uttered was his quote about then Italian premier Silvio Berlusconi, king of the bunga bungas: "I've learnt if the queen asks you to a party, you say yes, and if the Italian prime minister asks you to a party, it's probably safe to say no." The Brits of course came up with what many consider the classic scandal benchmark, the Profumo affair of 1963. Party girl Christine Keeler was supposedly sleeping with a Soviet spy and John Profumo, secretary of state for war, at the same time. Profumo lied about it to the House of Commons, got found out, and had to resign, seriously screwing up the Macmillan government. However, some Americans have done their best to sweep the disgrace stakes and you can read all about it here.

Finally we provide a stellar set of election talking points, mainly focused on the never-ending presidential race. Look on the bright side—at least America's taking the process seriously in electing the leader of the free world. Or keeping pundits like me in work. Please. You know you want to. Point is this, read Cheat Sheet 21 and you will be properly armed through every presidential debate and election-night drinking game.

Right, to the oldest and shortest written Constitution of any major government in the world. As a foreigner, I do have to hand it to you, America. You're not a country that's normally in need of an ego boost, so us outsiders don't usually hand you one, but in this next Cheat Sheet you do display unparalleled brilliance.

CHEAT SHEET 18—THE AMERICAN CONSTITUTION

BACKGROUND BRIEFING

Foreigners habitually perceive various American concepts as dubious. Football, to the rest of the world, is played with the feet. Yet Americans insist on calling their version of handball *football* and everyone else's football *soccer*.

However, there is little international (in fairly friendly places, at least) debate that Americans are justified in their pride in the United States Constitution. To remind you, it was written in 1787 and ratified in 1788, when Massachusetts became the ninth out of the thirteen original US states to agree, thus reaching a sufficient number to accept it. The Constitution has been in use since 1789, making it the world's longest utilized written national constitution. The supreme law of the United States, it's the source of all government powers—with built-in limitations that define the basic rights of citizens.

Why did it appear? When the Revolutionary War ended in 1783, there was the thought that the Continental Congress's powers via the Articles of Confederation, the United States's first constitution, weren't actually up to the job of governing the country. You know when it's not about money, but it is? It was. George Washington admitted as much: "No money," he said. The central government couldn't raise funds itself.

So the Constitutional Convention was called in May 1787 and the framers trotted off to Philadelphia to sort it all out. They were a collection of stellar names, with Thomas Jefferson going so far as to label them demigods. They included Benjamin Franklin, Alexander Hamilton, and James Madison, with George Washington as president of the convention.

KEY TERM: THE FOUNDING FATHERS

The Founding Fathers is an umbrella label. There are two important main groups within it: those who signed the Declaration of Independence in 1776 and those who framed the Constitution. Another group is made up of those who signed the Articles of Confederation.

The following is all deeply relevant for when you discuss the current crop of discordant politicians. For the US Constitution was drawn up with appropriate levels of falling-out and secret debate: splits between patriots and nationalists; the Virginia Plan (preferred by the big states) versus the New Jersey Plan (preferred by the small states). After much discussion between and within the thirteen states—Federalists supported, Antifederalists didn't—the Constitution was completely ratified when Rhode Island finally came on board in 1790. This was important, as everyone agreed that everyone should be seen to be agreeing.

NOTEWORTHY NUGGETS: THE SEVEN ARTICLES

The framers provided the framework of America's government via the preamble and seven articles. Whichever way you look at it, the separation of powers between the three branches of government is pretty genius. The headlines:

Article I—Legislative branch (Congress).

Article II—Executive branch (president, veep, cabinet).

Article III—Judicial branch (Supreme Court, lower courts).

Article IV—Relationship between states and the federal government. Also rules about admitting new states to the union.

Article V—Allows amendments.

Article VI—Constitution is the highest law of land.

Article VII—Ratification rules.

The Constitution began a tradition that lives to this day in American politics—the need for compromise, for it was a Great Compromise. Representation in the House would be based on population and members could serve two years; each state got two senators who could serve for six.

NOTEWORTHY NUGGET: THE FEDERALIST PAPERS

- In an attempt to convince New York that the Constitution should be ratified, between October 1787 and August 1788 Alexander Hamilton, James Madison, and John Jay published eighty-five articles in New York newspapers under the pseudonym Publius.

- They came to be labeled *The Federalist Papers* and have become a key source in understanding some of the framers' motives.

- Especially notable: No. 10 (warns against factions) and No. 51 (justifies the Constitution's structure).

WHY IT MATTERS TODAY

The demigods were self-aware enough to know they were not perfect, that they could not be the be-all and end-all and that the Constitution needed to be a living document. Hence Article V exists. Amendments.

WISE WORDS

The United States Constitution has proved itself the most marvelously elastic compilation of rules of government ever written.

—Franklin D. Roosevelt

America can amend the Constitution and it has managed to do so twenty-seven times. Although only twenty-six are in effect, as the Eighteenth, prohibition, beginning in 1920, is trumped by the Twenty-first Amendment of 1933. Thank goodness. I clearly wouldn't have bothered to go through the American immigration process if I couldn't have had a drink at the end of it.

The first ten amendments were all ratified in 1791 and are collectively known as the Bill of Rights. They were done in a speedy fashion, as for many it was somewhat a sticking point that there wasn't a Bill of Rights in the first place.

Since there have been only seventeen subsequent amendments, it is obviously not an easy process. Basically, an amendment can be proposed by a two-thirds vote of BOTH Houses of Congress or if two-thirds of the states request one. Ratification requires three-quarters of the states.

NOTEWORTHY NUGGETS: AMENDMENTS YOU NEED ON SPEED DIAL

NB: one through ten, part of the Bill of Rights, all 1791

1st: freedom of speech, religion, assembly, press.

2nd: right to bear arms. Been confirmed over time by SCOTUS, not going anywhere.

4th: right to be free from unreasonable searches and seizures.

5th: includes rights against double jeopardy and self-incrimination (so you can "take the fifth"). Also due process (which is also in the 14th).

6th: speedy trial by jury, etc. Right to counsel (also linked to 5th).

8th: "cruel and unusual punishments" banned. Gitmo, anyone?

13th: 1865, abolishes slavery.

14th: 1868, due process (linked to 5th). Equal protection. Citizenship and equal civil and legal rights to African-Americans. This amendment got applied for *Brown v. Board of Education of Topeka* (1954)—racial segregation in public schools unconstitutional—and *Roe v. Wade* in 1973.

15th: 1870, voting protection on race, color.

19th: 1920, women's suffrage vote.

26th: 1971, voting allowed for those eighteen and above.

TALKING POINTS

- The first three words of the US Constitution, "We the People," affirm that the US government exists to serve its citizens. Remind politicians of the preamble's beginning on a regular basis.

- The demigods got their inspiration from all sorts, including:

  * Right of due process came from England's Magna Carta (originally issued in 1215; the barons forced it on King John to protect their privileges—see Cheat Sheet 15).

  * The English Glorious Revolution of 1688, when Parliament told the monarchy that the concept of ruling by divine right was an absolute no-go.

  * The English Whigs Edmund Burke and William Blackstone were especially popular.

  * Thomas Hobbes on theory of government.

  * There were fans of Edward Coke's civil liberties and John Locke's philosophy.

  * It wasn't just the Brits. The French Montesquieu had some stellar thoughts on divided government.

- Controversial policies of racial profiling such as "stop and frisk" are always a case of demography versus the Constitution.

- As is true of every nutcase out there, the more extreme politicians' views are, the more they think they're right.

- The last amendment, the twenty-seventh, was in 1992 and was about Congress's salaries. If you sneer about this to your nearest politician and he or she retorts that the idea of it had been floating about since James Madison in 1789, just point out that American politicians taking 203 years to do something is about right.

- A couple of "crisp facts," as one of my Cambridge professors called them, to show your superiority: Neither House can meet anywhere else without agreement and a congressman cannot be arrested for misdemeanors on the way to the Hill.

RED FLAGS

- Article VI of the Constitution prohibits religious tests for office-holders. If you're trying to win votes at a Christian right meeting, best you don't bring that up.

- With a lover of the Second Amendment who claims that owning a gun is all-American? Probably wise not to mention that some suggest that it's actually a British idea and that the Brits later thought better of it while Americans failed to.

  * A case can be made that the right to bear arms stems from a proviso in the English Bill of Rights of 1689. Of course the Brits subsequently started introducing gun control laws in 1824, and since then they have developed to some of the strictest such laws in the world. Most limeys believe this is the reason why their gun deaths are around 150 a year and America's are at well over 30,000.

  * With an estimated 300 million guns in America, not worth bringing this up to a gun aficionado, who undoubtedly has immediate access to one.

∗ And just to throw it out there: The American per capita rate of gun ownership is nearly 50 percent, higher than any other country's.

WISE WORDS

The great enemy of truth is very often not the lie—deliberate, contrived, and dishonest—but the myth—persistent, persuasive, and unrealistic. Too often we hold fast to the clichés of our forebears. We subject all facts to a prefabricated set of interpretations. We enjoy the comfort of opinion without the discomfort of thought.

—John F. Kennedy

SOCIAL SURVIVAL STRATEGY

Argument: "Changing course is sometimes the right thing to do. Even the framers of the Constitution knew they were not perfect. Hence it is a living document and Article V exists and it can be amended."

This is to be utilized when someone is being inflexible. Monarchy still exists in Britain because it adapts. All men were created equal in 1776—unless they were female and/or had a skin color that wasn't white.

Crisp Fact: "America's Constitution is the oldest and shortest written Constitution of any major government in the world."

Subtly get this one in if you're an American feeling underappreciated amongst a bunch of foreigners—you've earned it.

Pivot: "Shall we make use of the Twenty-first Amendment and have another drink?"

Heading to the bar may be the oldest distraction in the book, but it's one of the best. How on earth did law-abiding people cope during Prohibition?

CHEAT SHEET 19—AMERICAN LAW

BACKGROUND BRIEFING

Stating the obvious, America's legal system makes its world go round. Much of American law can trace its roots to English common law, which was practiced at the time of the Revolutionary War. Fascinating as all this is (seriously, but admittedly I'm a nerd who regrets not doing postgrad law), this Cheat Sheet is not here for obscure bits of information you should be hiring a lawyer for. Apart from touching on some noteworthy legalese, we will focus on the headline bits of federal law enabling you to further compliment— or more likely criticize—Congress, POTUS, and SCOTUS.

Ostensibly Congress's job is to make the law, since it is the legislature. Which is why its approval rating hovers around that of Iran's and North Korea's. Congress is made up of the House of Representatives and the Senate, and both need to agree on the law to pass it.

The executive branch—POTUS, the vice-president, department heads (cabinet members), and heads of independent agencies—is responsible for ensuring that the law is carried out. Meanwhile the judiciary—the federal (not the state) courts, all the way up to SCOTUS—interprets the law. Whatever the Supreme Court says is the end, because there is no higher appeals court. If judicial review decides the law violates the Constitution, it prevents the law being enforced.

KEY TERM: HABEAS CORPUS

- Translated from the Latin: "that you have the body."

- A writ of habeas corpus is used to bring a detainee before a court to determine if the detention is lawful.

- The origins of habeas corpus can be traced in English law to as far back as Henry II's reign in the twelfth century.

WHY IT MATTERS TODAY

Congress has the capacity to improve or ruin your life—or at the very least, to confuse anyone who fell asleep in certain high school classes—with their vocabulary. Any member can introduce, or sponsor, a bill to create a new law. Once it is introduced, it is then assigned to the appropriate committee for review—perhaps hearings, testimony from special interests and the public—and revision, or markup. If the committee really doesn't like the bill, they table it so the House can't even vote on it. Otherwise they release it, reporting it out.

Now this doesn't necessarily mean that the bill will see a bit of floor action. In the House, that's down to the Speaker and the majority leader, and in the Senate, to the majority leader. If the bill makes it to debate, it may be passed, defeated, or amended. A vote passes by a simple majority—House 218/435 and Senate 51/100.

NOTEWORTHY NUGGETS: THE 113TH CONGRESS

- Ran January 3, 2013, to January 3, 2015.
- Had the lowest approval rating of any Congress since they began polling for it.

• The "Do Nothing" Congress denounced by Truman in 1947 passed 906 laws. The 113th Congress just beat the 112th Congress, passing 13 more—296. Be wary of pushing this point too much—it comes down to the quality of the laws, not just the number.

To put it simply, in the unlikely event that you think any of this procedure sounds simple, it isn't. Before a bill can become a law, both houses of Congress must pass identical versions of said bill. Thus most legislation ends up in conference committee, made up of representatives and senators trying to come up with a compromise solution. If they manage it and both houses agree, the bill is enrolled (printed) and the Speaker of the House and the vice-president, who is president of the Senate, sign it.

KEY TERMS: FILIBUSTER AND CLOTURE

- The word *filibuster* comes from a Dutch word meaning pirate. Originally both representatives and senators could try and hold the bill on the floor to prevent a vote, but now only senators have the right to speak as long as necessary on any issue.

- In 1917 Woodrow Wilson urged senators to adopt Rule 22, Cloture, which allows the Senate to end a debate with a two-thirds majority vote. They did, and it was reduced in 1975 to three-fifths, 60 of the 100 senators.

- Since 1980, neither party has ever held 60 percent of all the seats in the Senate, a filibuster-proof majority.

- The threat of filibuster (like a presidential veto) normally ensures it doesn't occur.

- South Carolina's J. Strom Thurmond holds the record for longest filibuster, which he used against the 1957 Civil Rights Act: 24 hours, 18 minutes.

- If one party is threatening to change the rules, wisely say that one day they will rue the day . . .

We're not done yet. For the bill to be promulgated, get to be a law, the president has to sign it. (S)he has ten days to put pen(s) to paper. If (s)he doesn't like it (s)he has two options. One is the veto, when the bill is sent back to Congress, who can override the president if two-thirds of both houses agree to. The second is just not signing or vetoing it, in which case the bill becomes law.

NOTEWORTHY NUGGETS: VETOES

- FDR holds the record for most vetoes—635.
- Bush II didn't veto at all until his second term. Stem cell research was definitely not his thing. It was, however, Nancy Reagan's, who sources tell me was furious with him when he vetoed a stem cell bill.

Crystal clear now why the government has issues governing?

Keeping an eye on those (not) governing, you've got SCOTUS. Made up of nine justices, including the chief justice, Article III states that with "good Behaviour" they may hold the position for life. Bearing in mind SCOTUS effectively determines what the Constitution means, it's clearly a BIG deal when one vacates the seat and the president gets to nominate one.

Of course, like all high-level executive positions (around 2,000), the nomination has to be confirmed by a Senate majority. Quite. Disastrous nominees who never made it onto SCOTUS include George W. Bush's "My Little Crony," Harriet Miers; Reagan's pot-smoking Douglas Ginsburg; and Nixon's G. Harrold Carswell, against whom there was evidence of racist conduct.

TALKING POINTS

- POTUS, under Article II, Section I, of the Constitution, can make legally binding executive orders to manage the operations of the federal government. They have been used by every president since George Washington.

* Executive orders are not all created equal, so it's a false comparison to compare a president's number of them. It's the content that counts. Some are innocuous—proclamations such as National Take Your Child to Work Day. Other executive orders are laws containing important policy changes: Truman integrated the armed forces; Eisenhower desegregated schools; Reagan barred federal funds advocating abortion, which Clinton reversed. National security directives (aka presidential decision directives) are not always made public in the interest of national security.

* One of the most notorious executive orders was FDR's transferring German-Americans and Japanese-Americans to internment camps during World War II.

* Issues arise when executive orders are contrary to Congress's liking. Normally Congress is okay when the president is wearing his or her "commander in chief" hat, since the Constitution does make the president America's chief diplomat. Domestic policy executive orders are more controversial. To do something about it, because of the presidential veto, two-thirds of each house has to agree more specifically on how the president should act. Tricky.

* It's rare, but SCOTUS of course can step in over executive orders. They did with Truman over nationalization of steel mills in 1952.

• Examples of SCOTUS's deciding lawmakers have been unconstitutional include 1996's Defense of Marriage Act, which barred the federal government from legally recognizing and extending benefits to same-sex couples. In June 2013 SCOTUS ruled that the federal government could no longer discriminate against same-sex couples, saying that to deny same-sex couples equal protection under the law was a violation of the Fifth Amendment. Go, liberty and equality.

• In 1935 and 1936, SCOTUS "handed down" twelve decisions voiding various New Deal acts of Congress. FDR was unimpressed and came up with a court-packing plan. Congress wasn't having it.

- It was the Warren Court (1953–1969) that okayed the trailblazing of civil liberties—against school segregation, limiting religion in schools, Miranda rights. Note that Earl Warren himself was nominated by Eisenhower, a Republican.

- FISC, the United States's eleven-member Foreign Intelligence Surveillance Court, has controversially been expanding its role behind closed doors. The eleven justices (all currently appointed by the chief justice of the Supreme Court) work in rotating shifts (so only ONE signs most orders) and have created a burgeoning secret body of law. This court allows the NSA to do what it does. Some believe it is stretching the Fourth Amendment (prohibits unreasonable searches and seizures) to the breaking point.

  ∗ The Supreme Court hears both sides of the case, FISC only one—the government's. Which is not the American way of doing things.

  ∗ The justices are all appointed by one justice. Doesn't sound like justice to me, at any rate.

  ∗ FISC was originally created by Congress as a check against government wiretapping abuse.

- An international perspective is always useful. You can point out that English-speaking nations—the Anglosphere, if you will—have a concept of liberty different from that of the nations of continental Europe. Anglos believe their rights are established by tradition and rooted in law. The Euros perceive their rights as being granted by the state.

RED FLAGS

- If you want to send your dinner guests to sleep, Article I, Section 7, of the Constitution will do the trick. It means that only members of the House can introduce revenue bills, ones that deal with taxes or spending. The reason being that until the Seventeenth Amendment was ratified in 1913, senators were chosen by state legislatures, while representatives had to be voted in by the people. Since there were more representatives, they were thought to be more representative of the people and also likely to be poorer than the senators and thus more mindful of the right for Americans to keep their hard-earned cash.

- If anyone is still awake and you really want to finish them off, you can talk about how impeachment proceedings have to begin in the House; it is the Senate that adjudicates them.

- Don't confuse Miranda rights with anything to do with your friend Miranda. They are the cop TV show rights. Exact wording can change, but the gist is always is "You have the right to remain silent. Anything you say can and will be used against you in a court of law. You have a right to an attorney. If you cannot afford an attorney, one will be appointed for you."

  * It was created in 1966 after the SCOTUS case *Miranda v. Arizona*. Ernesto Arturo Miranda was arrested and tried for domestic violence and had his Fifth and Sixth Amendment rights infringed on. He was later retried and convicted anyway.

  * Small print: You don't get Miranda rights until you're arrested. Also there is an exception for public safety if federal prosecutors think a public safety threat is imminent or if you're an "enemy combatant" and subject to military law.

  * There was a Big Drama over whether Boston bomber Dzhokhar Tsarnaev should be read his Miranda rights or not. Was he an enemy combatant? Several Fox News pundits believed they were vindicated when sixteen hours after the start of his interrogation he was read them . . . and stopped talking when he had been "singing like a canary until the judge showed up."

WISE WORDS

You should see what our Founding Fathers used to say to each other and in the early part of our nation. But what they were able to do, especially in Philadelphia in 1787, four months, they argued about what a House should be, what a Senate should be, the power of the president, the Congress, the Supreme Court. And they had to deal with slavery.

—Colin Powell

SOCIAL SURVIVAL STRATEGY

Argument: "The English-speaking nations, the Anglosphere, have a concept of liberty different from that of the nations of continental Europe. Anglos believe their rights are established by tradition and rooted in law. The Euros perceive their rights as being granted by the state."

This is one of the reasons the UK-US "special relationship" exists and why you probably feel more affinity with a sarcastic Brit than a sophisticated French(wo)man.

Crisp Fact: "*Filibuster* comes from a Dutch word meaning pirate."

This should calm a cantankerous conversation about politics, as you can then start talking about Johnny Depp's career and how his *Pirates of the Caribbean* costar Keira Knightley "has done well."

Pivot: "Let's talk about people and objects who do what our politicians can't—compromise. What do you make of the cronut concept?"

The croissant-doughnut hybrid will be something the person you're talking to adores, disapproves of, or hasn't heard of, in which case you can enlighten him/her. Whatever the case, you can stop talking about law in the highly likely event that you've run out of talking points.

CHEAT SHEET 20—POLITICAL SCANDALS

Power corrupts; absolute power corrupts absolutely. Politicians' tendency toward corruption is thus unsurprising, but the advantage of living in a democracy is that truth usually comes out sooner rather than later—and if it's a Republican, often them in the process.

Scandal has a long and undistinguished history, making the hit ABC television show seem positively tame in comparison. The ancient monuments of the Acropolis had as many question marks about them as the current Greek banking process. The Roman emperors had some particularly sordid predilections: Tiberius had a penchant for young boys, Nero an inclination toward incest, and Commodus (Joaquin Phoenix in *Gladiator*) not only had harems of concubines but regularly turned up in public wearing drag. Not that there's anything wrong in that per se, but his cruelty and megalomania were the stuff of legend.

They say the definition of insanity is doing the same thing over and over again. Many of our politicians can't have read their history books, for instead of learning from their predecessors' mistakes and thus gaining twenty-twenty vision, their myopic view lets us read about their embarrassing exploits on a daily basis. And yes, the cover-up is always worse than the crime.

We focus here on three case studies of more recent American scandals. For some reason, the politicians all seem to be male.

TIP 1

Vote for women. (Although between lost e-mails and all sorts of Clinton Foundation allegations, Hillary Clinton has been doing her best to jeopardize my rule before going to press.)

Although Republicans do have affairs with women—consider the governator Arnold Schwarzenegger shagging the maid and fathering a child or Mark Sanford doing a disappearing act because of his mistress soul mate's vintage—there is a conspicuous tendency for vociferously antigay Christian conservative types to be found in same-sex clinches. Case Study 1 reminds you of the names and shame of some of these hypocrites. Democrats have done their utmost to make their straight affairs anything but straightforward, so in Case Study 2 we see how men such as Bill Clinton and John Edwards made a valiant effort to keep their party down. Finally we end up with a case study of the standard non-sexual-corruption variety.

TIP 2

Congressmen, don't use your congressional e-mail to send pictures of yourself stripping and flexing your muscles to a random soul you meet on Craigslist, as Republican Chris Lee did in 2011.

CASE STUDY 1. REPUBLICANS AND MEN

Millennials of all political persuasions and most of the rest of us (including SCOTUS) have concluded the ancient Greeks were spot-on and same-sex relations are absolutely acceptable. However, there are still some Republicans out there who claim you can pray the gay out. The noisier they are, the more likely shining a spotlight into their closets will reveal a sticky stack of *Playgirl,* not *Playboy,* magazines.

David Dreier, a representative from California, was particularly vociferous in his antigay stance—so only naturally it transpired in 2004 that he was having a relationship with his male chief of staff. That same year, Ed Schrock, a Republican from Virginia, had to abort his run for a third term—something to do with a male prostitute. Then there was Mark Foley, a Republican congressman from Florida, who in 2006 was discovered sending sexually explicit e-mails to underage male pages. Not only did it ruin his career but some blamed him in part for the Republican loss of control in Congress later that year. Who can forget big Bill Clinton critic Larry Craig, a veteran eighteen-year senator from Idaho, who was allegedly found up to George Michael shenanigans in an airport bathroom in 2007? And a dishonorable mention should go to Robert Bauman, representative from Maryland, and his male prostitute moment in 1980.

SUGGESTED VIEWING

Outrage, the 2009 documentary starring David Dreier.

There is always a path to redemption. Jon Hinson, a representative from Mississippi, who was repeatedly linked to and denied homosexual activity, eventually resigned after performing some oral action on a male Library of Congress employee in 1981. He became a gay rights activist.

TIP 3

Don't have sex in a public bathroom. There are other (more hygienic) locales and ways to have non-vanilla sex.

CASE STUDY 2. DEMOCRATS AND WOMEN

Before the modern political party dividing lines as we know them, Thomas Jefferson kicked off the presidential sex scandal tradition, supposedly fathering a child with his slave Sally Hemings. DNA testing in 1998 concluded his denials were likely a lie. By the twentieth century, although JFK did his utmost to degenerate the office to such depths, it was Bill Clinton's dalliance with Monica Lewinsky that ruined her life and in the end didn't do much to his that really caught the public's imagination. And gave politicians all over America the hope they could Get Away With It If Found Out—which is what you say the motivation today is whenever a man is caught up to no good and refuses to resign.

Bill, of course, had public previous—Gennifer Flowers had come and gone claiming a twelve-year affair during the 1992 Democratic primary campaign. Three years or so later he was having sexual relations in the Oval Office with Lewinsky, a White House intern, which she confided to her pal Linda Tripp. Tripp recorded the chat, because that's what you—and the NSA—do to your friends. The tape ended up in the paws of special prosecutor Kenneth Starr in 1998, and the sorry sordid situation eventually led to an impeachment vote—the first since Andrew Johnson in 1868—by the House of Representatives. Although Bill had lied about the affair under oath, the Senate bailed him out. Whatever the rights or wrongs of Bill's behavior, in a particularly startling display of duplicity, a significant number of wife-deceiving Republicans were among those who tried to get rid of the 42nd president. Examples include Newt Gingrich (had an affair with an intern himself while married to his second wife), John Ensign (later resigned for cuckolding a close friend's wife), Pete Domenici (son outside marriage), Stephen C. LaTourette (shagging his female chief of staff), Henry Hyde (former affair revealed while fronting impeachment), Robert Livingston (extramarital affair), Dan Burton (illegitimate love child), and Ken

Calvert (champion of the Christian Coalition—and caught with a prostitute allegedly going down on him in his car).

Dodgy Democrats weren't above reprimanding Clinton either. Especially notable was Gary Condit, a representative from California, who later had an affair with intern Chandra Levy, who disappeared and was found murdered. Years later an undocumented immigrant was subsequently convicted.

TIP 4

People in glass houses shouldn't throw stones.

Clinton, by virtue of his position as president, may still be the pinnacle Democratic philanderer charlatan, but it would be remiss not to mention John Edwards, the veep on John Kerry's 2004 presidential ticket and cheater on his cancer-stricken wife. Indeed, he became baby daddy to his mistress Rielle Hunter. The 1980s of course had Gary Hart, initially the front-runner for the Democratic presidential nomination, who had a fling with Donna Rice, she of the splendid hair. More recently political men in New York have lived up to the cliché that men in the Big Apple are bad apples.

Eliot Spitzer, the governor of New York State and scourge of Wall Street, was undone by an IRS investigation and the *New York Times* then reporting he had been an enthusiast of the Emperors Club, a prostitution ring. What made client No. 9's appearance on this client list so especially jaw-dropping is that while Spitzer had been New York's attorney general he had himself PROSECUTED prostitution rings.

Also doing his utmost to boost circulation for the ailing *New York Post* was Anthony Weiner, the congressman caught sexting over Twitter. The headline writers at the publication probably never dreamed they would ever owe so much to a conservative enfant

terrible, the late Andrew Breitbart, who was key in exposing Weiner's exposing and then Weiner himself, for reappearing—and
reoffending—in public life so swiftly.

CASE STUDY 3. MONEY AND POWER

Of course, American political scandals have not all just been about
the sex factor. One of the worst presidencies, corruptionwise, was
that of the eighteenth president, Republican Ulysses S. Grant. Its
1867 Crédit Mobilier Scandal—dodgy stocks and railroads—was the
first significant post–Civil War display of depravity. The administration then followed it up with the Whiskey Ring scandal, in which
it emerged that cabinet members were up to tax evasion and bribery.

In modern times, the benchmark every transgression is measured against is Watergate. The suffix *gate* is added onto incidents
on a regular basis. Indeed, if we had a dollar for every time Fox
News compared something Obama had done as being the most disgraceful event "since Watergate," we could all retire.

It is thus worth reiterating that Watergate so far has been the
modern political pinnacle of deceit. Perhaps interesting to remind
ourselves that Republican president Nixon didn't actually start it
himself. Five members of his reelection campaign team broke into
the Democratic headquarters inside Washington, DC's Watergate
Hotel. However, in a classic case of the cover-up being worse than
the crime, Nixon discovered the scandal and did everything he
could to hide it. It broke him—and was the big break for many a
media career. Hollywood has even immortalized the *Washington
Post's* Carl Bernstein and Bob Woodward along with their source
Deep Throat for their work uncovering the story, and also David
Frost, the late, great British broadcaster who later interviewed the
disgraced president.

TIP 4

Monica Lewinsky attempted to hide at the Watergate Hotel for a time at the height of her scandal. Possibly the place to go if you're trying to make a statement, not disappear, no?

That said, the Reagan administration's Iran-Contra foray was pretty jaw-dropping. It was secretly selling arms to Iran and using the profits to fund, expressly against Congress's wishes, the Contra rebels in Nicaragua. Fourteen people faced criminal charges for the situation, including Lt. Colonel Oliver North. He was initially convicted on three felony counts in 1989, but they were to all intents and purposes overturned the following year.

This is where one bows down in admiration to the Founding Fathers and the Constitution. For the separation of powers and the freedom of the press, which will be needed more than ever to keep an eye on the evolution of the Foreign Intelligence Surveillance Act, FISA. Introduced by Democratic senator Ted Kennedy in 1977, the way it has been used by both a Republican and a Democratic president since 9/11 should cause eyebrows to be raised. Politicians across the political spectrum have to be checked and balanced.

WISE WORDS

It is not the young people that degenerate; they are not spoiled till those of mature age are already sunk into corruption.

—Montesquieu

SOCIAL SURVIVAL STRATEGY

Argument: "The cover-up IS always worse than the crime."
Lob this one into a chat about someone's naughty behavior and nobody will be able to disagree—all that's left for you to do is take an elaborate sip of your beverage and look wise.

Crisp Fact: "It amazes me how people in glass houses are always throwing stones. Remember the big Bill Clinton critic Larry Craig, the veteran senator from Idaho, who was allegedly found up to George Michael shenanigans in an airport bathroom in 2007?" If someone in the public eye is being attacked by the baying media mob, inevitably if any of those doing the criticizing looked in the mirror, perfection wouldn't be gazing back. Appear sophisticated with your measured criticism; hysterical heckling is beneath you.

Pivot: "Sometimes I think sex scandals exist to keep tabloid headline writers happy. What's your preferred news source nowadays? Still get papers, or is it all about the tablet?" A little technology talk normally distracts anyone, since it impacts everyone. Safe terrain and also useful in helping anyone left out of a conversation back in.

CHEAT SHEET 21—ELECTIONS

BACKGROUND BRIEFING

"Government by the people" was initially a euphemistic term—when the Constitution was penned, only 10 to 16 percent of the US population got the vote. You had to be white and male and own property. Things did improve in the early 1800s. By 1810, all religious prerequisites for voting had been dropped, and by 1850, property ownership and tax requirements had been eliminated.

However, despite all this, the states do have a long history of disenfranchisement shenanigans, which you should bring up whenever someone starts talking about voter ID laws.

First, we saw literacy tests for voting to discriminate against those nontraditional Americans known as Irish-Catholic immigrants, in 1855 in Connecticut, followed by Massachusetts in 1857. Take note, Bill "Fox News" O'Reilly. Of course the Fifteenth Amendment in 1870, giving former slaves the right to vote and protecting the voting rights of all adult males, really put the cat among the pigeons amongst the "traditional" fans. Cue segregation and the Jim Crow laws in the southern states of the former Confederacy, which continued all the way until Dr. Martin Luther King's fight for civil rights and the Voting Rights Act of 1965. Many an institutional roadblock had appeared to prevent African-Americans from voting. There was the 1890 Mississippi literacy test, which inadvertently impacted whites too, so "grandfather" clauses were added—descendants of those who could vote before 1870 got to vote, no questions asked. Eventually SCOTUS ruled the grandfather clauses were against the Fifteenth Amendment.

It took until 1920 for women and 1924 for Native Americans to get the vote. This was all for people over the age of twenty-one, mind. It was only when American teens were being shipped off to Vietnam to die that the voting age was brought down to eighteen in 1971 with the Twenty-sixth Amendment.

At last everyone could have a stake in picking the president, who has to be an American citizen over thirty-five, resident for fourteen years within the USA, who hasn't been elected to the Oval Office twice before. Of course, via the Constitution, American voters vote via the Electoral College.

KEY TERM: ELECTORAL COLLEGE

- The Electoral College is a Founding Fathers compromise between Congress's voting for the president and every "qualified" citizen voting for the president.

- Every state (and the District of Columbia) has an allocated number of Electoral College members, aka electors. There is one elector for each senator (which means two, as there are always two senators) and one for each representative (which is determined by the census's population count).

- There is a minimum of three members, in states such as Alaska and Montana, and a maximum of fifty-four members in California.

- To win the American presidency today requires 270 votes or more, out of 538.

- You can win the electoral contest and lose the popular vote—as experienced by Al Gore in 2000. The last person that had happened to was Grover Cleveland in 1888, who lost the presidency to Benjamin Harrison.

- If no candidate gets to 270, in steps the Twelfth Amendment. The president is decided by a ballot of the House of Representatives—and for this, each state gets one vote. Although it has happened only in 1800 and 1824, pundits can get VERY excited about the possibility during campaign season. The Senate chooses the vice-president, although it has done this only once, in 1836.

WHY IT MATTERS TODAY

Well, we are talking about the leader of the free world here. Grateful cable news producers owe millions of hours of programming to the fact that identifying him or her is such a lengthy process. But do keep this in mind: A fundamental political truth is that almost everything that "strategists" do or say doesn't count. Most voters are not remotely impacted by political strategy—the campaigns, the speeches, the events, the punditry. Especially the punditry. One network I appeared on was always calling me a political strategist in my introduction. Of what, precisely? How to get to the nearest bar after my segment was over? Elections are won because of basics such as the economy and the political cycle and whether you'd be willing to sit down and have a beer with the politician, as he or she is "authentic."

So actually maybe the strategist label was the right one for me after all.

That being said, you will undoubtedly be dragged into a political chat. Although the presidential election is every four years on the first Tuesday after the first Monday in November—set around harvest, weather, and worship schedules—the whole process basically takes two long years.

NOTEWORTHY NUGGET: SECRETARIES OF STATE AND THE PRESIDENCY

Serving as secretary of state between 1801 and 1841 meant you'd probably end up president—five of the six had been. This has happened only once since then, with James Buchanan in 1856.

About two years before an election, a would-be president forms an exploratory committee. If all goes well, a candidacy is declared and the candidate campaigns in key states. Summer through to the end of the preelection year, there are primary and caucus debates. January through June of election year is primary season, in which candidates fight for the Republican or Democratic nomination. Some states have primaries; others have caucuses (a local meeting system); some have both.

NOTEWORTHY NUGGETS: REPUBLICAN TICKETS

• The last time the Republicans won a presidential election without a Bush or a Nixon on the ticket was 1928.

• Worth noting that George H. W. Bush, aka Bush I, was one of the most qualified men to be president. Ever. Not just because he had been veep to Reagan, but because prior to that he had been DCI, director of Central Intelligence. That is to say, Bush I had been head of the CIA, had coordinated intelligence activities between all the US intelligence agencies, and had been the main intelligence advisor to the president and National Security Council.

• I have observed that half of America appears to believe that Bush II was the opposite of his father on many levels.

Historically Iowa holds the first caucus and New Hampshire the first primary, which is why we hear about them All the Time. This means that although they are tiny, they have more influence than a larger state such as California, whose primary is later. Some pundits have even gone as far to label Iowa akin to one of the UK's "rotten boroughs"—constituencies with tiny electorates that had disproportionate power. These were stopped by the Brits with their 1832 Reform Act. Not so by Americans yet, but there have been mutterings that ultraconservatives in Iowa may drive more mainstream candidates away, thus diminishing its impact.

Rules vary state by state, but basically if you win a state primary, the state party delegates will be on your side at the national party convention held in the summer. There are some technicalities involving unpledged delegates, or superdelegates, that some commentators get their knickers in a twist about, but normally we know who has the party's nomination by then.

Candidates finally square up against each other, the high (or low) points of which are the much hyped and talked about debates between late September and October.

KEY TERM: OCTOBER SURPRISE

- A news event late in a political campaign that can influence an election.

- Label appeared in 1972 with the announcement that peace was at hand in Vietnam. Helped the already favorite incumbent Nixon take every state but Massachusetts.

- A famous example is 1980 over the Iran hostage crisis. The GOP worried throughout the fall that Jimmy Carter would sort out a last-minute deal and it would give him a bump to defeat Reagan.

- Wrong to label Hurricane Sandy in 2012 an October Surprise (supposedly helped Obama as he looked presidential and Chris Christie hugged him, while Romney, well, looked out of it/touch), as it wasn't man-made. Well, it probably was indirectly through climate change, but you know what I mean.

In practice, not all votes are created equal and not every vote counts. Because of the Electoral College, it all depends on swing states, aka purple states, aka battleground states. Politicians basically move there on the campaign trail unless they're going to raise money in a stinking rich state to spend on an interminable round of ads in purple-land.

NOTEWORTHY NUGGETS: OHIO IN 2012

• "As Ohio goes, so goes the nation." Ohio has the seventh most electoral votes of all states, and since 1964, it has always voted the way of the winning president. The only swing states that have more electoral votes than the Buckeye State are Pennsylvania and Florida, and they don't have its track record.

• 219,414 political ads were run.

• Romney visited fifty-one times, Obama twenty-two.

• Final Ohio vote split: Obama 50.1 percent versus 48.2 percent for Romney.

And then finally, thankfully, especially if you live in a swing state, the election.

NOTEWORTHY NUGGETS: VOTES

• Russia—the candidate who receives the most votes (lately if your name's Putin or he has your approval) wins.

• Florida's famous disputed vote came down to 537 votes, or 0.01 percent.

You may think that the American presidential election is a long process, but it has sped up. It used to take so long to sort out who actually had won the presidential election that up to 1937 presidents were sworn in on March 4. Now it's noon on January 20. Which is so much warmer for an outdoor event in the Northeast.

KEY TERM: GERRYMANDERING

- When electoral districts are set so one party has the advantage. Term has its roots from the 1812 redistricting antics of Massachusetts governor Elbridge Gerry and the word "salamander."

- In 2012, Democrats received 1.4 million more votes for the House of Representatives, yet Republicans won control of the House by a 234 to 201 margin.

TALKING POINTS

- Throwing in the following phrases will get you through the campaign season. As will playing drinking games every time you watch the news and a pundit utters one of them:

  * British Labour Party Prime Minister Harold Wilson coined the phrase "A week is a long time in politics." Utilize this regularly, as it's so true—anything can happen to derail a politician.

  * "All politics are local."

  * "The electorates are different in off-year cycles." (Voters are older, whiter, and thus more Republican leaning.)

  * "On some levels we get the politicians we deserve."

  * "Enlightened self-interest is a powerful motivator."

  * "You can't beat something with nothing. It must be about proposition, not opposition."

  * "A plague on all their houses."

  * "You don't win campaigns by playing defense."

  * "It's easier to campaign than govern."

  * "Wall Street likes certainty."

  * "The biggest threat to the economy is Washington."

  * The get-out-of-jail-free card if you want to change the subject? "Wake me up on November [the day after the pres-

idential/midterm election]" and switch the chat to something else.

- For everyone but a second-term president, one campaign ends and the raising money and jockeying for next nominations begin.
- Americans get the worst political campaigns that money can buy.

  * The total amount of money spent on the 2012 elections was $7.3 billion, and 2014's midterms were the most expensive in history, with $4 billion splurged. Politicians have to raise that money and it will have a corrosive influence. One politician's loophole to close becomes another's constituent's special interest to defend.

    —During the Obamacare debate, over 3,300 lobbyists registered to work on the issue. There are only 535 members of Congress. That's six lobbyists for each member.

    —Say "There is a revolving door between Capitol Hill and K Street" (where the fancy lobbyists are based). Also note sagely, "Follow the money."

- The Supreme Court's 2010 Citizens United ruling allowed "Super PACs." Corporations and unions can spend unlimited cash on a political action committee that aims to influence voting.

- If a party's candidates are having a competitive primary season, always proclaim:

1. The other party's front-runner is the winner of whichever primary has just occurred. So during the 2012 election where Romney was fighting it out with Santorum, Gingrich, Perry, et al., the winner of each Republican primary was always Obama.

2. Winning a primary is completely different from winning a presidency. Candidates have to go to the extreme to win primaries and then retreat to the center, where national elections are always won.

- In general, Americans are more moderate than both Republicans and Democrats would have us believe—around 40 percent identify themselves as independents. Come election time, America's basically a 51/49 percent country—thus the tendency for results to always be for divided government. Means gridlock? Yes, but it does prevent extremism, which is a big tribute to the Founding Fathers.

TOPIC FOR DEBATE

- Are the Republicans in a "demographic death spiral"? In the six presidential elections since 1988, Republicans have won a majority of the vote exactly once, in 2004.
- Romney would have won the 2012 election with 501 electoral votes and 45 states . . . if only white men voted.

- Voter ID laws touted by Republicans arguably give a bigger boost to Democrats, who can portray them as a symbolic issue and use them to mobilize their base.
- When it comes to conventions, the convention is to say that "neither convention will be too bold." There'll be some "red meat" for the base, but they're playing to independents in swing states and the aim of the party's game will be to create lots of positive sound bites and images and *not* to give ammunition to the other side.

  ＊The keynote address may well be given by a Rising Star earmarked for Great Things. Obama at the Democratic National Convention (DNC) in 2004 being the prime example.

  ＊Urban legend has it that during the course of their conventions, Republicans spend about three times more on strip clubs than Democrats do.

- Defeating an incumbent will always be tricky, as a number of voters will have to admit that they were wrong in voting for him/her in the previous election. Charisma is normally essential to succeed in this situation. Jimmy Carter and George Bush I were defeated by Ronald Reagan and Bill Clinton respectively, who both had bucketloads of the stuff.

- Presidential debate talking points don't change. The following will get you through:

  * "Debates are rarely game changers that decide elections—the exceptions being 1960 (tanned JFK versus sweaty Nixon, but even then, he won on radio and nobody can remember what was said) and 2000 (Gore invading Bush II's space and sighing). They're so close to the elections most people have decided and some already voted."

  * "Hope the moderator has packed his tin hat."

  * "You'd be surprised what blows up. Remember Romney and his binders full of women?"

  * Obama prepped by debating John Kerry in 2012. Reagan converted his garage into a TV studio and hired congressman David Stockman to stand in for Jimmy Carter. Stockman was rewarded with a job as budget director once Reagan was elected. Ohio congressman Rob Portman spent years pretending to be a Democrat for GOP prep.

- Midterm voters tend to be fewer in number, older, and whiter. It's also perfectly usual, especially if in the second term of a two-term presidency, for the opposing party of the president to win Congress. So in 2014, the GOP got control of the Senate (they already had the House) . . . for the first time since 2006. When Bush I was president.

RED FLAGS

- The concept that blue states subsidize red states and blue counties subsidize red counties. This debate always gets ugly, with questions thrown in as to accuracy of data. Unless you have said data at your fingertips, you may end up on the losing end of this argument.

- Be wary of the "get money out of politics" claim; if you're up against a smart person, he or she will press you as to what you replace it with. In the UK, campaign spending has been strictly limited since 1883 and the total cost of elections for all parties is around $50 million. But every prime minister since Thatcher has needed the support of Rupert Murdoch and his media empire to get elected, which is why the phone hacking scandal got as scandalous as it did. Politicians were in bed with the press, who were in bed with the police. Just corruption of a different kind. Also, there's a free speech element: Why can't Americans spend their money how they choose?

   * If you must grandstand, throw the word *transparency* around a lot. You don't mind the money in politics, but it's got to be transparent so you know who's trying to buy votes and politicians.

- There is much talk about how in America voter turnout—at around 60 percent, where it's hovered for decades—is very low compared to other countries. Although mandatory voting, as they have in Australia, has its advantages, it won't work in the USA. It quite possibly violates the freedom of speech concept, as Americans have the freedom not to speak and often believe that voting is a civic right rather than a civic duty.

- The Republican acronym GOP stands for Grand Old Party, in case you were confusing it with Good Operating Practice or Gross Operating Profit. (I'm being very good and not making a joke here.)

- A RINO is not an animal. Well. No, it means "Republican in Name Only"—normally what Tea Party types label old-school conservative compromise types.

- Now, on the subject of animals, don't get these confused: The GOP is represented by an elephant, the Democrats by a donkey. This dates back to a *Harper's Weekly* cartoon in 1874.

- There is a line of reasoning that Texas (thirty-eight electoral votes) could become a swing state thanks to shifting demographics. But it's controversial and dependent on your statistics being better than your adversary's.

- Not worth proclaiming that the 1960 Nixon-Kennedy election was disputed. The Kennedys may have been up to naughtiness in Chicago, but JFK had a MASSIVE margin of victory overall—303 to 219.

- Remain healthily skeptical of the idea of a third party. Washington's political duopoly is entrenched, although you can always throw in the concept that in 1992, Ross Perot helped throw the election to Bill Clinton. That is why the Republican establishment was so wary of the Donald Trump surge in the GOP presidential nomination polls in summer 2015 and his threats to run as a third-party candidate.

WISE WORDS

Democracy is the worst form of government except all the others that have been tried.

—Winston Churchill

SOCIAL SURVIVAL STRATEGY

Argument: "Oh, as the former British Labour Party Prime Minister Harold Wilson said, 'A week is a long time in politics.'"
Anything can happen, especially in this day and age of modern technology—one tweet can ruin your life. Say this sagely and nobody can contradict you.

Crisp Fact: "The last time the Republicans won a presidential election without a Bush or a Nixon on the ticket was 1928."
This is one of those mind-boggling, jaw-dropping truths that always adds spice to a political discussion.

Pivot: Say: "Wake me up on November [the day after the presidential/midterm election]" and simply switch the chat to anything else. I used to use this line live on MSNBC when all the panel was regurgitating talking points. Fortunately for me, I was working for a host whose frustration with the vast majority of politicians was legendary.

GEOGRAPHY SUMMARY

This subject is actually incredibly simple to navigate. Live by the theme that "there are no foreign lands; it is the traveler only who is foreign," never confuse Austria and Australia, and if you need to pivot out of a chat about distant climes, say: "My sense of direction is so bad, a member of One Direction's would be better." You can then talk about boy bands, where your lack of knowledge is a badge of honor, as opposed to one of shame. Unless you are a twelve-year-old girl, and I somehow doubt, dear reader, that you are that.

It may be unfair, but those who live elsewhere are likely to assume that, as an American, you need to read up on this subject. The myths about Americans and their grasp of geography are the stuff of legend. And by geography, I'm talking internationally—I'm not going to stoop so low and print a map of the United States here. And BTW, make this a maxim to live by: "There are no foreign lands; it is the traveler only who is foreign." I KNOW. Genius. And as a foreigner in the United States I try to remember it daily.

The first big myth, of course, is passports, and Americans' lack of possession of them. Which actually I've got some more positive news on than you thought I would. Urban legend has it that only about 10 percent of Americans have them, and this little nugget is repeated by many millions of the 6.8 billion or so people in the world who aren't American. Fairly recent figures suggest about a third of you do. Could be worse.

However, by some rather more complex math, it is estimated that only 3.5 percent of all US residents travel overseas in any given year. And by overseas, I don't mean Canada or Mexico, which don't count. Really, they don't count—you don't have to travel over any seas to get there. I almost screamed when I was told I had no US credit rating (read: no ability to get a mobile phone, credit card, do anything), as the only international country that counts was Canada. FFS.

What is true is that Americans have a worldwide perception problem when it comes to their grasp of geography. Now most of this, if any, is not your personal fault. There's the face in various key locales of the Obama administration's foreign policy being drones, over a decade of war waged in the Middle East; the fact that it's John McCain who always seems to be on a plane (has he ever gone to a country apart from perhaps Monaco where he doesn't think US military action is required?); not to mention McDonald's, Coca-Cola, and Starbucks. However, do you know the difference between England and Britain? Where's oil-rich Brunei? What's the capital of Turkey? It's not Istanbul.

For those of you who weren't flawless in your responses, you'll know all by the end of this subject. And if you were stumped, you are not alone. Remember the Boston Bombers back in 2013? In response to so much social media activity incorrectly identifying the suspects as having Czech, rather than Chechen, origins, the Czech ambassador to the US had to issue a statement. Yes, a statement. Pointing out that "the Czech Republic and Chechnya are two very different entities—the Czech Republic is a Central European country; Chechnya is a part of the Russian Federation."

What are the answers to the questions? I cover Brunei below. Ankara is Turkey's capital. And Great Britain?

Well, Britain includes England (capital: London), Scotland (capital: Edinburgh) and Wales (capital: Cardiff). It does not include Northern Ireland (capital: Belfast). Read the Cheat Sheet on the royals and you know that these areas didn't always get along. Britain is the ninth largest island in the world. Now, here's the complicated bit. Britain is part of the sovereign state of the United Kingdom of Great Britain and Northern Ireland. In 1922, most of Ireland seceded from the United Kingdom of Great Britain and Ireland. So just the Northern part remained. The UK also has a ton of islands, but I'm not going to overly confuse you right now. Just remember a Scottish or a Welsh person is not an English person. And most important, remember the same thing goes for someone from Northern Ireland.

I leave you with these thoughts, as it does come with geography, after all: climate change. I used to be asked on another Fox Business host's morning show twice a month. And then he decided we should debate climate change. I skewered him. Never been invited back since. Because I'm right and showed him up. I know all too well when I suck, and I didn't that day.

First of all, always call it climate change. Please, if you're in the Caribbean and it snows, don't ask where the global warming is now. It's causing the freak weather, you muppet.

There is no scientific controversy over this. We can't just live in the short term. Most experts believe in climate change and that it can cause future generations serious problems. Don't believe me? Look at the NASA website. I have no idea how they put a man on the moon; I'm somewhat inclined to believe them when they red-flag this as a problem. Still not good enough? In 2013, 900 scientists reviewed 9,000 studies and concluded there was a 95 percent chance climate change is man-made. Even if you don't buy into climate change, there's a cost-benefit analysis here. Reagan phased out our ozone-depleting chemicals as his economists discovered that the costs for doing so were less than for not doing so—basically because various cancers would be avoided. Climate change will equal more expensive natural disasters. It would be cheaper for the international community if it reduced greenhouse gas emissions and avoided natural disasters (Sandy cost $50 billion; the 2011 and 2012 heat waves and droughts added $10 billion to farm costs) than if it did nothing.

Although feel free to point out that Hollywood types who drive a Prius made in Japan or fly around on a private jet and start spouting save-the-planet stuff are complete hypocrites.

Geography is actually just really depressing. What's next? Biology! Excellent, sex.

No, abortion, the death penalty, that sort of thing. If I were you I'd just switch to culture and all those hypocritical celebrities. I'm losing patience with myself.

Right, before I strop (see Cheat Sheet 3) anymore, let's get to our two maps, shall we? They are really all you need.

WISE WORDS

War is God's way of teaching America geography.

—Ambrose Bierce

CHEAT SHEET 22—MAP ONE: WORLD MAP

First of all, a world map. Please can you note my top ten of the following:

1. **Brunei.** One of the top five richest nations in the world. Public debt hovers around 0 percent of national GDP. (US—around 70 percent). Not in the Middle East. Not even close. Southeast Asia.

2. **Oman and Amman.** Oman is an Arab state that is situated at the mouth of the Persian Gulf. It has a marine border with Iran and also borders Saudi Arabia, UAE, and Yemen. Vital, wouldn't you say? Amman is the capital of Jordan.

3. **United Arab Emirates,** aka UAE. The UAE is made up of seven emirates (including Abu Dhabi and Dubai), each of which has a hereditary emir governing it. The emirs form the Federal Supreme Council, which runs things, and one of the emirs is chosen as the president of the United Arab Emirates.

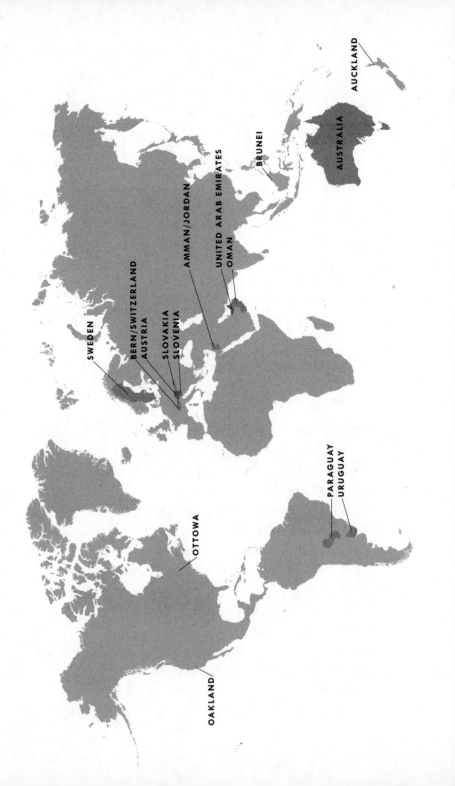

4. **Austria and Australia**. Please God no, don't confuse them. Apparently this is a thing. Apparently some Americans do so much that in tourist shops in Austria they actually have T-shirts for you to buy saying "No kangaroos in Austria." And then Bush II (it wouldn't have been I), who thanked the AUSTRALIAN premier for calling on AUSTRIAN troops in Iraq. Iraq. That war—it doesn't get any worse. No, no, no, I can't cope.

5. **Oakland and Auckland.** This is also a thing. A California student in 1985 was in Germany and wanted to return to Oakland. He ended up in Auckland. New Zealand.

6. **Switzerland and Sweden.** Supposedly actress Jessica Alba got these confused back in the day, before she was a big businesswoman. However, whether you are model or mogul, it is completely unacceptable to not know the difference between Sweden and Switzerland.

7. While we're in the vicinity, neither **Geneva nor Zurich** is Switzerland's capital city. *Bern* is. And it's a charming town complete with its own bear pit.

8. **Toronto** isn't Canada's capital either. *Ottawa* is.

9. *Paraguay* **(landlocked)**. *Uruguay* (on the Atlantic, FFS).

10. **Slovenia and Slovakia.** Not just you getting it wrong for these two independent 1990s nations, so feel better. The UN. World leaders. Olympic officials. It's so bad, embassy staff meet once a month to switch mail. For the record: Slovenia is right down by Italy and split from Yugoslavia. Slovakia split from Czechoslovakia (duh!) and is right up near Poland.

SOCIAL SURVIVAL STRATEGY

Argument: All the world's a stage, not just the USA.

The world doesn't revolve around America but around the sun, so turning the dialogue to the big picture will make you look open as opposed to small-minded.

Crisp Fact: Ottawa is Canada's capital.

Often the obvious place is not a country's capital. Be wary of looking like a muppet and getting it wrong.

Pivot: Can you believe some people confuse Austria and Australia? Have you been to either country?

This pivot will spark a chat about travel, which should be safe and sometimes even enlightening.

CHEAT SHEET 23—MAP TWO: NUCLEAR WEAPONS

Only one country has ever used nuclear weapons in combat—the USA. What does every permanent member of the Security Council have in common? Nuclear weapons. Of course they do. The "nuclear club" is the most exclusive, powerful club in the world. Muammar Gaddafi dismantled his nuclear program in 2003 to end his status as international pariah. Eight years later, look what happened. The only security guarantee for dictators is nuclear weapons; just ask North Korea. Why would anyone ever want a bomb? America continues to prove dictators have only one true security guarantee: nukes. Now from 1970 the NPT (Non-Proliferation Treaty) has been in force, which is supposed to stop the spread of nukes, promote the peaceful uses of atomic energy etc., etc.

The good news: most states have signed up to it! Including Iran!

The bad news? There have been some disputes about Iran's status, hence all those negotiations in 2015. And North Korea, India, Israel, Pakistan, and South Sudan have never joined it.

Those designated by the ⚛ symbol officially have nukes. Those with the ▲ symbol have access via NATO. Those with the ✳ symbol

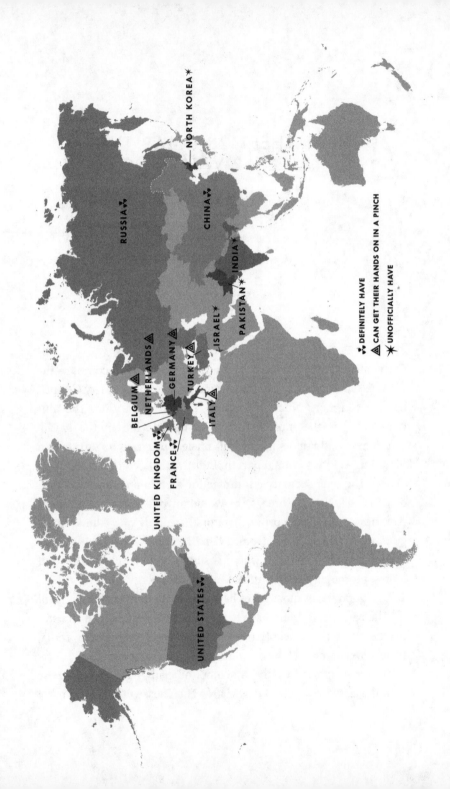

unofficially do. Note that Israel is always ambiguous on the topic, but we know.

DEFINITELY HAVE (☢)

USA

Russia

UK

France

China

CAN GET THEIR HANDS ON IN A PINCH (⚠)

Belgium

Germany

Netherlands

Italy

Turkey

UNOFFICIALLY HAVE (✳)

India

Pakistan

North Korea

Israel

SOCIAL SURVIVAL STRATEGY

Argument: The only security guarantee for dictators is nuclear weapons.

Every permanent member of the Security Council has nuclear weapons. Nukes equal power, so it is unsurprising that countries that currently don't have them try to attain them. Ask the assembled company if they think it's hypocritical that we attempt to prevent them from doing so. It should provoke an interesting debate.

Crisp Fact: Only one country has ever used nuclear weapons in combat.

If nuclear weapons come up, the fact that nations have shown sense about their deployment should always be acknowledged before delving into a discourse about the dangers of proliferation and terrorism.

Pivot: Ask "Have you been to India?"

Another solid travel pivot. India is somewhere people have had the most life-changing experience in or would like to go to—or will never visit. They will have a view on it, though.

BIOLOGY SUMMARY

The key theme to keep in mind when discussing anything related to this subject is that the personal is political. People can possess firmly held "old-fashioned" views about feminism and same-sex marriage, but if they have a daughter who wants to be paid the same as her male coworkers for identical work or a son who comes out of the closet, perspectives can change. Think about dropping in this brilliant fact—it's uncontroversial, as you can't even offend the Swiss on it, it's so disgraceful: In Switzerland, women were only granted the right to vote in 1971. That's right. 1971. Even Iran had managed to do it in 1963. And if you need to pivot the conversation somewhere else, which is highly likely with any of these topics, pronounce: "As Errol Flynn once said, 'Any man who has $10,000 left when he dies is a failure.' Let me buy you another drink."

You may be hoping that with our penultimate subject we will put the fun into that most fundamental of topics—biology. Somewhere between the sensitive topics of abortion and the death penalty, this proves unfeasible.

From this you will deduce that the next Cheat Sheets are not comprised of the biology we were fed at school. There will be no discussion of amoebas or plant cells. There will be a bit about the birds and the bees, but quite frankly there's more to life than sex. There has to be, bearing in mind how many single people there are out there. To be precise, almost 50 percent of American adults, and they can't be doing it all the time, as otherwise 1.7 billion swipes a day wouldn't have occurred on Tinder in February 2015.

At this point, in the manner of a leading economist, I issue a disclaimer. I am a European-born feminist and I work in the Broadway community. Biology's first Cheat Sheet covers contraception, abortion, pregnancy, and the death penalty. The second takes on feminism, and the third, the lesbian, gay, bisexual, transgender, and questioning (LGBTQ) sphere. Impartial perspective? What do you think? I may have attempted it in previous chapters, but I well and truly give up any semblance of it here.

Now, dear reader, I completely understand that you are entitled to be of another persuasion and I don't want to leave you cross. For those who suspect that the next three Cheat Sheets may rub you up the wrong way, over the rest of this biology introduction I cover various uncontroversial nuggets you can take away. I suggest then skipping straight through to the last subject, culture. If we ever meet, I'll buy you a drink by way of an apology that you couldn't read a few thousand words. Here goes on my apolitical points.

- Cellphones carry ten times more bacteria than most toilet seats.

- According to the National Sleep Foundation, adults need seven to nine hours sleep, so it's no wonder parents of newborns are nuts.

- The oldest dildo was made about 30,000 years ago.

- Orgasms can cure hiccups.

- Lemons ripen after you pick them, while oranges don't.

- Obesity is an American public health-care catastrophe—it costs so many billions a year to treat that if you sorted out obesity, it is fair to contend that you would seriously help the problem that is American health care. In that vein, Spanx has nothing on our ancestors for quick fixes. In the seventeenth and eighteenth centuries, whalebone corsets and "anti-corpulency belts" were in vogue, as were laxatives and eating a bar of soap before bed every night. Celebrities have also always been proponents of the diet du jour. We have Kirstie Alley waging a perpetual weight war, while history had Lord Byron. One of his diet regimens included drinking only claret and water—more appealing than the cabbage soup diet of the 1990s, it has to be said. What has been called "the best diet ever invented" was the British diet during World War II. My embattled home isle was forced to become self-sufficient. For my grandmother and her generation, there was no snacking or suspect fats. The Brits' food was rationed and they strictly adhered to War Office nutritional guidelines. Following the Dig for Victory campaign, they grew as much of their own food as they could. The British population emerged healthier than it had ever been before. Well, but for one area. What they were imbibing.

- Alcohol has been the crux of society for centuries. Without it, the fittest would never have survived. Or at least the free world as we know it—Winston Churchill freely admitted: "I have taken more out of alcohol than alcohol has taken out of me." The limey's love of alcohol is nothing new. The discovery of late Stone Age beer jugs has established the fact that purposely fermented beverages existed at least as early as c. 10,000 BC. It has even been suggested that beer may have preceded bread as a staple. The Egyptians believed that the important god Osiris invented beer, a beverage that was considered a necessity of life. Pure distilled alcohol was first produced by Muslim chemists in the Islamic world during the eighth and ninth centuries. Yes, you read that right. Muslim chemists. The Puritans brought more beer than water on the *Mayflower* as they departed for the New World. In colonial America, it was perfectly acceptable for those over the age of fifteen to consume the equivalent of seven shots a day. It took until 2011 for Russia to view beer as an alcoholic beverage. Before then, anything under 10 percent volume of alcohol was categorized as a soft drink. Celebrity teetotalers include: Marie Antoinette (the "let them eat cake" queen of France during the French Revolution) and Donald Trump. Oh, and drink too much? It is thought that the hiccup may be an evolutionary remnant of earlier amphibian respiration.

- Ebola has been around bats and marsupials for more than 10 million years. We get a global viral outbreak every generation or so, ergo we're due one, but ebola needs intimate contact to transmit and a true pandemic, such as the 1918 Spanish influenza, is spread through the air or by touch.

  * The next pandemic is likely to come from animals (we're hanging out in their environs more, as there are seven billion of us), and thanks to air travel we'll probably all get it.

- The recent rise in measles cases in the West and the immunization "debate" (how can there even be one?) brings out the worst sort of liberals (organic and alternative medicine only) and conservatives (liberty!). If you don't immunize your child, you are putting them, their friends, and those with compromised immune systems such as cancer patients at risk. That discredited 1998 report by Dr. Andrew Wakefield about the links between MMR and autism has a LOT to answer for.

Right. If you think you might agree with a theatrical European-born feminist, read on. Otherwise best not. I could really do without any more one-star reviews on Amazon.

CHEAT SHEET 24—LIFE AND DEATH

This book has always been nothing other than ambitious. However, the spectrum covered in this Cheat Sheet is perhaps the most dramatic.

Ideology has been kept away as much as possible from this tome. But in this Cheat Sheet I write mini reports on contraception, abortion, pregnancy, and the death penalty. And as I tackle them, it is not the first time and certainly won't be the last time that a pundit has let the fair and balanced concept fly right out the window.

MINI REPORT 1. CONTRACEPTION

In the beginning there was sex. Which means that contraception methods are as old as time. One of those scientific studies proving what we already know has shown that out of a list of eight reasons for having sex, for the majority having a baby is the least frequent motivator. Other recent studies indicate that 99 percent of American women aged fifteen to forty-four who've had sex have used contraception at some point. No, I don't know how Congress managed to hold a hearing on contraception in 2012 with NO WOMEN WITNESSES either, although Democratic strategists knew precisely what to do with that. Along with various "gaffes" by other old white male Republicans, "war on women" blazed the liberals' election talking point, as they cemented their hold on America's biggest voting demographic. Republicans = muppets sometimes. Why give the opposition such potent ammunition?

Sorry. I told you this independent observer thing was going to be a challenge. Actually, no, I'm not sorry. As a UN agency has pointed out, birth control is a human right. Why is it so controversial that a woman has control over her own body and life? That a woman has jurisdiction over whether she's pregnant or not? Back to Hillary Clinton's 1995 declaration in China: Women's rights are human rights. Women who use contraception are better educated and healthier. What's the problem? That they're empowered? That society benefits as a whole? Oh, FFS.

On the basis that men don't always want to reproduce either, birth control methods have been used in one form or another for thousands of years. Egyptian men wrapped their penises in linen sheaths. Other approaches varied from crocodile dung and honey before sex, to sea sponges and beeswax, to drinking postcoital hot mercury. Not up your street? Some used alcohol made from stewed beaver's testicles. In the majority of American states, diaphragms and condoms were illegal from 1873 through World War I, and it could be tricky to get hold of them for decades more.

Myths surrounding the use of contraceptives have also been around forever. It seems we still believe a fair few of them if the conversations I've had with highly educated people are anything to go by—and the fact that some male Republicans believe women's reproductive organs can shut down on a whim and that aspirin prevents pregnancy. Small surprise that half of all pregnancies in the United States are unplanned.

NOTEWORTHY NUGGETS: STDs

- STD stands for sexually transmitted disease, formally known as venereal disease (VD).

- Some pedants prefer STIs, sexually transmitted infections, as not all STDs are diseases.

- These have been common for centuries. If you have an STD, you are actually in the highest brow company you will ever keep. We are talking geniuses such as Mozart, Beethoven, and Van Gogh; wits like Oscar Wilde; and mighty men, including Napoleon (allegedly), Winston Churchill, and Al Capone. The late great Robin Williams was sued by an ex for not telling her he had herpes.

- Around 1 in 5 Americans have an STD, and about 80 percent of them do not know it. Symptoms can remain hidden for years. So don't automatically assume you have been cheated on . . .

- Don't sleep around in Mississippi. Last figures I was able to get my hands on, this state has the highest rates in America of both chlamydia and gonorrhea, while the death rate from AIDS is more than twice the national average. If you want to irritate the resident of a red state, you could also make a general statement that those who are flagrantly moral are often more clandestinely libertine . . .

Thus, in the interest of avoiding unwanted C-section scars and/or child support payments, here is a swift round of contraceptive clear-ups. Douching, showering, or bathing (even in Coca-Cola) cannot prevent pregnancy, however quickly you leap out of bed. Pregnancy will not be thwarted by jumping up and down. Or by having sex standing up. And you can't prevent a bun in the oven by either sex's not having an orgasm (the penis leaks, people). Whoever invented the latter lie was clearly just a lazy lover.

NOTEWORTHY NUGGET

Sperm can live inside a woman's body for up to five days, so if you ovulate any time within seven days of having unprotected sex, you could become pregnant.

Modern medicine has managed to produce contraceptive choice. Marvelous. We'll be here all day if we go through every type, but interesting to note that 1844 brought the first mass-produced condom, made of vulcanized rubber, which we use in car tires. The latex condom made its first appearance in 1880.

NOTEWORTHY NUGGETS: THE PILL

- About 100 million women worldwide use the pill. Since women are always right, they cannot all be wrong.

- The pill was approved in the USA on May 9, 1960.

- It is safer to use the pill than to have a baby. Recent statistics have 18.5 moms dying for every 100,000 births in the US (more than triple the rate in the UK, more than double that in Saudi Arabia and Canada—and more than in China. Go figure). I can't even unearth the statistical likelihood of women dying from the pill. What about probably the most talked about side effect of the pill, DVT (blood clots)? Being pregnant increases the risk of DVT more than any brand of pill.

- Take note, anti-Obamacare types: Studies indicate that around 50 percent of women use the pill for its noncontraceptive advantages (regulating periods, protecting against ectopic pregnancy, treating acne, noncancerous breast growths, and pelvic inflammatory disease).

It would be remiss of me to not clear something up here. The morning-after pill, taken within seventy-two hours of sex, is a contraceptive. It is not an abortion pill. It BLOCKS ovulation, so THERE IS NO EGG TO BE FERTILIZED. Its only link to abortion is that it PREVENTS it. And yes, those are capital letters and I am shouting. I've got friends that call it the "pro-life pill." But then I would, wouldn't I?

The morning-after pill's roots are in the 1920s; vets discovered that a dose of estrogen could prevent pregnancy in horses and dogs. In the 1960s, doctors adopted this technique to help a thirteen-year-old who had been raped. Of course it should be used only for emergencies. But still. Scientists have written in the *New England Journal of Medicine* that the morning-after pill has proven to be "more dangerous to politicians than to adolescent girls." See, if they can't keep sarcasm out of their arguments on the issue, what hope do I have?

There is a pill that causes abortions for pregnancies eight weeks or earlier. But that is *not* the morning-after pill. So please, for the final time, let's take Plan B off the table. The next report is the one that makes the blood boil on all sides of the argument.

MINI REPORT 2. ABORTION

The emotional issue of abortion has been one of public and private debate throughout history. From China under Shennong (c. 2700 BC) to ancient Egypt to ancient Rome. It was the main form of birth control for Russian women in the Soviet era, while in America, abortion became legal nationwide with the Supreme Court ruling of *Roe v. Wade* in 1973.

STUNNING STATISTICS

- 97 percent of unsafe abortions are carried out in developing countries.
- Legal abortion in developed countries is one of the safest procedures in medicine.
- Abortion is banned in Ireland unless a woman's life is endangered. Since 1980 around 150,000 women are known to have traveled to Britain for the procedure.

Arguably abortion has gotten more divisive since the 1970s. To be antiabortion became a moral must for Republicans. However, until the 1990s, Republican voters remained *more* likely to be pro-choice than Democrats. Five conservative appointed justices were on board for the 7 to 2 Roe vote. A 1972 Gallup poll had 68 percent of Republicans and 59 percent of Democrats believing the decision to abort should be between doctor and patient ONLY. However, Republican strategists used the issue as a tool to entice evangelicals and Catholics to the GOP from 1979.

So here we are today. Americans remain conflicted, politicians divided, on the issue, ESPECIALLY WITH SCIENTIFIC PROGRESS. Polls consistently show three-fifths of Americans are not pro-life or pro-choice—they are somewhere in between. Studies have shown the following:

- Nearly half of all pregnancies in the US are unplanned, and of those, more than 40 percent end in abortion.

- Just under a quarter of all American pregnancies end in abortion—and the vast majority of the women have already had a baby.

- Some statistics suggest about a third of American women will have an abortion in their lifetime.

- Thirty percent of those who do have an abortion have at times identified themselves as Catholic.

- A woman who is denied an abortion is three times more likely to end up below the federal poverty line.

- Out-of-wedlock births are soaring—is this the irony of the pro-life movement?

There has been increasingly vitriolic debate on the around 1 percent of abortions performed after twenty weeks. So what makes a woman delay the decision for that length of time? It should be noted that physicians say this is just after the time when comprehensive fetal testing is performed—and devastating fetal defects discovered.

In 2006 $11.1 billion of America's public funds were spent on the births of unintended babies.

I will leave you with the below wise words and this thought: No child should be unwanted.

WISE WORDS

If men could get pregnant, abortion would be a sacrament.

> —Apparently told to Florynce R. Kennedy and Gloria Steinem in an old Irish lady's taxicab

Abortion should not only be safe and legal, it should be rare.

> —Bill Clinton

I think life is sacred, whether it's abortion or the death penalty.

> —Tim Kaine

MINI REPORT 3. PREGNANCY

A normal pregnancy is forty weeks. Ten months. They lie to you about the nine-month thing. Just saying.

A female is born with the total number of eggs she will have throughout her lifetime, normally around 2 million. They age with you and are never replaced. Indeed, you start losing eggs while you are still a fetus. Fertility tails off slowly during your early thirties and then basically goes into free fall the nearer you get to forty, although American mothers are getting older. This is a good thing. It shows society's progress. So you can tell anyone who criticizes you for not breeding yet to go shove it up their a**.

You were warned that I would spend my time coming over all *Jezebel* with this.

NOTEWORTHY NUGGETS:
OLD WIVES TALES VERSUS THE FACTS

People see a woman with child and become instant know-it-alls—but usually they are know-nothings. Here is a roundup of the most common misconceptions doing the rounds postconception.

Tale	Fact
You can tell from the shape of the bump what sex the child is. Carrying it low=boy; high (and/or fast heartbeat/morning sickness)=girl.	Myth. Without an ultrasound you won't know which you're having.
Heartburn means your baby will be born with a full head of hair.	Myth. Pregnancy hormones loosen the muscles of your esophagus, causing heartburn.
Spicy food and raspberry leaf tea in late pregnancy will bring on labor.	Myth.
Computers or cell phones can harm a baby.	They can't, but jury's out on microwaves.
You can eat for two.	Myth. Calorie needs are basically the same until late pregnancy, when you need an extra 300 calories or so.
Caffeine is bad for your baby.	True! Starbucks will unfortunately survive without you.
You can't dye your hair.	Avoid in first trimester.
Tanning beds and reflexology should be avoided throughout pregnancy.	True. What did Snooki do?

Tale	Fact
You can't drink when you're pregnant.	Our parents did. Look how we turned out. Best stick with the Poland Spring.
You can't eat sushi.	Stay off the raw fish—something to do with parasites.

Although you must NEVER ask a modern woman when she is due (social suicide if she isn't), it is in fact quite obvious to tell. She won't be drinking caffeine or cocktails in her normal fishlike way and will be off the raw-fish sushi, and her normally immaculate hair will have roots.

NOTEWORTHY NUGGET: BOYS VERSUS GIRLS

You have to feel sorry for Henry VIII's wives. It is in fact men who determine the sex of a baby, depending on whether the sperm that hits the jackpot is carrying an X or a Y chromosome. An X chromosome combines with the mother's X chromosome to make a baby girl (XX) and a Y chromosome will combine with the mother's to make a boy (XY).

MINI REPORT 4. DEATH

We begin this report with the death penalty. But since that's not a good place to bid our adieus on a Cheat Sheet, we then touch on the afterlife and finish up with some thought-provoking quotes from wise women and men on the subject of moving on.

Capital punishment, when the state puts a person to death, remains a divisive issue around the world. It has, as with abortion, existed throughout history. As of May 2013, 140 countries were abolitionist in law or practice. In 2014, at least 22 countries around the world carried out executions.

In 2015, the USA was the only source of executions in the western hemisphere (Japan still has it, if that makes you feel any better). You cannot be a member of the European Union and have the death penalty. However, surveys have long shown the majority of Americans are in favor of it. Since 1976, over 80 percent of all American executions take place in the South, less than 1 percent in the Northeast.

STUNNING STATISTICS: COUNTRIES WHO EXECUTED THE MOST PEOPLE IN 2014

1. China

2. Iran

3. Saudi Arabia

4. Iraq

5. USA

6. Sudan

7. Yemen

8. Egypt

9. Somalia

10. Jordan

Amnesty International has proclaimed that "the death penalty is the ultimate, irreversible denial of human rights." But if you're comfortable hanging out with the company America's keeping in the list of countries who execute the most, so be it.

Told you so. European liberal feminist. There's another matter that Europeans differ from their American counterparts on—the acceptance of the right to die and suicide tourism. "Going to Switzerland" has become a euphemism for assisted suicide.

There is no end in sight for the debates on these issues in many nations. However, we have the end in sight with this Cheat Sheet, so we now turn to the concept of the hereafter/life after death/the next world/the afterlife, which has rather obviously been around about as long as procreation.

Ancient cultures were terribly thoughtful for future archaeologists. The ancient Egyptians saw death not the end of life, just as an interruption, so the physical form needed to be preserved—hence mummification. Ancient Greek souls needed to give a ferryman some gold, so coins would be put under the deceased's tongue.

As we saw in the religion section, many adhere to the belief of reincarnation, including Buddhists and Sikhs, while the whole megillah of heaven aka paradise/hell with a bit of purgatory thrown in can be found in religions from Catholicism to Islam.

Science remains skeptical of the existence of the afterlife, although it has become somewhat less so. Hundreds of scholarly articles have been written over the last few decades about near-death experiences.

Fundamentally no one can know. You can't interview dead people. Well, those who are considered sane can't.

Thus we conclude by considering some wise words of people who are living—and have lived—some renowned lives.

WISE WORDS: DEATH

Do not pity the dead, Harry. Pity the living, and above all, those who live without love.

—J. K. Rowling

A man who won't die for something is not fit to live.

—Martin Luther King, Jr.

While I thought that I was learning how to live, I have been learning how to die.

—Leonardo da Vinci

> Any man who has $10,000 left when he dies is a failure.
> —Errol Flynn
>
> When you're dead, you're dead. That's it.
> —Marlene Dietrich

SOCIAL SURVIVAL STRATEGY

Argument: "I think we can all agree on one thing about Hillary Clinton from the 1990s, 'Women's rights are human rights.'"
Hillary Clinton has been a lightning rod in American conversation for decades. This comment will at least cool down the debate long enough for you to figure out how to change the topic—or come up with some better facts to win it.

Crisp Fact: "We, the USA, are the only source of executions in the western hemisphere."
You need to be aware of this one because if you're with foreigners, they probably are, and you need to stake your position, whether you are proud or ashamed of it.

Pivot: "As Errol Flynn once said, 'Any man who has $10,000 left when he dies is a failure.' What's on your bucket list?"
All of us have a fantasy list of things we want to do before we die. This will keep others occupied and your tête-à-tête out of trouble and strife.

CHEAT SHEET 25—FEMINISM

BACKGROUND BRIEFING

Feminism.

Pretty much ever since Socrates's wife was painted as a jealous shrew by one of his pupils, women have had it tough in philosophy. Thinkers from Aristotle to Kant questioned whether women were fully capable of reason.

CEO Marissa Mayer, Carla Bruni, Katy Perry, and Carrie Underwood have all distanced themselves from the F word. Susan Sarandon has muttered something along the lines that it's old-fashioned and prefers "humanist."

One might facetiously suggest that these women, unlike Emma Watson, Beyoncé, Lena Dunham, and Taylor Swift (who was assisted by Dunham in coming to terms with feminism), don't have access to a dictionary. According to the *Oxford English Dictionary,* the word *feminism,* which first appeared in its tome in 1895, is "the advocacy of women's rights on the grounds of political, social, and economic equality to men."

In this day and age, surely it should be uncontroversial, at least in developed nations, to believe that women should be treated as social and intellectual equals to men. Something has surely gotten lost in translation when you have women who believe in that concept but deny feminism.

However, rightly or wrongly, there can be no doubt that the label has become stigmatized. Which is annoying. As there is nothing that gives a misogynist greater pleasure than a female not deigning to call herself a feminist.

WISE WORDS

I've thought about what is an alternative word to feminism. There isn't one. It's a perfectly good word. And it can't be changed.

—Annie Lennox

Feminism is of course an umbrella term that includes a number of movements. Perhaps the roots of the controversy concerning it lie in the fact that it has never been a cohesive entity. It means different things to different people, sometimes unifying on certain issues.

The issue of women's rights first seriously cropped up during the French and American revolutions in the late eighteenth century. The word itself comes from the French word *féminisme,* and was supposedly invented by a man in 1837—Charles Fourier, a philosopher. However, the term became widespread in the West during the late nineteenth and early twentieth century, in what was subsequently labeled the first wave of feminism, which particularly focused on suffrage—the right to vote. US superstars of this era included the triumvirate of Susan B. Anthony, Elizabeth Cady Stanton, and Lucy Stone. American women won the right to vote in 1920.

The second wave of feminism is believed by many to have been kicked off by Betty Friedan's 1963 book, *The Feminine Mystique,* wherein she discussed "the problem that has no name"—women's discontent with their role in life. So came the fight for legal and social equality. "The Personal Is Political," wrote Carol Hanisch. Australian-born, British-based Germaine Greer penned the international 1970 pivotal bestseller *The Female Eunuch,* in which she argued male entitlement and female repression reduced women to the status of eunuchs.

Front and center in the second wave of all these trailblazers was the legendary Gloria Steinem, who founded *Ms.* magazine—its first 1972 issue of 300,000 rapidly sold out and became the landmark feminist American publication. Politicians included Bella Abzug, the first Jewish congresswoman (1971–1976), who was key in getting the Equal Rights Amendment as far as it did.

KEY TERM: THE EQUAL RIGHTS AMENDMENT (ERA)

- The ERA actually wasn't started by second-wave feminists, oh no. There was a 1923 draft by suffragist Alice Paul, and from then until 1970 it was introduced in some form in EVERY Congress session—and held up in committee EVERY time.

- Fast-forward to 1970, Martha Griffiths, a Democratic (surprise!) representative from Michigan, managed to get it to the House. Where it passed. Only to be killed by the Senate.

- Griffiths reintroduced a redraft, which was approved by the House in 1971 and the Senate in 1972, where it went to the states for ratification.

- The ERA was ratified in "only" thirty-five states—it needed three more in order to become a constitutional amendment.

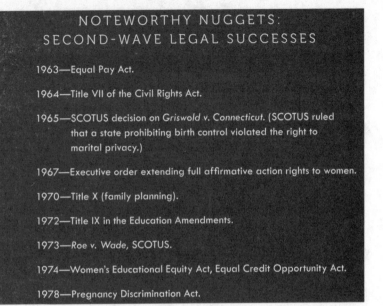

NOTEWORTHY NUGGETS:
SECOND-WAVE LEGAL SUCCESSES

1963—Equal Pay Act.

1964—Title VII of the Civil Rights Act.

1965—SCOTUS decision on *Griswold v. Connecticut.* (SCOTUS ruled
        that a state prohibiting birth control violated the right to
        marital privacy.)

1967—Executive order extending full affirmative action rights to women.

1970—Title X (family planning).

1972—Title IX in the Education Amendments.

1973—*Roe v. Wade,* SCOTUS.

1974—Women's Educational Equity Act, Equal Credit Opportunity Act.

1978—Pregnancy Discrimination Act.

There is debate over whether the second wave has ever really ended—it sort of goes along with the third wave of feminism, which hit in the 1990s. The third wave basically filled in the gaps that the second left. It was more inclusive of women of color and from diverse backgrounds (the second wave had been predominantly white and middle class). Poster girls—or should that be women?—of this era included the African-American academic and defiantly uncapitalized bell hooks and culturally Queen Latifah and Madonna, along with the Spice Girls and Girl Power.

WHY IT MATTERS TODAY

There are still some rather large outstanding difficulties that exist for women here, even in America. The ERA never passed, so these words have never made the Constitution: "Equality of rights under the law shall not be denied or abridged by the United States or by any state on account of sex."

Girls may get better grades in school, but in no small part because of the unfair division of domestic labor, the glass ceiling is still present. Oh, and unequal pay, violence against women, social inequality—plus women's portrayal in the media. Boys no longer have to buy a *National Geographic* to see breasts—they just Google porn. And what does that do to America's daughters?

Flip side is, there are *Fifty Shades* to the issue. Women may be, as ever, their own worst enemies—for instance, buying into airbrushing and even promoting the body fascism that breeds anorexia and bulimia.

NOTEWORTHY NUGGET

Hitler and Mussolini claimed they opposed feminism.

Still unconvinced feminism has no place today? What about these words from Mr. Rush "Feminazi" Limbaugh, No. 1 American radio talk-show host, 14 million listeners a week: "Feminism was established to allow unattractive women easier access to the mainstream."

Or perhaps these of Pat Robertson, media mogul: "Feminism encourages women to leave their husbands, kill their children, practice witchcraft, destroy capitalism, and become lesbians."

Even if you think there is no more work to be done on equal rights for women in the developed world, you surely cannot argue that far more needs to be achieved in the developing world. Prime example: Malala Yousafzai, the schoolgirl shot by the Taliban for championing girls' education. Hillary Clinton has called women's rights "the unfinished business of the twenty-first century." Sums it up for me. But it would, wouldn't it?

TALKING POINTS

- Feminism's first wave was not just about suffrage. In 1918, Marie Stopes published *Married Love*. It was a bestseller. Women were desperate for access to material about their own health.

- We would be remiss if we didn't mention Simone de Beauvoir's 1949 existentialist, Marxist look at feminism, *Le Deuxième Sexe*, *The Second Sex*.

- No surprise that Saudi Arabia was the last country to grant partial suffrage for women in 2011 for 2015 (we're still waiting on Brunei—for men and women), but note that Switzerland only did so in 1971. Iran had managed it in 1963. New Zealand was first, in 1893.

- Marital rape was not illegal in all US states until 1993. North Carolina was last to get on that bandwagon.

- The second-wave bra-burning thing? There's a big debate over whether or not it actually occurred at the protest outside the 1968 Miss America pageant. However, it was from this that the media moniker "bra burners" originated.

  * The bras are definitely off now for Femen members. Femen originated in Ukraine in 2008, with topless demonstrators protesting against sex tourism. The movement snowballed.

  * Unfortunately for Femen, Putin in 2013 showed exactly how to invalidate their actions. He enjoyed them.

- We do all love *Sesame Street,* but along with the whole Elmo dubious-sex thing, why did it take until 2006 to get its first female lead, Abby Cadabby?

- The average woman smiles sixty-two times a day, the average man only eight. How can you not love the fairer sex?

RED FLAGS

- Mary Wollstonecraft was around in the eighteenth, not the nineteenth century. Her *A Vindication of the Rights of Woman* was first published in 1792, where she came up with the revolutionary concept that women are not naturally inferior to men, suggesting that they should be educated. Fancy that.

- Although Emmeline Pankhurst and her daughters Christabel and Sylvia were notorious British militant suffragettes, they were not the ones who died throwing themselves under the king's horse at 1913's Derby. That was Emily Davison.

- The least interesting thing about Gloria Steinem is that *Batman* is her stepson. She married David Bale, Christian's dad, age sixty-six. Sadly he died three years later.

WISE WORDS

The idea of being a feminist—so many women have come to this idea of it being anti-male and not able to connect with the opposite sex—but what feminism is about is equality and human rights. For me that is just an essential part of my identity. I hope [*Girls*] contributes to a continuance of feminist dialogue.

—Lena Dunham

I'm a feminist because I believe in women . . . it's a heavy word, feminism, but it's not one I think we should run from. I'm proud to be a feminist.

—Sheryl Sandberg

SOCIAL SURVIVAL STRATEGY

Argument: "There is nothing that gives a misogynist greater pleasure than a female not deigning to call herself a feminist."
The debate about the label of feminism is counterproductive—this should shut that down and open a more constructive dialogue.

Crisp Fact: "Switzerland didn't let women vote until 1971; even Iran managed it in 1963 (the USA was 1920)."
This still staggers me every time I read it. 1971? If you feel like making jaws drop, this will do it.

Pivot: "The average woman smiles sixty-two times a day, the average man only eight. Who couldn't love women? You have a beautiful smile, who's your dentist? I'm not sure I entirely trust mine."
It is rare you will find someone who hasn't had a dental drama, and sensitive teeth will be a safe topic to turn to if feminism is proving a little too sensitive a topic.

CHEAT SHEET 26—HOMOSEXUALITY

BACKGROUND BRIEFING

Labels, labels. It wasn't until 1869 that the term *homosexuality* even made its appearance—it was coined by Karl Maria Kertbeny, an Austrian litterateur who was against sodomy laws. *Homo* comes from the Greek *homos,* which means same, and the root word for *sexuality* is the Latin *sexus,* which means male or female sex, gender. Thus the hybrid's literal translation is "of the same sex or gender." Meanwhile the word *gay* has been in the English language since about the thirteenth century, with the word taking on sexual connotations—for lively and merry activities got up to by everyone— by the seventeenth century. It wasn't until the twentieth century that gay was applied to homosexual behavior.

ALPHABET CITY

A: Ally, usually applied to straight people who supports LGBTQ rights

B: Bisexual

G: Gay

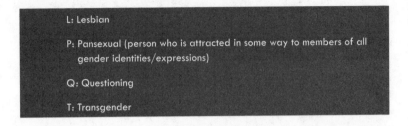

Science has no specific unanimity about why someone is LGBTQ—other species are noted to be so as well. Nature and nurture are believed to play a complex part. What is certain is that the majority of us feel only a modicum, if that, of choice about what we are when it comes to our sexuality and that homosexuality is not a mental disorder. In 1973 the American Psychiatric Association removed homosexuality from its list of mental illnesses—"praying the gay out" is not something that professionals condone. What is also for sure is that homophobia can cause serious psychological damage. It is notoriously tricky to put a specific number on those who are LGBTQ, but studies indicate anything between 2 to 11 percent of us have same-sex sexual contact in our lives and that around 4 percent of Americans consider themselves as LGBTQ.

Same-sex attraction has thus always existed. There is evidence that same-sex marriages were tolerated in parts of Mesopotamia and ancient Egypt. Plato's *Symposium* discussed same-sex relations in a philosophical manner, arguing that there should be an army made up of same-sex lovers. There are depictions of same-sex relations on Greek artwork and vases. The Greek god Zeus had stories of same-sex exploits attributed to him. In real life there was Alexander the Great and Socrates and then the Roman emperors Hadrian and Nero, who both reportedly married men. Apparently when Nero wed his freedman Pythagoras, the emperor was the bride.

The Roman empire got more intolerant over time and the more Christianity took hold. Abrahamic religions frowned on sodomy. Sodomite was understood as an act, rather than as a type of person.

But same-sex attraction never went away—think Venice during the Renaissance. As cities flourished, so gay communities grew; people could be themselves without family constraints. The Napoleonic code even decriminalized sodomy. Oscar Wilde became a poster boy of sorts in the late nineteenth century. Before Nazism took hold in Germany, there was a tremendously influential homosexual movement there. The Nazis murdered hundreds of thousands of LGBTQ people in concentration camps. The Nazis' pink and black triangles, used to demarcate for persecution homosexual men and lesbians respectively, were reclaimed by the gay movement in the 1970s as a symbol of commemoration and inspiration to battle persecution.

NOTEWORTHY NUGGET: THE RAINBOW FLAG

- The iconic symbol for gay pride was originally designed in 1978 by Gilbert Baker, a Vietnam vet who had settled in San Francisco.

- Baker knew Harvey Milk.

- Baker has said about the flag: "It's beautiful, all of the colors, even the colors you can't see. That really fit us as a people because we are all of the colors. Our sexuality is all of the colors. We are all the genders, races, and ages."

- Baker assigned a meaning to each of the original eight colors he used: hot pink (sexuality), red (life), orange (healing), yellow (sunlight), green (nature), turquoise (magic/art), indigo/blue (serenity/harmony), and violet (spirit).

The year 1950 saw the foundation of one of America's first homosexual political organizations, the Mattachine Society. McCarthyism helped restrict its impact, and it was the Stonewall riots in the summer of 1969, just after Judy Garland's death, that marked the real turning point for the gay rights movement. Patrons at the Stonewall Inn, a working-class lesbian and gay bar situated in Manhattan's Greenwich Village, resisted what was then a routine police raid. The riots and protests it sparked proved a watershed moment. In 1970 came New York's first gay pride parade, and it spread to other cities and countries. June is now Gay Pride Month around the world. Pride, being the opposite of shame.

NOTEWORTHY NUGGETS: HARVEY MILK

- Milk, a former US Navy man, teacher, Wall Street banker—and associate on Broadway musicals—was elected to San Francisco's board of supervisors in 1977, becoming the first openly gay person to hold high public office in a main American city.
- Sean Penn won the 2009 Academy Award for his portrayal of Milk.
- Milk was assassinated in 1978 by Dan White, who also shot and killed San Fran mayor George Moscone. There has been some conjecture that White, a former city supervisor, was in the closet. The contentious trial went down in history as White utilized what became known as the "Twinkie defense"—his judgment was impaired because he ate too many Twinkies. He was convicted only of manslaughter and served just five years in jail. Described as "perhaps the most hated man in San Francisco history," he later took his own life.

The appearance of AIDS in the early 1980s caused the nature of the LGBTQ community's campaigns to change. If you've not yet watched Ryan Murphy's HBO adaptation of Larry Kramer's award-winning play *The Normal Heart,* do so. A public backlash against the movement in Reagan's America took hold, although perception was aided through the community's work and with films such as Tom Hanks's *Philadelphia,* for which he won the 1993 Oscar for Best Actor.

KEY TERMS

- **Don't Ask, Don't Tell.** In 1982 Reagan issued a defense directive saying homosexuality was incompatible with the military. Bill Clinton promised to lift the ban when campaigning in 1992. In 1993 came the compromise—a defense directive from him stated that military applicants should not be asked about their sexual orientation, DADT. Obama repealed it in 2011. Arguably the military, as they did with integration, was leading the way on LGBTQ rights.

- **The Defense of Marriage Act,** of 1996. DOMA banned federal recognition of same-sex marriage and defined marriage as "a legal union between one man and one woman as husband and wife." Bill Clinton signed this into law, saying later that he regretted doing so, finding it "incompatible with our Constitution." On June 26, 2013, SCOTUS rejected parts of DOMA in a 5–4 decision.

- California's **Proposition 8,** of 2008. Defined marriage as between a man and a woman. This stemmed from San Francisco's 2004 decision to begin issuing same-sex marriage licenses. After campaigns that cost around $72 million, Prop 8 passed. Legal challenges commenced. Also on June 26, 2013, SCOTUS dismissed a case to overturn a lower-court decision striking Prop 8 down, paving the way for same-sex marriages to resume in California.

WHY IT MATTERS TODAY

In 1980, polling data indicated that only 11 percent of Americans supported same-sex marriage. By June 2015, with poll after poll confirming that same-sex marriage is supported by the majority of Americans, the Supreme Court ruled that same-sex marriage is a constitutional right. States can no longer ban gay couples from marrying. The decision was the most significant ruling made on marriage since *Loving v. Virginia* in 1967, which struck down laws that banned interracial marriages, and there are striking parallels. Since nobody has shown that interracial or same-sex marriage harms anyone, discrimination against it cannot be justified by the government.

It's an incredibly swift advance. President Obama's evolving on the topic somewhat reflected the nation's; he went from publicly, at least, opposing same-sex marriage for religious reasons in the 2008 election, to saying that states should decide (thanks to some "prodding" from Vice-President Joe Biden) in 2012, to declaring that the 2015 SCOTUS decision has "made our union a little more perfect." Most Americans, such as the Republican senator Rob Portman, know or are related to someone who is gay and realize that gay people are not social revolutionaries, they just want to participate in the same institution already open to their straight fellow citizens. The personal is the political, as the maxim goes. Millions of American kids are being brought up with gay parents. The arguments that same-sex marriage is "nontraditional" and marriage should be about procreation were also used against mixed-race marriage and women owning property. Popular culture is also making same-sex marriage acceptable. *Will & Grace. Modern Family. The Simpsons. Sesame Street* . . .

There are of course fights still to be fought both inside and outside the United States. It took until 2013 for a first openly gay player in the four major North American professional sports to come out, NBA player Jason Collins. It would be mischievous of me to point out that studies show homophobia is more common among those who have a hidden desire for others of the same sex, right?

WISE WORDS

I don't support gay marriage in spite of being a Conservative, I support it because I am a Conservative.

—David Cameron, prime minister of Britain

Internationally, same-sex marriages are now legal in more than twenty countries around the world. However, as of 2015, in sixty-six countries homosexuality is still criminalized; in more than 10 percent of those, it's punishable by death. We still have a ways to go.

TALKING POINTS

- "Friend of Dorothy" is a term that became popular in the 1950s, as Judy Garland reached the status of quintessential gay icon. Garland's seminal role as Dorothy Gale in *The Wizard of Oz* gave gays and lesbians a secret code phrase to use to identify each other in public. Some speculate that the "Dorothy" actually refers to satirist and poet Dorothy Parker.

- Early gay icons include the shirtless Saint Sebastian (Oscar Wilde used the name Sebastian after he got out of jail) and Marie Antoinette.

  * To attain gay icon status, one has to demonstrate appropriate levels of flamboyance and triumph through tough times. An extraordinary approach to fashion and a powerhouse voice doesn't hurt. So Barbra Streisand, Liza Minnelli (Judy's daughter), and Diana Ross with her "I'm Coming Out" anthem all qualify.

  * Actually looking like a drag queen really cements status—think Cher (who then went on to have an LGBTQ child) and Dolly Parton.

  * A dose of tragedy definitely helps the cause—Maria Callas lost her voice and died.

  * It's very possible to be male and a gay icon—the Latino community has provided the classics of Ricky and Enrique.

- Gays are good for the economy—they tend to be DINKY (Dual Income, No Kids Yet). As of 2013, conservative estimates of the Dorothy Dollar market put it at around $830 billion in the US.

  * Targeting the LGBTQ community in marketing can seriously bring in the big bucks. American Airlines focused on

getting gays on board in the 1990s, seeing earnings from the community rise from $20 million in 1994 to $193.5 million in 1999.

   ∗ The Dorothy Dollar is one of the top-level political contributors to . . . Democrats.

- One of the reasons the LGBTQ community in San Francisco became so vibrant is that at the end of World War II, many lesbians and gays were dishonorably discharged from the military—and were left in port cities. Not wanting a shameful return home, they remained.

- In 2014 Laverne Cox was the first openly transgender person to get nominated for an Emmy in an acting category, for her performance in the hit Netflix series *Orange Is the New Black*. Caitlyn Jenner's 2015 *Vanity Fair* cover was a further sign of a cultural revolution in America.

RED FLAGS

- When in doubt, don't use the moniker *gay*, use *LGBTQ*—the former can be a minefield, while the latter is seen to accurately represent everyone.

- Some American states really were very backward in decriminalizing homosexuality, although the argument is that there are many rules on the books that now make no sense. It took until 2003 for SCOTUS to finally invalidate the sodomy laws that still existed in fourteen states (which included Florida and Texas).

- Homosexuality was decriminalized in Poland (1932), Denmark (1933), and the UK (1967). It was actually decriminalized in Russia in 1993, BUT then came Vladimir Putin's war on gays . . .

- It is discourteous, to say the least, to comment or be turned off by any of the following if you've got someone naked. So just in case you're really wondering what is going on in your (male) date's pants, here's some clues before it gets to the point of rude return:

* Approximately 75 percent of men in the US are circumcised, whereas those in Canada take a more European perspective on the issue and the numbers are estimated at 30 percent. Across the Pond we're talking less than 20 percent.

* The first evidence of circumcision comes from early Egyptian wall paintings that are more than 5,000 years old. Estimates of the proportion of males that are circumcised worldwide vary from a sixth to a third and have been mostly for religious and cultural reasons.

* Religious perspectives vary widely. In Judaism, religious male circumcision is considered a commandment from God, representing the covenant made by God with Abraham and his descendants. On the other end of the spectrum, you have the Catholic Church, which condemned the observance of circumcision as a mortal sin and ordered against its practice in the Ecumenical Council of Basel-Florence in 1442. In 2012 a debate emerged about circumcision in Germany, of all places—the definition of inappropriate.

* The health debate is not really worth having with someone who isn't circumcised. Circumcision may be able to prevent some diseases, including penile cancer (if done in childhood) and some STIs. Views conflict on whether circumcision can prevent HIV infection. There is an argument that circumcision may be appropriate as a routine preventive measure only in regions that have a high rate of HIV infection, such as sub-Saharan Africa. But the foreskin is not simply a useless piece of skin; it is very rich in nerves and provides some of the pleasurable sensation experienced during sex. Adult males that were circumcised as infants do not usually report sexual problems linked with their circumcision, but those who are later frequently do. Studies have shown that penile warts and urethritis are more common in circumcised men. The evidence is inadequate to recommend

circumcision as a preventive measure against cervical cancer.

* Since we're in the area, know that globally, the average flaccid penis is 3.61 inches long, while the average erect penis is 5.16 inches.

- With someone LGBTQ? Don't mention and don't take them to Chick-fil-A. There was a debacle of a debate about the place after its president and COO came out as basically not for those coming out in 2012.

WISE WORDS

Jesus never said a word about homosexuality. In all of his teachings about multiple things, he never said that gay people should be condemned.

—Jimmy Carter

SOCIAL SURVIVAL STRATEGY

Argument: "The personal is the political on gay rights. Most Americans, such as the Republican senator Rob Portman, know or are related to someone who is gay and realize that gay people are not social revolutionaries."

There is inexorable change in the air. If people even try to disagree with you on this, they are swimming against an unwinnable tide, and at some point they will have to acknowledge this.

Crisp Fact: Approximate circumcision numbers if you're trying to work out what's going on in your date's pants: 75 percent of American men, 30 percent of Canadian men, Brit blokes less than 20 percent.

Useful information for quite possibly more than 50 percent of you reading this to have in your mind.

Pivot: "Let's play sleep with, marry, or kill these gay icons: Judy Garland, Madonna, and Barbra Streisand."
Everyone will have an opinion. And it should be amusing. Thus the perfect pivot out of anything prickly, one might say.

SUBJECT EIGHT—CULTURE

CULTURE SUMMARY

The key theme to think about when discussing anything related to this subject is Nietzsche's maxim: "There are no facts, only interpretations." The phrase is actually applicable in all sorts of situations, but the arts are everything to do with interpretations. Often people ignored or pilloried in their own lifetimes later undergo entirely different analyses—El Greco, Puccini, Tchaikovsky, even Gershwin. Of course, those who can't, criticize, so one should always be wary of the reviewer. A wonderful, mind-bending fact to drop into chat is that supposedly, of the 17,000 words Shakespeare used, he invented about 1,700 of them. And a pivot to get out of a cultural conversation? Ask those you're speaking with to name the people they'd thank in an Oscar acceptance speech. It will be telling, even if they lie and say they haven't thought about it. Everyone at some point or other has looked in the bathroom mirror and uttered the phrase: "I would like to thank the Academy . . ."

It was my editor's idea that I write about this subject. He was right, of course, culture being the bedrock of civilization and all. It reflects us as we are today. And since I've spent my entire adult life working in it, most recently as senior editor at Broadway.com, panelist on Imus's *Hollywood and Vine*, and my whole life observing it (yes, I'm one of those Lloyd Webbers, the cat phans), I actually know something about it. For a change.

Of course, if you're a sophisticated type, you may not find the next Cheat Sheets to your taste and believe that I've made it too philistine friendly. Wait, before you go, though, do you know who composed the British Airways signature tune or the now-defunct *X-Factor* theme music (you definitely saw a promo for it if not the show itself)? If you're wavering, then I suggest having a quick skim of this subject. I did even come up with something about Puccini that his greatest fan (my dad) didn't know about . . .

Our first Cultural Cheat Sheets are comprised of a series of grids: authors, artists, and composers you should have on your radar. We follow this with a standard Cheat Sheet on theater before having some fun and ending the book on awards season conversation.

In regards to authors, I am presuming some level of ability here. I'm not going to go on about Agatha Christie, Roald Dahl, or even Charles Dickens. You've seen *Oliver!* F. Scott Fitzgerald recently got the Baz Luhrmann treatment with *The Great Gatsby,* so I'm sure you've got a semblance of a talking point on that one. Jane Austen does make the cut on the basis that I'm concerned you might confuse her with Charlotte Brontë in front of a Janeite, who are up there with *Star Trek* fans for unhinged behavior. I've also neglected those authors who crop up elsewhere—the feminists have their day in the sun in their own Cheat Sheet, as does George Orwell and *Nineteen Eighty-Four* in Cheat Sheet 16.

The art Cheat Sheet is—well, to put it bluntly, I'm here to remind you that Leonardo, Donatello, Raphael, and Michelangelo are not turtles. And unlike the turtle creators, you always knew that Michelangelo isn't spelled Michaelangelo. No, really, I'm not joking there. It is also worth noting that an Old Master is a painter who was renowned before 1800. And if you want to placate someone who is really arty when you quite clearly know nothing, simply quote

Oscar Wilde: "The artist should never try to be popular. The public should try to be more artistic." They'll probably snog you on the spot.

In regards to composers, I keep it old school. We take a quick tour of some notable composers from the Medieval, Renaissance, Classical, and Romantic periods and from the twentieth century. Embarrassingly, I have to say, they are all men, which has thoroughly raised my feminist hackles, but at the same time, the most prominent of these eras had a Y chromosome. Of course they did.

Bearing in mind my current occupation and the fact I actually produced a play in the West End and wish to do so on Broadway, the theater Cheat Sheet does go on a bit. If you really can't be bothered to read it, merely mutter something about the Brunetière law of the theater—drama must deal with an exercise of the human will, and therefore a struggle of some sort is an essential element in the pleasure we take in a production.

Why no film, modern music, or television? you ask. These all come under awards season conversation. If you bump into someone who goes to Sundance or Toronto for the film festivals or is into the Grammys or Emmys, this Cheat Sheet will see you through. If it feels like too much of a challenge, then just sprinkle your chat with them with the following phrases: "Oscar/Emmy/Tony/Grammy bait," "shrewd marketing campaigns," "Harvey Weinstein," and "whisper campaigns against early front-runners." Oh, incidentally, do what you can to become friends with someone who can vote for the Golden Globes, BAFTAs, or Oscars. They get screeners and you'll save a FORTUNE on movie tickets. What this Cheat Sheet doesn't cover is the MTV Video Music Awards. Seriously. Are you twelve? No. All you need to remember for them is that you don't have a leg to stand on if there's a "shocking" performance. Madonna started that. It's de rigueur for that awards show.

Before we start, I will take pity on you as these composers didn't make it onto Cheat Sheet 29, as there were too many others we needed to cover. The British Airways signature tune is the "Flower Duet" from *Lakmé* by Leo Delibes and the *X Factor* theme music is from *Carmina Burana* by Carl Orff.

WISE WORDS

No culture can live if it attempts to be exclusive.

—Mahatma Gandhi

CHEAT SHEET 27—AUTHORS YOU NEED TO KNOW ABOUT

NAME DATES ALIVE	CLAIM(S) TO FAME FOR PHILISTINES	QUIRK(S)	TALKING POINT(S)
Homer Nobody's sure. Eighth, ninth, and twelfth century BC have all been suggested.	Not Homer Simpson. Instead, the greatest poet of ancient times. According to Plato, Homer was the educator of Greece. As the author of the epic poems the *Iliad* and the *Odyssey*, Homer began Western literature. The movie *Troy*, with Brad Pitt as Achilles and the kidnapping of Helen, the world's prettiest woman? Adaptation of Homer.	Very little is known about Homer the man. Was he blind? Did he sing? Did he write his poems alone? Was he transcribing stories that had been handed down through generations?	You can ponder the Homeric Question: Did he actually exist at all? Also note that the influence of *Odyssey* can be seen in everything from the Coen brothers' *O Brother, Where Art Thou?* to James Joyce's *Ulysses*.
Miguel de Cervantes Saavedra c. 1547 to 1616	Cervantes (translated) invented terms including "wild-goose chase," "the sky's the limit," and "pot calling the kettle black." They came from his book *Don Quixote*, the first modern European novel and the world's first bestseller, although it didn't make him rich—at the time authors didn't get royalties.	Spent five years in slavery after being captured while serving in the Spanish navy.	Cervantes's impact on the Spanish language was so significant it has been dubbed *la lengua de Cervantes* ("the language of Cervantes"). He inspired other authors, including Flaubert and Dostoyevsky, along with Picasso. Who was an artist. A famous one.

NAME DATES ALIVE	CLAIM(S) TO FAME FOR PHILISTINES	QUIRK(S)	TALKING POINT(S)
François-Marie Arouet aka **Voltaire** 1694–1778	French Enlightenment writer, philosopher, and historian. You know him for his wit and his support of separation of church and state, freedom of expression, and freedom of religion. Yes. Those small things that America holds dear. Author of satirical novella *Candide*.	Constantly being arrested and exiled for writing his incendiary works. Voltaire lived in England from 1726 to 1728, learning the language by frequent visits to the theater. VIPs he was feted by during his stay included Alexander Pope and Horace Walpole. Voltaire in turn was deeply influenced by the works of such men as John Locke and Sir Isaac Newton.	The French public at the end of his lifetime began to perceive Voltaire as a literary genius. He was an incredibly versatile writer, as a poet (*La Henriade*), playwright (tragedy *Oedipus*) and historian (*The Age of Louis XIV*). In 1764, he published another of his most important philosophical works, *Dictionnaire philosophique*, an encyclopedic dictionary embracing the concepts of the Enlightenment and rejecting the ideas of the Roman Catholic Church.
Jane Austen 1775–1817	Georgian era author who had a rather impressive run: *Sense and Sensibility* (1811), *Pride and Prejudice* (1813), *Mansfield Park* (1814), and *Emma* (1816). Then the small matter of *Northanger Abbey* and *Persuasion*, published after her death. She did NOT write *Jane Eyre*. Charlotte Brontë did, publishing it in 1847.	Beware: The Janeites are up there with the Trekkies, so if you're in their company, joke that you are *Clueless* (the fun 1995 movie was based on *Emma*). Keep in mind that Austen never married, received some acclaim for her work in her lifetime, but it was only after she died that her brother disclosed that she was the author and it took until the 1920s and beyond before she was really recognized for her skill.	Austen was published in her lifetime, but the phenom part came later. Exclaim something along the lines of: "Well, of course, Austen bridges the gap between romance and realism. The irony! The social commentary!" And it's worth repeating so you never make this error: She didn't write *Jane Eyre*.

(cont.)

NAME / DATES ALIVE	CLAIM(S) TO FAME FOR PHILISTINES	QUIRK(S)	TALKING POINT(S)
Mary Ann Evans / **George Eliot** / 1819–1880	Not Jane Austen. English novelist of the Victorian era. Author of *Middlemarch* (which Martin Amis believes is the greatest novel in the English language) and *Daniel Deronda*. Check your Netflix.	Rule breaker. Lived with a married man, George Henry Lewes, for two decades (his wife was already having a thing with someone else when she met him). "Eliot" and Lewes played host to such leading lights of the time as German composer Richard Wagner, the Russian novelist Ivan Turgenev, and the American essayist Ralph Waldo Emerson.	Eliot could have been published under her own name—women were in the era—but she wanted to be taken seriously. Remark how Eliot's work was all about realism and human psychology. In provincial England.
Lev "Leo" Nikolayevich, Count **Tolstoy** / 1828–1910	You're reading *The Intelligent Conversationalist*, so I'm doubting *War and Peace* is your thing to get through, but he wrote it (war and peace are literally and metaphorically around us at all times). Also *Anna Karenina*, which recently had a very well-lit Keira Knightley play the titular role. Not to be confused with Chekhov (1860–1904), who wrote plays, including *Uncle Vanya* and *The Seagull*.	Tolstoy at one point decided he was an anarchist and in 1857 found himself in Paris. However, he burned through his cash and returned to Russia. Achieved critical acclaim in his own lifetime, though, especially after the publishing of *Anna Karenina*, although he struggled morally with what to do with the money after a spiritual awakening—he ended up an anarcho-pacifist and Christian anarchist type.	Tolstoy had a knack for expressing the unconscious motives of his characters. His thoughts on nonviolent resistance, as seen in works such as *The Kingdom of God Is Within You*, had an impact on later luminaries including Gandhi and Martin Luther King.

NAME DATES ALIVE	CLAIM(S) TO FAME FOR PHILISTINES	QUIRK(S)	TALKING POINT(S)
Friedrich Wilhelm **Nietzsche** 1844–1900	Critical, philosophical type. Wrote about the concept of a "superman" and how God is dead, arguing that religion was over as a serious force in modern life. Famously published *Thus Spoke Zarathustra* in four volumes between 1883 and 1885.	Became pals with Richard Wagner. And as with Wagner, there's a Nazi sting in the tale. The Nazis appropriated parts of Nietzsche's work as justification for their atrocities—despite the fact he had clearly criticized nationalism and anti-Semitism. Spent last ten years of his life insane.	Quote him regularly when you meet a know-it-all and can't remember anything at all: "There are no facts, only interpretations." Nietzsche's writings on morality and individuality had an impact on many renowned twentieth-century types like Carl Jung, Sigmund Freud, Jean-Paul Sartre, and Hermann Hesse.
Oscar Fingal O'Flahertie Wills **Wilde** (He was Anglo-Irish, can you tell?) 1854–1900	Jailed-for-being-gay playwright who wrote one novel, *The Picture of Dorian Gray*. Was a toss-up whether to put him here or in the theater section, but my literary agent had him on his list of top authors, so that settled the debate. He also, of course, crops up in Cheat Sheet 26.	Wilde actually married a rich woman, Constance Lloyd, and they had two sons. When things were going swimmingly for him and *The Importance of Being Earnest* was on stage putting lots of bums on seats, the Marquess of Queensberry, the father of Lord Alfred Douglas, the man Wilde was having an affair with, left an insulting calling card at Wilde's club. Wilde sued the Marquess, but evidence of his homosexuality came out and he ended up spending two years in prison. Died broke in Paris.	Whenever discussing Wilde's work, mention how he's a proponent of aestheticism. This school of thought maintains that art can exist for beauty alone and that it need serve no serious political purpose. This was a reaction in part to the apparent unattractiveness of the Industrial Age.

(cont.)

NAME DATES ALIVE	CLAIM(S) TO FAME FOR PHILISTINES	QUIRK(S)	TALKING POINT(S)
George Bernard Shaw 1856–1950	You'll know him for his play *Pygmalion*—the silver-screen adaptation of which won him the Oscar in 1938. It was adapted again as a musical, *My Fair Lady*.	Shaw is the only Academy Award winner to have also won the Nobel Prize in Literature. Along with his writing, he was cofounder of the London School of Economics.	A socialist, Shaw said: "A government which robs Peter to pay Paul can always count on the support of Paul." However, I can see both left and right in America using that statement to support their beliefs. Think about it.
Hermann Hesse 1877–1962	German novelist, poet, and painter who wrote *Siddhartha* (trials and tribulations of Gautama Buddha) and *Steppenwolf* (a man's struggle to cope with a divided society and a divided self).	Didn't have the quietest life. Labeled a traitor during World War I, and his work was banned by the Nazis in Germany in World War II. In 1946, Hesse won the Nobel Prize for Literature.	To understand Hesse, one needs to understand his family's religion, Pietism. Pietists believe the Bible should be experienced, not just read.
Franz Kafka 1883–1924	If someone says *Kafkaesque* to you, they mean a surreal situation. His writing was, well, full of surreal situations. Famous for his works such as *The Metamorphosis*, *The Trial*, and *The Castle*. Big influence on existentialism.	Kafka's dad was a bit of a tyrant, and the author later believed his subsequent struggles had their root in his complex relationship with his father. Inhibited, insecure, Kafka was engaged twice to his girlfriend Felice Bauer. They eventually split in 1917, and he later fell for Dora Diamant, with whom he shared a penchant for socialism, along with Jewish roots.	Died of tuberculosis. Self-doubting Kafka instructed his friend Max Brod to destroy his unpublished work—Brod ignored him. Kafka's success thus came posthumously. At a 1988 auction, his handwritten copy of *The Trial* was sold for at that point the highest amount ever paid for a modern manuscript—\$1.98 million.

NAME DATES ALIVE	CLAIM(S) TO FAME FOR PHILISTINES	QUIRK(S)	TALKING POINT(S)
David Herbert **"D. H."** **Lawrence** 1885–1930	*Lady Chatterley's Lover.* The most scandalous tome of the time. Oh yes, and *Sons and Lovers* and *Women in Love.*	Working class, didn't want to be a miner like his dad.	*Lady Chatterley's Lover* was published in Italy in 1928, but was banned in the US until 1959 and the UK until 1960, when a jury found Penguin not guilty of violating Britain's Obscene Publications Act. This was a big turning point for openly talking about sex and freedom of expression. The poet Philip Larkin infamously noted that sex really caught on in 1963: "between the end of the Chatterley ban/And the Beatles' first LP."
Ernest Miller **Hemingway** 1899–1961	The Hemingway family gene: His dad took his own life, as did he. Multiple wives. Nobel and Pulitzer Prize winner. Journalist and giant of twentieth-century American literature: *The Sun Also Rises, A Farewell to Arms, For Whom the Bell Tolls,* and *The Old Man and the Sea.*	In 1952 he was almost killed in not one, but two plane crashes. Adventurous in life, he was economical and distinctive in his writing.	Lived in post–World War I Paris and became a key player in what his mentor Gertrude Stein labeled the Lost Generation. Hemingway moved in the same circles as Picasso, James Joyce, and F. Scott Fitzgerald. Came up with the immortal phrase "Never confuse movement with action." Throw that one about at a party when you feel the need to condescend.

(cont.)

NAME DATES ALIVE	CLAIM(S) TO FAME FOR PHILISTINES	QUIRK(S)	TALKING POINT(S)
Vladimir Vladimirovich **Nabokov** 1899–1977	Published *Lolita* in 1955, the bestselling book that got made into a movie by Stanley Kubrick. You know, the one about an old man and a young girl.	A refugee of Russia, then Germany, then France, Nabokov ended up in America in 1940. He taught at Wellesley (!), Harvard, and Cornell. Died in Switzerland.	Wrote his first nine novels in Russian before switching to English (which *Lolita* was penned in). Nabokov was brought up in a trilingual household.
Jerome David **"J. D." Salinger** 1919–2010	The ultimate one-hit wonder turned recluse. Penned 1951's *The Catcher in the Rye*, then basically stopped publishing, although he continued writing. Mark David Chapman, who assassinated John Lennon, had a copy of the book on him when he was arrested and said the reason for the shooting was inside.	Son of a rabbi. Salinger's mother wasn't Jewish—he didn't find this out until after his bar mitzvah. Flunked high school.	Suffered a nervous breakdown after fighting in World War II. Possibly ended up marrying a former Nazi named Sylvia for eight months. Later married a Brit and had two kids before he then went into his much-younger-woman phase. Initially the critics weren't that into *The Catcher in the Rye*, but it became a literary phenomenon, with his character Holden Caulfield finding its way into the American psyche.

NAME DATES ALIVE	CLAIM(S) TO FAME FOR PHILISTINES	QUIRK(S)	TALKING POINT(S)
Truman Streckfus Persons aka **Truman Capote** 1924–1984	Wrote the 1958 novella *Breakfast at Tiffany's*. Also *In Cold Blood* (1966), his last fully published book. The late, great Philip Seymour Hoffman won the 2006 Oscar for playing him in the imaginatively titled *Capote*.	Capote had a thirty-five-year relationship with author Jack Dunphy. Hosted the infamous Black and White Ball at the Plaza in 1966, where Lauren Bacall danced with choreographer and director Jerome Robbins. Descended into substance abuse. Pals with Jackie Kennedy and got into the Studio 54 scene of the Liza Minnelli, Andy Warhol, and Bianca Jagger types. Died at Johnny Carson's ex-wife Joanne's house.	*In Cold Blood* was a big critical and commercial hit, groundbreaking in how it used techniques usually used in fiction to narrate the nonfiction tale. Also, quote him liberally—as he said, "I don't care what anybody says about me as long as it isn't true."
Nelle **Harper Lee** 1926–	Where the Harper in Vicky Beckham et al.'s daughter's names comes from. Wrote the 1960 Pulitzer Prize–winning bestselling novel *To Kill a Mockingbird*. Its 1962 movie adaptation won the Oscar.	After arriving in NYC in 1949, Lee struggled, taking a job as a ticket agent for Eastern Airlines and the British Overseas Air Corp (BOAC). For Christmas, in 1956 her friends the Broadway composer and lyricist Michael Martin Brown and his wife Joy said they'd support her for a year while she wrote.	Until 2015's *Go Set a Watchman*, *To Kill a Mockingbird* was the only novel she had ever published. Big pals from childhood with Truman Capote; helped him in his research for *In Cold Blood*.

SOCIAL SURVIVAL STRATEGY

Argument: "I'm with Nietzsche, 'There are no facts, only interpretations.'"
This will serve you in pretty much any setting, but he is a literary figure, so he may as well go here. It's a clever put-down when you're in the company of a bombastic buffoon.

Crisp Fact: "George Bernard Shaw is the only Oscar winner (*Pygmalion*) to have also won the Nobel Prize in Literature."
This is a good one to have up your sleeve as you can serve it up at multiple venues—from an Academy Award viewing party to a pretheater supper to a gathering of a bunch of scientists (the Nobel is their Oscar).

Pivot: "As Truman Capote put it, 'I don't care what anybody says about me as long as it isn't true.' Shall we go hover by the kitchen to see if we can be first to grab the hors d'oeuvres? I wouldn't want anyone to think that I'm all cardio, no carbs."
This works whether you're a gym god(dess) or not. You end a difficult discussion by seemingly putting yourself down, when of course you're not, since you've just cited Capote, plus you can go stand by the kitchen. And as every seasoned partygoer knows, you will always meet the best people by the kitchen; they, like you, have been through this rodeo before.

CHEAT SHEET 28—ARTISTS YOU NEED TO KNOW ABOUT

NAME DATES ALIVE ERA (IF APPLICABLE)	CLAIM(S) TO FAME FOR PHILISTINES	QUIRK(S)	TALKING POINT(S)
Giotto di Bondone c. 1266–1337	Some say he was the first real painter, the father of the Renaissance.	Quite the joker. Apparently, when the pope's messenger turned up at his house requiring proof of his genius, with one stroke he drew a perfect circle in red and sent the messenger packing. Despite (or perhaps because of) such cheekiness, Giotto became pals with the pope and King Robert of Naples.	Groundbreaking in his authenticity, the way he added emotion and physical accuracy in humans (as opposed to religious types) in his work. His frescoes later influenced such luminaries as Raphael and Michelangelo.
Donato di Niccolò di Betto Bardi aka **Donatello** 1386–1466 Renaissance	Don't mention the Teenage Mutant Ninja Turtles, FFS. You'll pretend to know him for his lifelike and emotional sculptures. Cite David.	Donatello's bronze statue Gattamelata was the first bronze equestrian statue to appear in a public place since the Romans.	Donatello's work drew heavily from reality and incorporated the new science of perspective.
Alessandro di Mariano Filipepi **Botticelli** 1445–1510 Renaissance	The actor Peter Ustinov said, "If Botticelli were alive now, he would be working for Vogue." Well, plus-size Vogue. The man was into painting curvy girls.	Had the misfortune of falling out of fashion, being somewhat eclipsed by the arrival of Michelangelo, Raphael, and Leonardo da Vinci. That said Botticelli did take part in the decoration of Rome's Sistine Chapel.	Say something along the lines of: "The old master's reputation has gone up and down over the years, but his use of color is really quite extraordinary." He was a big inspiration to the Pre-Raphaelites (Rossetti and co., Victorian era Brits).

NAME DATES ALIVE ERA (IF APPLICABLE)	CLAIM(S) TO FAME FOR PHILISTINES	QUIRK(S)	TALKING POINT(S)
Leonardo da Vinci 1452–1519 Renaissance	Also not a turtle, FFS. Or the star character in a Dan Brown novel. Painted the *Mona Lisa*. Arche-typal Renaissance man, a genius. Leonardo was an innovator, sculptor, architect, engineer, mathematician, and scientist. Designs of flying machines can be found within his 13,000 pages of notes. Yes, flying machines. And if we start on his studies of anatomy we'll hit 13,000 pages in this Cheat Sheet.	Illegitimate, Leonardo was raised by his dad. According to Florentine court records, at the age of twenty-two, Leonardo was charged with and acquitted of sodomy. His male "assistant" was his heir.	Madcap tales about the *Mona Lisa* include that she had jaundice, was pregnant, and actually a bloke in drag. What is true is that Leonardo never delivered the painting to its commissioner—he held on to it until he died. Neither full faced nor in profile, it was a pioneering portrait. If you get onto the topic of Leonardo's *The Last Supper*, note that it is all about the dramatic composition and the way the apostles are in interlinking groups of three.
Michelangelo Buonarroti 1475–1564 Renaissance	Not a turtle and also not spelled Michaelangelo. Michelangelo defined himself as a sculptor (*David*), but did a bit of painting on the side (the Sistine Chapel, anyone?). Also an architect and poet.	Loner, awkward. Leonardo was influenced more by him than the other way round. Raphael was a rival.	You should pose the rhetorical question: Where would the seventeenth-century Rubens be without Michelangelo? Then utter something about the remarkable construction of Herculean nudes in *The Last Judgment*.

NAME DATES ALIVE ERA (IF APPLICABLE)	CLAIM(S) TO FAME FOR PHILISTINES	QUIRK(S)	TALKING POINT(S)
Raffaello Sanzio da Urbino 1483–1520 Renaissance	**Raphael** was a painter and architect. With Leonardo and Michelangelo he makes up the high Renaissance trinity. Many of the master's works remain, because so many of them were for the Vatican.	While Raphael was in Florence, from 1504 to 1508, he had a bit of a thing for drawing naked fighting men. Never married his fiancée, had a mistress, supposedly died after a long night of sex with her at age thirty-seven . . . And apparently flirted with the idea of becoming a cardinal.	Aged twenty-three, was the first to respond to the *Mona Lisa* and essentially copied it for his *Maddalena Doni*. You should say that he missed the point of Leonardo's high viewpoint and tonal control of color in the work.
Tiziano Vecellio c. 1488–1576 Renaissance	**Titian** was the greatest Venetian artist of the sixteenth century. Into mythological themes, although his subjects were often secular and sexual. *Venus of Urbino* was less your goddess, rather more your courtesan.	First painter to have a mostly international clientele. Game changer in the sense he enabled royals and churchmen to commission sexual shenanigans as well as crucifixions.	Incredibly versatile—mastered portraits, landscapes, and so forth. Known for his remarkable use of color. Had an important influence on later artists such as Rubens and Velázquez.
Domenikos Theotokopoulos 1541–1614 Renaissance	Aka **El Greco ("The Greek")**. A prophet of modern art, he was not properly appreciated for 250 years. El Greco's works of exaggerated and often distorted figures and his contrast of color and light are precursors of Cubism and Expressionism.	El Greco criticized Michelangelo's artistic abilities, as you do, when he was in Rome. Which was not then and still isn't now what you do in Rome. Subsequently made his home in Spain.	Studied under Titian. Been suggested that his *Fifth Seal* influenced Picasso's *Les Demoiselles d'Avignon*, often considered the first cubist painting.

NAME DATES ALIVE ERA (IF APPLICABLE)	CLAIM(S) TO FAME FOR PHILISTINES	QUIRK(S)	TALKING POINT(S)
Michelangelo Merisi da **Caravaggio** 1571–1610 Father of Baroque painting	Not to be confused with Michelangelo. We know him as Caravaggio. The murderer.	Celebrity in his own lifetime. Lived hard, played just as hard. A brawler, Caravaggio went around brandishing his sword (as with guns today, you needed a license to have one), and in 1606 even killed a man. Kept brawling.	Remark how Caravaggio's technique was as spontaneous as his temper and note he utilized ordinary people as models for saints, along with his spectacular use of lights and shadows.
Peter Paul **Rubens** 1577–1640 Baroque	Nudes of curvy girls.	Prolific. Famous in own lifetime, Rubens had wealthy clients throughout Europe—and was also a diplomat. At age fifty-three, he married for a second time—to a sixteen-year-old. They had five children.	If you're feeling perky, you could muster up some enthusiasm and exclaim something along the lines of "His Counter-Reformation artworks were astonishing! Just look at the movement, the sensuality, the color!"
Rembrandt Harmenszoon van Rijn 1606–1669 Baroque	Rembrandt, the Dutch master, was probably the greatest master of the self-portrait in history. Known for his vivid realism.	Probably had over fifty students during his career. Went into a bit of a slump later on—some attributed it to the loss of his wife and a not very enthusiastic reception to *The Night Watch*, but that's been disproved.	Looking at his infamous *The Night Watch*? Well, you can see how it was influenced by Caravaggio's dramatic devices and Titian's use of color as well as having echoes of Raphael.

(cont.)

NAME DATES ALIVE ERA (IF APPLICABLE)	CLAIM(S) TO FAME FOR PHILISTINES	QUIRK(S)	TALKING POINT(S)
Francisco José de **Goya** y Lucientes 1746–1828 Romantic	Goya was the last of the Old Masters (painter who was renowned before 1800) and first of the moderns.	Painter of the court and the people. Famous for his brutally realistic dark prints and paintings in his own lifetime. Became deaf after an illness in 1792.	Observe that along with his commissioned portraits of the nobility, he created works that criticized the social and political problems of his era. His 1799 series of images, *Los Caprichos*, were a commentary on rampant corruption, greed, and repression.
Édouard **Manet** 1832–1883 Origin of Impressionism	Not to be confused with Monet. Instead, Manet was a key figure in the transition from Realism to Impressionism.	Bit of a scandal over his *Olympia*, which featured a naked courtesan and a black servant. Pregnant women were even advised to avoid it. Of course, this made him a leader of the avant-garde who hung out at the Café Guerbois. Avant-garde artists "of course" included Renoir, Degas, and Monet.	Paris's architectural makeover gave artists the opportunity to explore contemporary urban subjects in a way they hadn't before. Manet's bold use of paint may have inspired the future impressionists, but he never exhibited with them.
Hilaire-Germain-Edgar **Degas** 1834–1917	The one who painted ballerinas.	Degas met Manet in 1862 at the Louvre and they rapidly established a friendly rivalry.	Degas thought himself a realist, rejecting the term Impressionism, although he is seen as one of its founders. Joked he was the least spontaneous artist alive.

NAME DATES ALIVE ERA (IF APPLICABLE)	CLAIM(S) TO FAME FOR PHILISTINES	QUIRK(S)	TALKING POINT(S)
Paul **Cézanne** 1839–1906 Postimpressionist	French postimpressionist painter. You've probably seen his depiction of Provençal peasants playing cards, *The Card Players*.	Cézanne was friends from his college days with Émile Zola (later a French writer famous for his theories of naturalism) and Baptistin Baille (became a professor of optics and acoustics). Together they were known as *les trois inséparables* (the three inseparables).	Ahead of the curve, so mixed critical reception in his lifetime. Both Picasso and Matisse have been credited with the quote "Cézanne is the father of us all." His unique use of color and analytical approach precursor for Cubism and Fauvism.
Claude **Monet** 1840–1926 Impressionist	What the nouveau riche buy when they get "in the monet." You also know him for his water lilies.	The critic Louis Leroy mockingly employed the term Impressionism in reviewing Monet's work entitled *Impression, Sunrise*. The amount people pay for an impressionist painting now is serious.	Monet's fellow students in the Paris studio of academic history painter Charles Gleyre included Renoir. In the 1910s and 1920s, Monet pretty much exclusively focused on his water-lily pond at his place at Giverny.
Pierre-Auguste **Renoir** 1841–1919 Impressionist	Early pioneer of Impressionism. You know him for his pictures of pretty women and sensual nudes of curvy girls.	Founding member, with Monet, of the Society of Independent Artists.	The quote people use about him is that "Renoir is the final representative of a tradition which runs directly from Rubens to Watteau." Employ that line and most people will be excusing themselves to go the bar.

(cont.)

NAME DATES ALIVE ERA (IF APPLICABLE)	CLAIM(S) TO FAME FOR PHILISTINES	QUIRK(S)	TALKING POINT(S)
Vincent Willem **van Gogh** 1853–1890 Postimpressionist	You thought this Dutch painter was earlier too, didn't you? The *Sunflowers* and ear one.	Supposedly sold only one work in his lifetime. Tried out various jobs before deciding on artist—at the age of twenty-seven. The largely self-taught artist had a career that lasted only ten years, although he was incredibly prolific.	Every time you look at his work, remember this: Van Gogh had a breakdown in 1888, where he cut off part of his left ear with a razor. He voluntarily entered an asylum in May 1889, where he painted around 150 canvases, which are influenced by the hospital's surroundings. He shot himself in 1890.
Henri **Matisse** 1869–1954	Matisse is right up there with Picasso in the twentieth-century stakes. A French painter, printmaker, draftsman, and sculptor.	Trained as a lawyer before switching to art at age twenty-one.	Matisse eventually settled in Nice in the South of France, but he did visit the US in 1930, where he was commissioned by Dr. Albert Barnes of Merion to paint a massive mural for his mansion's picture gallery. You can go and visit it at the Barnes Foundation in Merion, Pennsylvania, if the mood takes you.

NAME DATES ALIVE ERA (IF APPLICABLE)	CLAIM(S) TO FAME FOR PHILISTINES	QUIRK(S)	TALKING POINT(S)
Pablo **Picasso** 1881–1973	You just might have heard of this Spanish painter, sculptor, printmaker, ceramicist, stage designer, and womanizer. Created (with Georges Braque) Cubism, where objects are broken apart and reassembled in abstract form. Picasso's 1907 *Les Demoiselles d'Avignon*, his depiction of five naked prostitutes, is viewed as a precursor to Cubism.	Legend has it that Picasso's first words were "piz, piz." The Spanish for pencil is *lápiz*.	Try throwing either of these comments into an art crowd: "Of course, the Picasso that really matters is the young Picasso of the Blue [1901 to 1904—blue dominated his work] and Rose [1904–6—used warmer colors] periods." "Arguably Picasso's masterpieces really stopped in 1937 with the grotesque surrealist masterpiece *Guernica*, after he experienced the monstrosities of the Spanish civil war."
Salvador **Dalí** 1904–1989 Surrealist	Spanish Catalan surrealist painter infamous for his flamboyant and somewhat atypical behavior. You've heard his quotes along the lines of: "Don't bother about being modern. Unfortunately it is the one thing that, whatever you do, you cannot avoid." You've also seen his work. Think of Hitchcock's *Spellbound*, starring Gregory Peck and Ingrid Bergman—his paintings are in the dream sequence.	Dalí's older brother Salvador died of gastroenteritis. According to Dalí, when he was five, his parents took him to Salvador's grave and told him he was his reincarnation. When his mother died of breast cancer, his father married her sister. Perhaps not surprising then that Dalí was an avid reader of Sigmund Freud.	When André Breton expelled Dalí from the surrealists, he shouted, "I am Surrealism!" History has proven Dalí had a point—his images are the most famous of the surrealist movement.

(cont.)

NAME DATES ALIVE ERA (IF APPLICABLE)	CLAIM(S) TO FAME FOR PHILISTINES	QUIRK(S)	TALKING POINT(S)
Frida Kahlo 1907–1954	Had to get a woman on here. She's the one with the eyebrows that Salma Hayek played in the 2002 Oscar-nominated film *Frida*. Mexican painter, feminist icon, and political activist known especially for her self-portraits after her terrible 1925 bus accident which broke her spinal column, pelvis, and right leg.	In 1929 married fellow communist artist Diego Rivera, who she'd spotted as a schoolgirl. The exiled Trotsky came to stay with the couple in 1937—apparently Stalin's nemesis and Kahlo had a fling-ette.	Kahlo's creations were not exactly the personification of fluffy. Observe that her work was "just so incredibly personal—when say you think of her painting, *Henry Ford Hospital* (1932), where she appears naked with items including a fetus after her second marriage."
Jackson Pollock 1912–1956	The drip one. The blob paintings. Sorry, your author subscribes to the view that they're a load of Pollocks. Others view him as a major figure of American Abstract Expressionism.	An alcoholic, he died at age forty-four in 1956 after drunk driving his car into a tree.	I suppose you could pronounce how fame seriously came his way in 1949 when Pollock was featured in *Life* magazine, which posed the question, "Is he the greatest living painter in the United States?" Not in my view, but what do I know? Peggy Guggenheim, who let's face it really understood art, was one of his patrons.

NAME DATES ALIVE ERA (IF APPLICABLE)	CLAIM(S) TO FAME FOR PHILISTINES	QUIRK(S)	TALKING POINT(S)
Lucian Freud 1922–2011	The Kate Moss naked pregnant and fraternal feuding one, who did THAT to the queen (an uncompromising portrait). Grandson of Sigmund Freud, the pioneer of psychoanalysis.	Serial seducer of women. Dated Greta Garbo.	Preferred to have a close relationship with his sitters, opting for friends and family, rather than random models. Exponent, along with Francis Bacon (1909–1992), of the so-called School of London. Gave the queen his portrait of her, partly in repayment for his freedom—his Jewish family had escaped to Britain from Germany in 1932 after being vouched for by the Duke of Kent.
Andy Warhol 1928–1987	Pop Art. Campbell's soup. The *Marilyn Diptych.* Certainly has had more than his infamous expression "fifteen minutes of fame."	The child of Russian immigrants; his surname was originally Warhola. A feminist tried to assassinate him in 1968.	Recall how he designed album covers for artists including Mick Jagger, Liza Minnelli, John Lennon, and the Velvet Underground, becoming the group's manager in 1965. As much as anyone could manage a band formed by Lou Reed and John Cale.

SOCIAL SURVIVAL STRATEGY

Argument: "Maybe it will take time to fully grasp the work of X. After all, it took two hundred and fifty years for El Greco to be properly appreciated as a prophet of modern art."
You may be looking at something you perceive as frightful and your neighbor delightful, or vice versa, but this concept works for both. It sparks a debate and yet takes the sting out of it.

Crisp Fact: "Leonardo never delivered the *Mona Lisa* to its commissioner—he held on to it until he died."
Drop this one in if you're with someone buying art (and by art, it could be a postcard in a gift shop). It's food for thought.

Pivot: "Legend has it that Picasso's first words were 'piz, piz,' from the Spanish for pencil. I'm sure mine was drink. Shall we go find (another) one?"
There are geniuses and then there's the rest of us, including the person you're talking to, who will have an opinion on the current status of their wineglass. They will either accompany you to find a refill or release you so you can both find someone more agreeable to talk to.

CHEAT SHEET 29—COMPOSERS YOU NEED TO KNOW ABOUT

NAME DATES ALIVE ERA	CLAIM(S) TO FAME FOR PHILISTINES	QUIRK(S)	TALKING POINT(S)
Guillaume de Machaut c. 1300–1377 Medieval	One of the earliest composers we have proper records about. Hung out with royalty and such.	Poet and a composer. Harder than it looks to do both—how many lyricists has my dad been through? Machaut's poetry was so admired by other poets they even imitated it. Geoffrey Chaucer was a fan.	Machaut was considered to be an avant-garde composer, and his style dominated the medieval era's Ars Nova period. Machaut's most famous work is the *Messe de Notre Dame*. It's a textbook example of medieval counterpoint (music with two or more melodic lines played at the same time and written in four-voice form).
William Byrd c. 1540 to 1623 Renaissance	Composer who hit the big time in Elizabeth I's reign. Known as the English Palestrina and the Father of Music.	Viewed as a master of European Renaissance music and one of England's greatest composers ever. Many believe him to be the first genius of the keyboard.	In 1575 Elizabeth I granted Byrd and his mentor Thomas Tallis a patent, the exclusive right for the importing, printing, publishing, and sale of music and the printing of music paper.
Claudio **Monteverdi** 1567–1643 Links Renaissance to the Baroque	Wrote one of the first dramatic operas, *La favola d'Orfeo*. You may still come across that and his *Coronation of Poppea* being performed today.	In 1632, he became a priest.	Appointed music director of St. Mark's in Venice in 1613.

NAME DATES ALIVE ERA	CLAIM(S) TO FAME FOR PHILISTINES	QUIRK(S)	TALKING POINT(S)
Henry **Purcell** c. 1659–1695 Baroque	Influenced the Who. Seriously. The introduction to "Pinball Wizard." Oh, and the theme of A Clockwork Orange. Wrote the chamber opera Dido and Aeneas for a girl's school situated in Chelsea. The Brit twentieth-century composer Benjamin Britten created a realization of Dido and Aeneas. It's still performed by upmarket London girls' schools.	Purcell's 1692 The Fairy-Queen score was an adaptation of Shakespeare's Midsummer Night's Dream.	One of the great Baroque—and English—composers. Labeled the English Orpheus. Became an organist in the Chapel Royal in 1682. He's buried under the organ in Westminster Abbey. Wrote "My Heart Is Inditing of a Good Matter" for James II's coronation (the Glorious Revolution one) and provided music for Queen Mary's funeral in 1695.
Antonio **Vivaldi** 1678–1741 Baroque	Composed the violin concertos The Four Seasons. Elevator and on-hold Muzak wouldn't be the same without it.	Had red hair and in his early career as a priest was nicknamed "The Red Priest."	More to the man than advertising music. Wrote upwards of 500 concertos. Believed to have come up with the ritornello form (translation: a little return—a snippet of music that comes back later). Was popular in his lifetime, then fell out of fashion until becoming seriously en vogue in the last century. Some would say ubiquitous.

(cont.)

NAME DATES ALIVE ERA	CLAIM(S) TO FAME FOR PHILISTINES	QUIRK(S)	TALKING POINT(S)
Johann Sebastian **Bach** 1685–1750 Baroque	Bach's music is perpetually used in movies, TV, and TV commercials. Especially his cello suites. Gatorade antiphysics commercial in 2007, anyone?	Bach had two wives and twenty children: not quite living up to how he started out, as a child with an angelic singing voice. Some of his offspring were seriously gifted musically and included composers Carl Philipp Emanuel Bach and Johann Christian Bach (who influenced Mozart's concerto style). Bach has more music on the Voyager golden record (sample of earthly things) that was sent out into space with the Voyager probes than any other composer. And he's got loads of streets named after him in Germany.	Successful organist during his lifetime—his compositions got full-on recognized after he died from around the nineteenth century on. Beethoven pronounced Bach to be the "original father of harmony."
Franz Joseph **Haydn** (known as Joseph Haydn) 1732–1809 Classical	His compositions are as prolific as his lengthy IMDB credits: *Boardwalk Empire*, *The Vampire Diaries*, *The Duchess*, *Save the Last Dance 2*, *Mission Impossible III* . . .	Haydn and Mozart were proper pals, and Haydn also taught Beethoven at one point.	Bequeathed many of his compositions amusing nicknames. Symphony No. 82, "The Bear," Symphony No. 83, "The Hen," and Symphony No. 103, "The Drum Roll."

NAME DATES ALIVE ERA	CLAIM(S) TO FAME FOR PHILISTINES	QUIRK(S)	TALKING POINT(S)
Wolfgang Amadeus **Mozart** 1756–1791 Classical	Amadeus. The movie. Won eight Oscars in 1985, for goodness sake. A child prodigy. His works included the Symphony No. 31 in D major, better known as the Paris Symphony, *The Marriage of Figaro*, *The Magic Flute*. Etc., etc., etc.	Mozart's dad, Leopold, was also a composer. His pitch-perfect son wrote his first opera at fourteen, had a crude sense of humor, and kept pets, including a canary.	Mozart was friends with Haydn and had a huge influence on Beethoven, who was fifteen years his junior. Mozart did what composers then and composers now can't do: wrote and shined in every one of the musical genres of the time.
Ludwig van **Beethoven** Classical into c. 1770–1827 Romantic	The deaf one. C. 1796, when Beethoven was about twenty-six, he began to lose his hearing. He wrote his third to eighth symphonies while he was almost completely deaf. Yes, he wrote that fifth symphony of his, which you've definitely heard, almost deaf. You've also heard the Ninth. He was deaf. Ladies and gentlemen, we have found our definition of genius.	Legend has it that when Napoleon attacked Vienna in May 1809, Beethoven hid in his brother's basement, covering his ears with pillows, terrified the noise would destroy the remnants of his hearing. Rumor also has it that his dad used to box his ears when he was little. Some sources say his last words were: "I shall hear in Heaven."	It's believed Beethoven was briefly taught by both Mozart and Haydn. A legend in his own lifetime; an estimated 20,000 Viennese citizens turned up to his funeral and one Franz Schubert was one of the torchbearers. The following year Schubert himself died and was buried next to him.
Franz **Schubert** 1797–1828 Romantic	Died at thirty-one, but had managed to write hundreds of compositions including "Ave Maria." Yes. That's Schubert.	His vocal talent as a boy caught the attention of Antonio Salieri, leading musical authority in Vienna, and the very same Salieri whom Mozart had a falling-out with. Just watch Amadeus, will you?	Died and then got famous—Brahms, Mendelssohn, and Schumann were also in that boat. As discussed, a torchbearer at Beethoven's funeral.

(cont.)

NAME DATES ALIVE ERA	CLAIM(S) TO FAME FOR PHILISTINES	QUIRK(S)	TALKING POINT(S)
Niccolò **Paganini** 1782–1840 Romantic	Such a virtuoso violinist (and somewhat strange looking) that it was rumored he'd made a pact with the devil. To the point where the church refused to let him be buried on sacred ground.	Paganini was partial to gambling and tried to open a Parisian casino, which left him in complete financial ruin.	Paganini's compositions (obviously) were all about the violin, most famously with the 24 Caprices for Solo Violin. Inspired composers including Rachmaninoff, Brahms, Schumann, and Chopin. Instruments he played on include some made by the famed Stradivari. A Stradivarius is a stringed instrument made by a member of the Stradivari in the seventeenth and eighteenth centuries. Many believe their sound has never been equaled.
Frédéric **Chopin** 1810–1849 Romantic	Jameson Irish Whiskey "disaster" averted TV commercial. Also the piano composer—chances are if you're listening to a classical radio station and it's a piano piece, it's Chopin.	Big love affair with George Sand. Who was actually female—a novelist, older, whose real name was Amantine-Lucile-Aurore Dupin.	Child piano prodigy genius type. Heard Paganini play in Warsaw in 1829. All Chopin's known compositions involve the piano. His will had his heart placed in an urn and brought back to Warsaw, being positioned in a pillar of the Holy Cross Church.

NAME DATES ALIVE ERA	CLAIM(S) TO FAME FOR PHILISTINES	QUIRK(S)	TALKING POINT(S)
Wilhelm Richard **Wagner** 1813–1883 Romantic	Hitler was a huge fan. Wagner pronounced himself: "I am the most German being, I am the German spirit." Author of anti-Semitic writings—his operas are littered with anti-Semitic stereotypes, although he did have Jewish friends and supporters. Performance of his music has been controversial in Israel.	Ahead of his time on psychoanalysis. Wagner's concepts, including about the Oedipus myth and dreams, were before Freud.	Most famous, apart from the Hitler connection, for his operas, for which unusually he wrote the libretto (the lyrics) as well as the music. You can go and see his four-opera cycle, *Der Ring des Nibelungen* (which he intended to be performed together), at the Bayreuth Festival, if your backside and brain are sturdy enough.
Giuseppe Fortunino Francesco **Verdi** 1813–1901 Romantic	Luciano Pavarotti's rendition of "La donna è mobile" from *Rigoletto*. Also the Drinking Song, "Libiamo ne' lieti calici," from *La Traviata* and the Grand March from *Aida*.	Verdi and Wagner are thought to be the two top nineteenth-century opera composers. Controversially, Verdi with his *Otello* was accused of copying Wagner's work.	Verdi was not too keen on putting in a high C in his tenor arias, as it was just too distracting for the performer. Although you may hear the high C in *Il Trovatore*'s "Di quella pira" aria, Verdi didn't put it in his score.
Pyotr Ilyich **Tchaikovsky** 1840–1893 Romantic	The ballets: *Swan Lake*, *The Nutcracker* (Sugar Plum Fairy, people), and *Sleeping Beauty*. Then the small matter of the 1812 Overture. Oh, and operas and concertos and a quite endless list . . .	His same-sex tendencies were originally suppressed by Soviet censors but are all out now.	The greatest Russian composer of his time, and the first Russian composer to really make a surviving international impression. The public has always loved him. The critics? Not so much. Probably due to his extraordinarily accessible melodies.

(cont.)

NAME DATES ALIVE ERA	CLAIM(S) TO FAME FOR PHILISTINES	QUIRK(S)	TALKING POINT(S)
Edward Elgar 1857–1934 Romantic	The *Enigma Variations*, including "Nimrod." The first of his five *Pomp and Circumstance Marches* is what those nutty Brits bop up and down to at the Last Night of the Proms in the Albert Hall.	Elgar's dad was a piano tuner. There are around sixty-five roads in the UK named after Elgar.	A success in his own time, knighted by Edward VII, Elgar was the first composer to really get to grips with the gramophone. His "Land of Hope and Glory" tune (in the first of the *Pomp and Circumstance Marches*) should be Britain's national anthem instead of the claptrap that is the dreadful melody "God Save the Queen" (composer—unknown).
Giacomo **Puccini** 1858–1924 Romantic	The *Room with a View* music— "O mio babbino caro." He's the *La Bohème, Tosca, Madama Butterfly* one. Emotional, melodic, and thus always being performed—then and now. So guess what? Consistent, critical condensation.	Puccini's wife claimed Puccini had been having an affair with a female servant who had taken her own life. Later proven false. He was buried with his wife and son at a chapel at his house, which you can go and visit, the Villa Museo Puccini.	Very influenced by Verdi, especially *Aida. Madama Butterfly* had an initially disastrous reception. Puccini's fifth version of it is the one that you probably know of. Nothing wrong with rewrites, people.
Claude **Debussy** 1862–1918 Twentieth century	A favorite of R-Patz in *Twilight*. He even plays "Clair de Lune" for K-Stew.	Created an alter ego called Monsieur Croche late in life whom he used to have imaginary chats with.	Detested his compositions being linked with the term impressionist music, although they were. Influenced composers from Igor Stravinsky and Maurice Ravel to George Gershwin and John Williams (*Jaws, Star Wars, ET,* and *Harry Potter*), along with jazz figures such as Miles Davis and Duke Ellington.

NAME DATES ALIVE ERA	CLAIM(S) TO FAME FOR PHILISTINES	QUIRK(S)	TALKING POINT(S)
Sergei Vasilievich **Rachmaninoff** 1873 to 1943 Romantic	Eighteenth variation of the "Rhapsody on a Theme of Paganini." Used a lot, including: *Somewhere in Time*, the Christopher Reeve/Jane Seymour movie, *Ronin*, *Sabrina* (1995 Harrison Ford version), *Groundhog Day* . . . Also known for his piano concertos. His second was featured in *Brief Encounter* and *The Seven Year Itch*, while his third was the basis of Geoffrey Rush's 1996 movie *Shine*. In *The Devil Wears Prada*, Meryl Streep's daughters play Rachmaninoff at the recital she can't make because of bad weather.	The last great Russian Romantic composer died in Beverly Hills. Had huge hands so could play large intervals on the keyboard. Lots of piano in his compositions.	Rachmaninoff had a nervous breakdown after the catastrophic performance of his First Symphony in D minor. It took him three years before he was able to compose again. "All by Myself," the Céline Dion warbled song, has Rachmaninoff elements. Also inspired the band Muse.
Sergei **Prokofiev** 1891–1953 Twentieth century	*Peter and the Wolf*!!! If you were a child, you should have been played it; if not, you were deprived. Also known for the *Romeo and Juliet* ballet.	Died the day Stalin's death was announced. As a result one of the major composers of the twentieth century, a master of multiple musical genres, had a small paragraph devoted to his obituary on page 116 of the USSR's main musical periodical. The previous 115 were all about Stalin's death.	Evacuated from Moscow during World War II, which was when he produced his opera *War and Peace* and the ballet *Cinderella*. Many of Prokofiev's works were banned by the Soviet authorities in 1948.

(cont.)

NAME DATES ALIVE ERA	CLAIM(S) TO FAME FOR PHILISTINES	QUIRK(S)	TALKING POINT(S)
George Gershwin 1898–1937 Twentieth century	*Rhapsody in Blue.* The United Airlines TV ad campaign song. Wrote *An American in Paris* and *Porgy and Bess*, and his songs, including "I Got Rhythm," have been recorded by everyone from Frank Sinatra to Diana Ross to Barbra Streisand to Madonna.	Was actually called Jacob Gershwin. At age fifteen, he dropped out of school and went to be a record plugger for a few years. The majority of Gershwin's song lyrics were written by his brother Ira.	Guess what? See a running theme here? *Porgy and Bess* opened to mixed reviews. Never believe what the critics say.
Benjamin Britten 1913–1976 Twentieth century	Somewhere, on a high school or amateur stage near you, some very keen people are wailing their way through Britten's *The Beggar's Opera.*	Born in Suffolk, England, the son of a dentist. In 1945, Britten and Yehudi Menuhin visited Germany to give recitals to concentration camp survivors. He saw Belsen and unsurprisingly his immediate subsequent works had a darker tone. There has been speculation that Britten was attracted to boys, but held his impulses under control. The future *Phantom* Michael Crawford, who sang treble roles for the composer in the 1950s, had nothing but praise for the man he had a strictly professional relationship with. Britten and his partner Peter Pears are buried side by side in Suffolk.	Collaborated with the poet W. H. Auden (the *Four Weddings and a Funeral* "Stop all the clocks" one), who wrote the libretto to Britten's early operetta *Paul Bunyan.* They then fell out, with speculation it was a result of a lovers' tiff. Britten, though, once said of Auden, that he was "in all my operas." Those in the know (Dad) say his great genius was with his orchestrations.

NAME DATES ALIVE ERA	CLAIM(S) TO FAME FOR PHILISTINES	QUIRK(S)	TALKING POINT(S)
Leonard Bernstein 1918–1990 Twentieth century	*West Side Story. Candide.* Score for *On the Waterfront.*	Graduated from Harvard in 1939. Married Costa Rican actress Felicia Cohn Montealegre. Their support of the Black Panthers helped Tom Wolfe coin the derogatory term "radical chic." In 1976 Bernstein left her for Tom Cothran. When she was diagnosed with lung cancer, he moved back in with her until she died.	Famous conductor, skilled pianist— often conducted piano concertos from the piano. Fused musical styles together—think of how he bridged the gap between classical and popular music in *West Side Story*. Worth noting that Stephen Sondheim, the greatest American theater composer of the late twentieth century, wrote the lyrics to *West Side Story*.
John Coolidge Adams b. 1947	*The Death of Klinghoffer,* his controversial 1991 opera that some claim is anti-Semitic. Rudy Giuliani and more were vociferous in their disapproval when the Met exercised their First Amendment right to mount a production of an American composer's work in 2014.	First Harvard student to be permitted to submit a senior honors thesis in the form of a musical composition. Origins in minimalism—think not too much embellishment, lots of repetition and structure.	He worked with director Peter Sellars on *Klinghoffer,* along with his 1987 opera *Nixon in China* (which won a Grammy) and 2006's *A Flowering Tree.* The latter was inspired by Mozart's *The Magic Flute.* After 9/11 he was commissioned by Lincoln Center and the New York Philharmonic to pen *On the Transmigration of Souls* in tribute to those who lost their lives, for which he won the Pulitzer and three Grammys.

SOCIAL SURVIVAL STRATEGY

Argument: "Don't be snobbish. Just because a piece of music is popular, it doesn't mean that it lacks artistic merit. Puccini, Tchaikovsky, even Gershwin all suffered at the hands of the critics, but the people loved their work."
You are within your rights to call out a music snob, and if you're being one, expect to be challenged. Don't be an elitist old fogy.

Crisp Fact: "It's believed Beethoven was briefly taught by both Mozart and Haydn. Greatness breeds greatness, they egg each other on."
Say this and you can then open up the exchange to other disciplines, such as sport—John McEnroe and Björn Borg in tennis being a classic example.

Pivot: "I'm hungry, it feels like I last ate a Wagner opera ago. What shall we do for food?"
The joke being, of course, that Wagner operas go on for days.

CHEAT SHEET 30—THEATER

BACKGROUND BRIEFING

I do on some levels respect Americans for their alternative use of spelling. I understand that you want to break free from the mother country, own your own language, and all that. But there is no justification for your implementation of the word *theater*. It's the bane of my life as the senior editor at Broadway.com. Because your use of the word *theater* isn't consistent. You name the bricks and mortar of so many of your theaters *theatre*. So you go to the theater at the XXX Theatre. Honestly. Even arty insiders don't get it right.

This is the American publication of my book, so however much it pains me to do it, I employ the word *theater*. Except when I can't, as it's about a building called *theatre*. Sigh.

The word *theater* comes from the Greek *theatron,* a place for viewing, along with *theasthai,* to look at, and is related to the Greek *thauma,* meaning wonder, miracle. It miraculously encompasses everything from plays to ballets to musicals to opera (the latter two forms having their own mini-drama about their differences and definition). Incidentally, the word *drama* also comes from a Greek word meaning action.

All that being said, theater actually predates the Greeks. For with civilization comes culture, which is the argument you deploy when a politician objects to artistic funding. Passion plays were performed in Egypt for the legendary king-divinity Osiris.

The Greeks, of course, is where theater really got going. They were all about the theatrical competition and loved pitting the talents of the time against one another. Drama was made up of tragedy, comedy, and the satyr play, with an emphasis more often than not on Greek mythology. The plays evolved so that however many characters there were, only three actors were allowed to perform, so there was also a chorus, which was often underscored by music. The actors wore masks (which they changed, along with their costumes, when they switched roles) so the audience could see them; comic masks were grinning, the tragic versions were, well, unhappy. The masks were actually a form of ancient microphone—they amplified the actor's voice.

Thespis (ah yes, you cry, you understand—*thespian* also comes from the Greek) has ended up with the reputation of being the first Greek "actor" and the originator of tragedy. Greek playwrights' names you should casually drop into conversation if discussing the origins of theater include the father of all modern drama, Euripides, along with Sophocles and Aeschylus.

The Romans, ever an empire about improving itself, latched onto Greek theater and got into the business of doing wholesale adaptations—think what Hollywood does to French cinema. That's not the only link between Roman theater and Tinseltown. Stock characters in Roman comedy included the parasite (*parasitus*), a selfish liar, along with the love interest, a young maiden (*virgo*), who has little personality and doesn't get much stage time. Nothing changes.

When the Roman empire fell around AD 600, everything did, well, fall apart a bit. The period between Rome and the Renaissance is labeled the Dark Ages for a reason (although some historians claim that *dark* is not an appropriate term for all of those centuries—but really, you don't want to be stuck with someone who's going to debate you on this point—they will be dull). The Catholic Church was the power of the day, so traveling troupes of performers who were viewed as potentially sinful suffered, but the staging of liturgical drama found a platform. This was the era of cycle plays, morality plays, that sort of thing.

We shouldn't write medieval theater and the church's penchant for script approval completely off. The period did contain some breakthroughs: Shows started to be done in the vernacular, not just in Greek and Latin. As the era went on, theater moved away from the religious. Farce—making fun of authority and getting away with it—began to be seen. Also the spectacle side of performances developed—sets, costume, music, and dance. All rather crucial to getting us to Broadway today.

When the Renaissance hit in the fifteenth century, so did a renewed interest in the Greeks and Romans—and professional actors took to the stage. And so we reach the sixteenth century. Now, Britain's Henry VIII loved a masque and established the Office of Revels in 1545, but let's face it, it was in his daughter's era, the first Elizabethan age, that everything got going. In 1567, almost ten years into Elizabeth I's reign, the Red Lion, the first English theater, opened. (Shakespeare would have been twelve.) As it had done in ancient Greece, theater developed rapidly. Since religion was not exactly the ideal talking point after Henry VIII split with Rome and all of that, a vacuum was created for . . . oh, I don't know, someone to write some tragedies, comedies, and histories. To completely revolutionize theater.

Hello, Shakespeare. And professional theater troupes. And healthy rivalry between theaters. Just watch *Shakespeare in Love*, it's one of those movies (or indeed, as of 2014, plays) that can be trusted for historically accurate brilliant asides—Tom Stoppard, playwright and intellect extraordinaire, cowrote the screenplay.

During Shakespeare's period, the plays were the property not of the author, but of the acting companies. Aside from the costly costumes, they formed the most valuable part of the company's capital. So Shakespeare was in pauper-ville? Well, not always. He did make some cash because he was also an actor and, more crucially, a shareholder in the company for which he acted and in the theaters they used. By 1595 he was actor and shareholder in the Lord Chamberlain's Company (later the King's Men). After 1599, he was a shareholder at the newly opened Globe Theatre, which now has a fully functioning replica that you can visit in London today.

An important footnote that's appearing in the main body of the text, as maybe it's not a footnote. Despite the fact there was a woman successfully ruling England, there were no female professional dramatists or actresses.

NOTEWORTHY NUGGETS: SHAKESPEARE (1564–1616)

- Shakespeare produced fewer than forty solo plays in a career that spanned more than two decades.

  Play names you should throw about include the histories, such as *Henry IV, V, VI, VIII, Richard II, Richard III*; the tragedies—*Romeo and Juliet, Othello, Hamlet, King Lear, Macbeth*; and the comedies—*Twelfth Night, As You Like It, Comedy of Errors*.

- His reputation during his lifetime was probably lower than that of, say, Ben Jonson (1572–1637). There was also Christopher Marlowe, who died a premature death at age twenty-one, supposedly in a pub brawl. Marlowe's big work was *Doctor Faustus*, who sells his soul to the devil.

- The first publication of Shakespeare's plays came in 1623, called the *First Folio*.

- Shakespeare was all about great stories, illumination of the human experience, compelling characters, and oh, his ability to turn a phrase. He came up with the following lines: We band of brothers. The green-eyed monster. What's in a name? Now is the winter of our discontent. If music be the food of love. Beware the ides of March. We are such stuff as dreams are made on. It's Greek to me. More sinned against than sinning. Salad days. Act more in sorrow than in anger. Refuse to budge an inch. Tongue-tied. Played fast and loose. Laughed yourself into stitches. Had short shrift. The long and the short of it. Teeth set on edge. If the truth were known.

- Supposedly, of the 17,000 words Shakespeare used, he invented about 1,700 of them. My name, Imogen, is one of them.

- Shakespeare was born and died on April 23 (1564 and 1616, respectively).

Shakespeare died in 1616, well into King James I's reign. Mirroring what went on in other arenas (see Cheat Sheet 15), the theater of the period under James I and his son Charles I (the one who managed to get his head chopped off, so England was a republic for a bit) was far from the Elizabethan glory days. Theatrical works from this time are referred to as Jacobean and Caroline drama, and their decadence is exemplified in, for instance, John Ford's *'Tis Pity She's a Whore*.

The Puritans (the ones who didn't like Charles I) were not theater's biggest fans. Nutty religious types have always had a problem with art. And fun. Theaters were closed in 1642. And Christmas was canceled in 1644.

English theater was restored along with the restoration of Charles II to the throne in 1660. Much of the drama had French influences, since Charlie had been stuck with the "frogs" for so long in exile. The French Molière had made a name for himself with his satiric comedies—his plays, such as *The Misanthrope*, are still performed today. The Restoration play *The Plain Dealer* by William Wycherley was an English version of *The Misanthrope*. And naturally there was that extraordinary back catalogue of Elizabethan drama to tap into.

It was also at this time that the red-blooded male Charles II allowed women to play women's parts on stage. Before then, adolescent boys (to much acclaim) had. A French company had tried to put women onstage in England in 1629, but they were pippin-pelted and hissed off. A few women playwrights rose to prominence—Mrs. Aphra Behn (1640–1689) saw some success.

What you need to know from there is that theater, after flirtations with melodrama (eighteenth and nineteenth centuries—the characters end up in danger) and Romanticism (peak time 1800–1850—a counterreaction to the Industrial Revolution and the rise of science, emphasizing the imagination, the irrational, and the individual), plays (as opposed to opera) and stagecraft began to move toward realism, which continued into the twentieth century.

WISE WORDS

The stage is not merely the meeting place of all the arts, but is also the return of art to life.

—Oscar Wilde

WHY IT MATTERS TODAY

Theater has been an important part of human culture for more than 2,500 years, so it's not going anywhere. You need to have a basic grasp of the concept of this multibillion-dollar industry that millions of people attend every year. Odds are that you are one of them and will find yourself holding a conversation about the genre.

We will begin with the pinnacle. And it is Broadway, which is comprised of around forty professional theaters, which seat more than five hundred, in New York's Theater District AND Lincoln Center. It gets around 13 million bums on seats per year.

After America's Civil War ended, theaters began to make their presence felt in New York, especially downtown. Lower Manhattan was the location for P. T. Barnum's entertainment empire by the 1840s. Big Apple theater began its migration from downtown to midtown around 1850, looking for cheaper real estate prices. In midtown. Quite. Some things do change.

It wasn't until the 1920s roared that theaters began to really consolidate on Broadway as we know it today, when the Shubert brothers started pulling their strings. They were helped by the fact that this was the era of the Gershwin brothers, Irving Berlin, and Rodgers and Hart—you can own the venue but you need the product to put derrieres on seats.

KEY TERM: THE GREAT WHITE WAY

Situated in one of the first New York districts to be electrified, Broadway shows installed electric signs outside the theaters. Since colored bulbs rapidly burned out, white lights were used for the marquees. It is thought the nickname originated in a 1902 edition of the *New York Evening Telegram* newspaper.

Broadway has had its ups and downs over the years. Talkies and the Great Depression did nothing for its box office receipts in the 1930s, although it did wonders for artists' creativity. The example to throw about is the playwright Eugene O'Neill—some of his finest work, such as *The Iceman Cometh,* comes from this period.

KEY TERM: STANISLAVSKI

- Constantin Stanislavski (1863–1938) was a Russian theater director and actor who basically came up with what we know as method acting. Performances should be all about keeping it real.

- Stella Adler studied with Stanislavski, the only American actor to do so. Marlon Brando ended up in her class. She also taught Warren Beatty and Robert De Niro.

- Lee Strasberg (who famously fell out with Adler over technique) tailored the Stanislavski concept for American actors. His students included Marilyn Monroe, Al Pacino, and Jack Nicholson.

There were still struggles for the industry by the 1940s, but the birth of the mega musical came into play. The Golden Age of the Broadway musical is usually considered to have begun with Rodgers and Hammerstein's huge hit *Oklahoma!* in 1943 and to have ended with the cast stripping off in *Hair* in 1968 (although some argue it stopped with Lerner and Loewe's *Camelot* in 1960). Rodgers and Hammerstein followed up *Oklahoma!* with *Carousel* (1945), *South Pacific* (1949), *The King and I* (1951), and *The Sound of Music* (1959). Lerner and Loewe's *My Fair Lady*, adapted from *Pygmalion*, made its appearance on the Great White Way in 1956. Laurents, Sondheim, and Bernstein's *West Side Story* made its debut in 1957, while *Chicago* penners Kander and Ebb had everyone coming to the *Cabaret* from 1966.

All that being said, by 1969 only thirty-six playhouses remained, compared to the around seventy-five in the 1920s. Despite the bright lights of *A Chorus Line* in 1975 and *Annie* in 1977, Broadway was not the most salubrious of areas. Then in part courtesy of the British Invasion and later mayor Rudy Giuliani and Disney, the area became Disneyland. The upstarts' names from across the pond? Well, to name a few: Cameron Mackintosh, Tim Rice . . . and Andrew Lloyd Webber (Dad!). Homework at this point: Although it personally pains me to say it, Michael Riedel's *Razzle Dazzle: The Battle for Broadway* will be the best work you will ever read on this transformation.

If one thinks about it, it's not that surprising that these Brits appeared and conquered. My tiny island nation does have the pedigree. The British equivalent of Broadway, the West End, is hardly to be sniffed at. The first West End venue opened in Drury Lane in 1663. The theater burnt down in 1672, but the theater district went on to become the world's largest, and it still garners about the same number of bums on seats a year as Broadway. In a country with a population of . . . Not that we're counting or anything.

In London and New York, beyond the "commercial" theater of the West End and Broadway, you have subsidized (UK) or not-for-profit (US) theater. Now, here's what you need to know about this: The subsidized sector can obviously take more risks—they are not beholden to angels, investors, in quite the same way. So in the not-for-profit sector, you will see more avant-garde productions with actors you've never heard of. In London it's places like the National Theatre, and in New York, the Roundabout Theatre, the Public Theater, and the Manhattan Theatre Club (and I've spelled all those correctly, *knocking head on desk*). You should never be too disdainful of obscure or, on the other end of the spectrum, jukebox musical productions. The existence of each helps the other flourish.

Of course, Broadway and the West End do not contain every significant theatrical venue. The Royal Opera House in London and the Metropolitan Opera House in New York being two that come to mind. And so we reach the argument that is of great importance to only a few, but that we should have on our radars. 'Twas ever thus.

The term *musical* took hold in the early twentieth century. The precise differences between operas and musicals do keep getting blurred. There's the case of *West Side Story,* which has been performed in both genres. Basically, in musical theater, words are the driving force; in opera, music is. Thus musicals tend to be performed in the language of their audience.

It is perfectly forgivable if you are on shaky ground in regards to your operatic knowledge. America's Metropolitan Opera puts the average age of its audience as over sixty. But if someone has paid for your very expensive ticket, read Cheat Sheet 29 so you're up on your significant composers and note the types of singing voices in existence on the next page.

NOTEWORTHY NUGGETS: OPERATIC SINGING VOICES—HIGH TO LOW

Soprano: Since the late eighteenth century tends to be the female lead. Classical period brought in the high notes/range (before then it was about vocal virtuosity).

Mezzo-soprano.

Contralto: Lowest girl.

Countertenor: Highest boy.

Tenor: High male voice. From classical era on, normally male lead.

Baritone: Normal male voice. Term took hold in mid-nineteenth century.

Bass-baritone: High-lying bass or low-lying classical baritone.

Bass: Low voice. Supporting type. Often the comedic turn.

TALKING POINTS

- If you're with theater buffs, say, "A dramatic literature is necessarily conditioned by the audience for which it is intended," and you won't have to utter another word as those in the vicinity debate the point.

- Colonial America first got a theater presence of note in 1752, when a company of actors established a theater in Williamsburg, Virginia. That's right, Virginia.

- The notable Shakespearian Broadway actor Edwin Booth's brother, John Wilkes Booth, assassinated Abraham Lincoln. Edwin's *Hamlet* in 1865 was a particular success at the Winter Garden Theatre just a few months before his brother made the family infamous.

- Improvisation has been a consistent feature of theater, first emerging with commedia dell'arte, which began in northern Italy in the fifteenth century before spreading throughout Europe. By the turn of the seventeenth century some theatrical troupes that practiced it, such as the Comici Confidènti, attained international celebrity. A master of improvisation today is Mike Leigh, a British playwright who for more forty years has been creating plays that encompass it, including 1977's *Abigail's Party*.

- In Shakespeare's time, acting companies played in rep, rarely doing the same show every night. Long runners were alien.

  * The first recorded long-running production was *The Beggar's Opera*, which ran for sixty-two successive performances in 1728.

  * The world's longest-running production is *The Mousetrap* by Agatha Christie, which opened in London's West End on November 25, 1952. If you see a stellar show, declare that you "think it's going to *Mousetrap* it."

- The Majestic Theatre on Broadway is considered by many to be the home of the musical. Originally built in 1927, it has played host to *Carousel, South Pacific* (starring musical theater legend Mary Martin), *Camelot* (starring Julie Andrews and Richard Burton), *Mack and Mabel* (a Jerry Herman piece—the infamous American composer also behind *Hello, Dolly!* and *La Cage aux Folles*), and *Phantom of the Opera*, which has turned into a bit of a *Mousetrap*—*Phantom* is currently the longest-running musical on Broadway, having opened in 1988.

- Musicals were undoubtedly improved by sound technology, so don't be too sad you didn't see Ethel Merman, the first lady of musical theater for decades, do Cole Porter's *Anything Goes* in 1934. Radio mics didn't happen really until the 1970s. The original *Superstar* staging was all done around microphones with leads.

- Stephen Sondheim, that somewhat significant (he's won more Tonys than any other composer) American musical force of the late twentieth century (his shows include *A Funny Thing Happened on the Way to the Forum, Company, Follies, A Little Night Music, Sweeney Todd,* and *Into the Woods*) and the British equivalent(!), Andrew Lloyd Webber, were both born on the same day—March 22 (1930 and 1948 respectively). Take that, astrology doubters. Or something. But it is odd.

- Dad cowrote the musical *Evita* with lyricist Tim Rice and there are two fascinating—no, really—backstories that aren't very well known about it.

  * Tim had the bright idea to do a show about Eva Peron. Dad, when he was a boy, had seen Judy Garland turn up wrecked and late to perform at the London Palladium. Her rendition of "Over the Rainbow," her signature anthem, was abysmal. It later became Dad's way of getting to grips with Tim's brainwave. Dad gave Eva an anthem that subsequently turns against her, which you know as "Don't Cry for Me, Argentina."

  * According to Dad, Mrs. Thatcher, before she was prime minister and while she was still leader of Britain's opposition, used to turn up and stand at the back of *Evita* for the end of the first act and the beginning of the second. So the future Iron Lady stayed for the big, conquering numbers—"A New Argentina," "Don't Cry for Me, Argentina" (the balcony scene with the arms), and "Rainbow High." And then left before things went pear shaped for Eva. All deeply ironic considering the subsequent Falklands crisis (when Thatcher's Britain went to war with Argentina over some small islands near Argentina).

- The *Chicago* revival, which opened in 1996, in 2014 became the longest-running American musical on Broadway and the second longest-running overall, beating *Cats*. The original production opened in 1975 and closed in 1977. Why has it been so successful? Tunes that people know, sexy dancers in black lace, occasional stunt casting, and a hit movie—what more can you want from a tuner?

- Particularly in musical theater, there is a fine line between success and failure and no such thing as a sure thing. Cite legendary flop *Anyone Can Whistle*. It paired Arthur Laurents with

Stephen Sondheim in his first outing as both composer and lyricist and starred Angela Lansbury and Lee Remick. It played twelve previews and just nine performances at the Majestic Theatre in 1964.

- Space has prevented me from talking ballet in any great detail. However, please be aware of the groundbreaking cultural figure that is Misty Copeland. In 2015 she finally became the first African-American principal ballerina in the seventy-five-year history of American Ballet Theatre. A queen of social media, like the Williams sisters in tennis, she has pushed the boundaries in an arena once perceived as limited for African-Americans.

RED FLAGS

- Running late for a Broadway show? You've probably got seven minutes from the advertised time until curtain up. Anything past that and you're annoying to actors and audience alike. And turn off your phone, FFS. Otherwise Patti LuPone may walk off with it.

- If you've just witnessed a dreadful show on Broadway you can say, "They're doing it for the tour," but not within earshot of anyone involved with the production.

- At an opening night? Do not repeat legendary theater owner Jimmy Nederlander's words of wisdom: "There's no limit to the number of people who won't buy tickets for a show they don't want to see." Instead say something along the lines of David Ives's brilliant line: "Ultimately one has to pity these poor souls who know every secret about writing, directing, designing, producing, and acting but are stuck in those miserable day jobs writing reviews. Will somebody help them, please?"

- Tennessee Williams wrote the mid-twentieth-century American classics *The Glass Menagerie, A Streetcar Named Desire,* and *Cat on a Hot Tin Roof.* He did not write *Death of a Salesman.* That was Arthur Miller. Or *Who's Afraid of Virginia Woolf?,* which was actually penned by Edward Albee later, in 1962.

- I don't think Shakespeare's comedies are funny, but I do rate his tragedies. This is not something one should utter while at the opening night of a Shakespeare comedy on Broadway. It can get you into trouble. Just saying. Your author has never done such a thing, slightly tipsy, obviously.

- *Show Boat* premiered in 1927 at the Ziegfeld Theatre. Yes, that early. Don't confuse it with later shows, which it is easy to do, as it was written by Jerome Kern and Oscar Hammerstein II. The very same Hammerstein who went on to collaborate with Richard Rodgers on *The Sound of Music* and the like.

- Andrew Lloyd Webber didn't compose *Les Misérables* or *Miss Saigon*. You'd be surprised.

- You are within your rights to complain about another dreadful jukebox musical, but be warned. Someone in the vicinity may counter with the examples *Jersey Boys* and *Mamma Mia! Jersey Boys* won four 2006 Tony Awards, including Best Musical, while *Mamma Mia!*, which was based on Swedish pop sensation ABBA's songs, is a global phenomenon that has made its producer Judy Craymer (who used to work for Tim Rice, who wrote the musical *Chess* with ABBA members Benny Andersson and Björn Ulvaeus) a very rich woman indeed.

- A show is ON Broadway and IN the West End. If an entertainment journalist makes that mistake more than once, you should never read them again, for they are ignorant and not to be trusted.

WISE WORDS

All the world's a stage,
And all the men and women merely players;
They have their exits and their entrances,
And one man in his time plays many parts.

—William Shakespeare, *As You Like It*

SOCIAL SURVIVAL STRATEGY

Argument: "A dramatic literature is necessarily conditioned by the audience for which it is intended."
As a rule of thumb, always consider whom the writer was writing (or indeed, the artist was drawing) for, for it is key to understanding the work. If you don't know the answer to this and you're with someone who considers themselves a know-it-all, ask—it's acceptable not to have the answer at your fingertips, but the question should always be posed.

Crisp Fact: "Supposedly, of the 17,000 words Shakespeare used, he invented about 1,700 of them."
Use this either to impress someone with your knowledge or to commiserate with them if they are complaining they don't understand the Bard, since probably nobody ever fully has.

Pivot: "Where are the best places to go in New York pre- and post-theater? It's hard to find a gem of an eatery amongst all the irritable Elmos in Times Square."
Anyone who has ever been to New York has been accosted by a grumpy Elmo and wondered if there was anywhere decent to dine in the Theater District. The person you're with will agree with you and may even reveal a secret night spot that will change your life.

CHEAT SHEET 31—AWARDS
SEASON CONVERSATION

Awards season, in the traditional sense, refers to the film awards season, which runs November through February every year, culminating with the Oscars. But this book is a collection of Cheat Sheets. We covered British history in a few pages, so it's child's play for us to also include here the Tonys (theater), Emmys (TV), Grammys (music), and most important, fashion. What? you say. Sartorial selection is the one theme that runs through all of them, people.

Now, you might scoff and ask why you need to know about such fluff. Because it's fun. And if you want to be a boring person who understands only the inner workings of the Electoral College, fine, skip this bit. But for those of us who want to be well rounded, it's amusing to look at people who couldn't get remotely rounded over the festive season—instead starving themselves for months to fit into their awful outfits. To laugh at their inability to do anything unscripted, such as make an acceptance speech or be interviewed on E! And if you're into the concept of being an entertaining individual, you probably know someone who's holding an Oscar viewing party containing attractive people whom you want to sleep with. But to get them into bed, you need to look like you know something about culture.

I'm not going overboard here. We're concentrating most of our energies on the Oscars, as quite frankly, who holds a soiree to watch the Golden Globes? Other film awards we mention during the season are merely to see you through Academy Awards tweeting or viewing. We mention the Tonys for any same-sex dalliances you might be cooking up, along with the Grammys and Emmys so you can survive any water-cooler chat the following morning.

Awards ceremonies do attract the naysayers. Those who complain about the "marathon" awards season. They grumble that prizes ruin the magic of cinema, theater, TV, and music and make them a means to an end, rather than an end in themselves. Yes, we know that they are all about marketing. And to be fair, it is annoying that in the case of films, there's a glut of good ones at the end of every year to make the Oscar nominations cutoff point, so we're stuck with sequels the rest of the time. But these grouchy types are missing the joy one can gain from watching celebrities involved in a ruthless, *Survivor*-esque battle. And even the winner is still a loser in most instances.

Because what celebrities want most of all is the EGOT. All of them. The Emmy, Grammy, Oscar, and Tony. It was Tubbs from *Miami Vice* that coined that phrase (he didn't achieve it). Those that have done the EGOT include composer Richard Rodgers, Rita Moreno, Audrey Hepburn, Whoopi Goldberg, Scott Rudin (producer who puts an equal level of fear into the Broadway and film communities), and Bobby Lopez (theater guy who was involved in the penning of the *Book of Mormon* and a small movie you might have heard of called *Frozen*).

So, here we go, awards season conversation coming right up.

PEOPLE'S CHOICE AWARDS

BACKGROUND BRIEFING

Started in 1975, voted for by the general public (sort of). All about pop culture.

WHY IT MATTERS TODAY

First ceremony of the season, still voted for by the masses (sort of), so a lot fairer than the Golden Globes. Dares to mix movie, TV, and music stars and have awards such as Favorite On-Screen Chemistry and Favorite Movie Franchise.

TALKING POINT

Nothing will beat 1977 when *Star Wars* won Favorite Picture, Barbra Streisand and John Wayne picked up the main actor categories, and Farrah Fawcett-Majors won for Favorite Female Performer in a new TV show.

RED FLAG

The voting is complex, done by all sorts of market research and online polls, and OH, JUST DON'T BE CYNICAL THAT ONLY THE WINNERS SHOW UP AND THEY OFTEN HAVE CBS SHOWS AND IT'S BROADCAST ON CBS.

GOLDEN GLOBE AWARDS

BACKGROUND BRIEFING

Hollywood Foreign Press Association started awarding it in 1944.

WHY IT MATTERS TODAY

The bastard stepchild of the Oscars. Usually the third most watched awards show after the Oscars and the Grammys. There are fewer than a hundred voters who have a huge amount of influence. They also dare to mix movie and TV stars—and to sit them down and serve them alcohol. This means there's plenty of scope for amusement. Since they split the film categories into musical or comedy and drama, there's also more of a chance for A-listers to win, so they're even likelier to (a) turn up and (b) imbibe. Note that this division means that Madonna has a Golden Globe. For acting. For *Evita* in 1997. Which to be fair she was good in, for her, but still.

TALKING POINTS

- The awards used to be given out by journalists (dull) until an inebriated Rat Pack stormed the stage in 1958 (Frank Sinatra, Dean Martin, Sammy Davis, Jr.). They were invited back the next year to officially be on the stage and the tradition of celebrity involvement continued.

- Both Renée Zellweger (2001) and Christine Lahti (1998) were in the bathroom when they won. Someone online will bring that up.

- 2009—Kate Winslet started listing her fellow nominees when she won for *Revolutionary Road* but didn't manage to remember Angelina Jolie.

RED FLAGS

- The Vegas Trip controversies. I'm not sure remembering this level of detail will help you attract a date. Recalling the 1981 Pia Zadora hullabaloo will show your age. (Pia had a rich husband who supposedly went above and beyond what was strictly necessary campaignwise by offering voters a trip to

Vegas. Zadora beat out Kathleen Turner and Elizabeth McGovern for Newcomer of the Year.)

- Too obvious to instigate a Ricky Gervais as host versus Tina Fey and Amy Poehler debate.

- Any joke involving Globes and women's breasts. Bette Midler made the obvious pun in 1980. It's just, well, too obvious.

You then have in quick succession the Critics' Choice Awards, Screen Actors Guild (SAG) Awards, Producers Guild of America Awards, Directors Guild of America Awards, and the Writers Guild Awards. And when I say quick succession, by now we're not even really into February. The only thing you need to know about these is that the SAG Awards is the only TV awards show that just awards thesps—that's where you've seen the cast of *Modern Family* all onstage. In regards to the Writers Guild Awards, just repeat the following conversation from *Argo*:

John Chambers: Can we get the option?

Tony Mendez: Why do we need the option?

Lester Siegel: You're worried about the Ayatollah? Try the WGA.

At this point any celebrities that are still in the running (or hold a British passport) have to get on a plane to the UK and stand on a red carpet with no coat in the freezing rain.

THE BRITISH ACADEMY FILM AWARDS (BAFTAS)

BACKGROUND BRIEFING

Started in 1947 by such luminaries as David Lean.

WHY IT MATTERS TODAY

It didn't, merely being a consolation prize for some Oscar losers and Brits who are big fish in the UK and tadpoles across the pond in America. However, in 2002 the BAFTAs moved from after the Oscars to before them. They thus now occur at a critical juncture: By the time you get to them, there are only three or four films with a remote chance of Oscar success.

TALKING POINT

When BAFTA voters deviate from the Oscars, history shows that they tend to go for an unexpected European or an overlooked American. Case in point: In 2013 Ben Affleck got best director for *Argo*, when the academy didn't even nominate him in that category.

RED FLAG

Don't insult Stephen Fry, who has hosted about a thousand BAFTA awards; he's much loved in Blighty and it's not worth the upset you may cause to anyone with any British blood.

We then come to the big one. The one you're probably going to have to watch. And need enough talking points to get you through the evening, which is about five hundred hours long. So take what you can above and study the information below.

ACADEMY AWARDS

BACKGROUND BRIEFING

Started in 1929, making it the granddaddy, the oldest, of media awards ceremonies. The statuette is 13.5 inches tall and weighs 8.5

pounds, and the naked dude is modeled on Mexican actor and director Emilio "El Indio" Fernández. Worth noting that during World War II the Oscars were made of plaster and were traded in for gold ones when the war was won. Controversy surrounds where the Oscar nickname came from. Some say it was after Oscar Wilde, others after a staff member of the academy's Uncle Oscar, others after Bette Davis's first husband Harmon Oscar Nelson, Jr.

WHY IT MATTERS TODAY

There's about six weeks of relentless campaigning between nominations and the ceremony. It will come across your radar because you don't live under a rock, you are someone who's out and about, and as discussed, you want to have sex.

TALKING POINTS

- There are around 6,000 members of the academy. Basically to get a vote, just win or get nominated, it's that easy. The most recent statistics available reveal that it is 94 percent white, 77 percent male, with an average age of sixty-three. Which was cited often when the academy shut out African-Americans and women in 2015.

- Surprisingly, although we all complain about the ceremony, the broadcast has won the most Emmys in history, at around fifty wins.

- Although the academy does get it wrong, they can also hand out justice. Julie Andrews, who starred in the stage version of *My Fair Lady*, lost out on the movie role to Audrey Hepburn. Andrews then beat Hepburn to the Academy Award in 1965, for *Mary Poppins*. Hepburn, whose singing had been dubbed, wasn't even nominated for *My Fair Lady*.

- Winners aren't supposed to talk longer than forty-five seconds. You may have to repeat this talking point a fair amount.

- The Animated Feature Film Award was added in 2001, with *Shrek* taking the prize.

- The cool kids all go to the Independent Spirit Awards the Saturday before the Oscars. The coolest kids go to the Golden Raspberry Awards, aka the Razzies, which since 1980 has been presenting honors to the worst films, but often cult classics, of the year. This is where you give kudos to Halle Berry, who actually turned up to pick up her Razzie for *Catwoman*—clutching her Oscar.

- Pulp Friction: What you label an Oscar going to the wrong person, or a tight race in any category. You note that in 1994 *Forrest Gump*, with Hanks being stupid is as stupid does, beat out *Pulp Fiction* and *The Shawshank Redemption* for Best Picture. Come again?

- Oscar at time of press has snubbed: Tom Cruise, Brad Pitt, Marilyn Monroe, Johnny Depp, Glenn Close, and Richard Burton. Of these, those that are alive will probably win for the wrong thing. Al Pacino won his Oscar for *Scent of a Woman* in 1992, not the *Godfather*. Or *Scarface*.

- We do like a good performance by a Grammy type trying to pick up the Oscar for best song and get closer to the EGOT. It won't get any better than the 1991 ceremony when Bon Jovi did "Blaze of Glory" for *Young Guns II* and Madge did "Sooner or Later" from *Dick Tracy,* winning the Oscar for Stephen Sondheim. Theater buffs will note that she later performed the same favor for Sondheim's sharer-of-birthday Andrew Lloyd Webber for "You Must Love Me" from *Evita*. Oh, and Michael Jackson did "Ben" in 1973, at age fourteen—but lost Best Original Song. Still a performance to remember and watch on YouTube, though.

RED FLAGS

- Bit obvious to bring up Marlon Brando refusing his Oscar for the *Godfather* in 1972 and sending Sacheen Littlefeather to collect it. Or Michael Moore's political diatribe against George Bush II in 2002. Go with the George Bernard Shaw anecdote. Shaw refused to pick his Oscar in person for *Pygmalion*, saying something along the lines of "It's perfect nonsense! To offer me an award of this sort is an insult, as if they had never heard of me before—and it's very likely they never had." His Oscar was found to be in such bad condition when he died that it was initially used as a doorstop when his home was turned into a museum.

- Conspiracy theories: Marisa Tomei's 1992 best supporting actress win for *My Cousin Vinny,* when she managed to beat out Judy Davis in *Husbands and Wives* and Vanessa Redgrave (who had all sorts of supporting Palestinian controversy swirling around her when she picked up the gong in 1977) in *Howards End.* A discredited rumor has it that presenter Jack Palance misread the winner from the back of the envelope, instead of from the contents. One feels sorry for Tomei that it's still swirling.

- Never bet against a movie about show business—Hollywood loves giving its top honor to films about itself. In recent memory, think *Birdman* (2015), *Argo* (2013), *The Artist* (2012), *Chicago* (2003), and *Shakespeare in Love* (1999).

TONY AWARDS

BACKGROUND BRIEFING

The American Theatre Wing established an awards program to celebrate excellence in the theater in 1947. They were named for actress, director, producer, and the dynamic wartime leader of the Theatre Wing, Antoinette Perry. Initially there was no physical Tony Award; the winners got a scroll and a mini-memento such as a money clip. The medallion has been around since 1949. After World War II ended, the Tonys were born in order to improve the quality of the performances by introducing the element of competition and to attract a broader audience.

WHY IT MATTERS TODAY

The Oscars of the theater. The Broadway community, who, let's face it, never shy away from a theatrical moment, quickly took to the concept. And it is a community, which is why everyone HAS to thank it in their speeches. To be fair, the Tonys help keep Broadway alive. A good performance on the Tony broadcast or some high-profile wins can save a show and thus the jobs of an awful lot of people. There are around nine hundred Tony voters drawn from the Broadway community.

TALKING POINTS

- What works for the Tony broadcast might not necessarily tie in with where the community's heads are at. But since the community wants CBS to keep broadcasting the show, they lump it. Thus you saw Harry Potter himself singing and dancing his way through a number from *How to Succeed* . . . in a prominent position in 2011's broadcast—when he'd been snubbed and not even nominated for his starring role. Hats off to Daniel Radcliffe for turning up.

- In 2011 and 2012 the Tonys moved from Radio City Music Hall to the Beacon Theatre. This upset some in the community. Size matters. They returned to Radio City in 2013.

- *The Producers* in 2001 managed to win twelve awards, including Best Musical. *The Scottsboro Boys* was nominated for twelve Tonys in 2011 . . . and won none. It had closed months before the Tonys, though.

- Hal Prince, the director/producer, isn't known as the Prince of Broadway for nothing—he's got twenty-one Tonys and counting.

- Five actresses have won a Tony and an Oscar in the same year. They include Audrey Hepburn in 1954, with a Tony for *Ondine* and an Oscar for *Roman Holiday,* and Judi Dench in 1999, winning a Tony for *Amy's View* and an Oscar for *Shakespeare in Love.*

- Tony-winning best plays and musicals that were adapted into Oscar-winning best pictures include *My Fair Lady* (Tony, 1957; Oscar, 1964), *The Sound of Music* (Tony 1960; Oscar 1965), and *Amadeus* (Tony, 1981; Oscar, 1984).

- Patti LuPone has given some legendary Tony Award number performances, for example, in 1980 with "A New Argentina" from *Evita* and "Anything Goes" from *Anything Goes* in 1988.

- The British invasion of Broadway seriously took hold with the *Les Misérables* performance "At the End of the Day"/"One Day More" (1987).

- You will invariably be able to say about the telecast: "A second-rate tribute to a first-rate season."

RED FLAGS

- Broadway shows are incredibly expensive, so in recent years Wall Streeters have suddenly become "producers," who then win Tony Awards when all they've done is written checks. One such type admitted to me he'd invested in a musical to win a Tony so he had something to brag about on dates. You need to watch out for such kinds—they will not be kind to you after you've slept with them.

- Shows you think won for certain awards didn't. *Wicked* didn't win Best Musical in 2004—that went to *Avenue Q. Phantom of the Opera* didn't win Best Score. Dad was up against Stephen

Sondheim, who isn't at Hal Prince levels of Tony wins, but is highly decorated.

- The *Wicked* performance of "Defying Gravity" really weren't the best vocals Idina Menzel has ever produced. If watching the Tonys, however, you might find yourself with a *Wicked* fan, at which point, best to keep schtum. *Wicked* fans (and indeed Fanzels), well, they're up there with Janeites and Trekkies.

GRAMMYS

BACKGROUND BRIEFING

Originally called a Gramophone Award, it's presented by the National Academy of Recording Arts and Sciences of the US for outstanding achievement in the music industry. The first awards were held in 1959 and it's a peer honor, not based on chart positions or sales.

WHY IT MATTERS TODAY

Money, money, money—it comes streaming (geddit?!) in. The post-award weekly sales bounces for the following say it all: Adele 2012: 207 percent, Dixie Chicks 2007: 714 percent, Norah Jones 2003: 331 percent.

TALKING POINTS

- If you work in the music industry and you don't have a Grammy, well, what's wrong with you? They hand out about 80 (at one point it was 109). Of course, you can't air all that, so only the big ones make it to the small screen.

- Those behind the Grammys telecast know what they're doing. The low ratio of awards (about a dozen) to performances = ratings and as discussed, purchases.

  * There are endless sparkling performances to choose from that will be better than someone you're watching this year: Michael Jackson in 1988 with "Man in the Mirror"—seven minutes reminding everyone of his talent. In 1999 Ricky Martin crossed over with "La Copa de la Vida"/"The Cup of Life" and the Ladies Marmalade belted it out in 2002.

  * When anyone does something controversial, note how Elton John sang with Eminem in 2001 after critics labeled the rapper a homophobe.

  * When somebody does something eccentric, remind them how Gaga made an "eggcellent arrival" and then performed "Born This Way" in 2011.

- Grammy voters can verge on the conservative side. As a result, seminal records from those such as Bob Dylan, the Rolling Stones, Marvin Gaye, and Bruce Springsteen didn't win. Specific snubs:

  * Note that in 1992 Nirvana managed not to win Best Rock Song for "Smells Like Teen Spirit." It went to Eric Clapton's unplugged version of "Layla." Which should have won in 1972. In 1992? Not so much.

  * In 1966 the Best Rock and Roll Recording went to "Winchester Cathedral." Wait? What? It was a novelty single, up against, wait for it: "Eleanor Rigby" (the Beatles), "Good Vibrations" (the Beach Boys), "Last Train to Clarksville" (the Monkees), "Cherish" (the Association), and "Monday Monday" (the Mamas and the Papas).

RED FLAGS

- The difference between Album, Record, and Song of the Year is as follows:

* Album goes to the performer and production team of a full album.

* Record goes to the performer and production team of a single song.

* Song goes to the writers/composers of a single song.

* Not sure if that's really any clearer. Sorry. I tried.

- Milli Vanilli lip-synched their way to the Best New Artist award in 1990's show. They eventually, of course, lost their Grammy. Bit obvious to remember that.

- US immigration prevented Amy Winehouse from turning up in 2008, so she was in London performing for the broadcast. Debating the pros and cons of this is going to get dull and possibly turn a fun evening into a discussion about politics, drug addiction, and death. Leave it.

- Justin Timberlake apologized for Janet Jackson's Nipplegate Super Bowl scandal in 2004. Just painful to watch. Can we not do that again, please?

PRIMETIME EMMY AWARD

Now there are lots of different types of Emmy awards and as a result various awards ceremonies throughout the year. You've got the Daytime Emmys, the Sports Emmys (I once interviewed for a sports hosting job in an office that contained loads of these—I didn't, unsurprisingly, get the gig), International Emmys, and it just goes on. Unless you work in television, the only Emmys, dear reader, that you need to concern yourself with are the Primetime Emmys.

BACKGROUND BRIEFING

They started in 1949, and the winged woman holding an atom on the actual award was the designer's wife. Emmy comes from *immy*, a term used for the image orthicon tube in early cameras. Actually you don't need to know that. Sorry.

WHY IT MATTERS TODAY

The Primetime Emmys, which are held in September, are, as with all awards ceremonies, about promotion. They're usually on the Sunday before the official start of the fall TV season, so hopefully ratings will get a boost from actresses prancing about in nice clothes attempting to step it up and look like a movie star. Trust me, watch any red carpet coverage and some emaciated pundit will trot out that line.

TALKING POINT

Quite rightly for an egalitarian medium, the Primetime Emmys are decided on by—wait for it—more than 16,000 Television Academy members. Take that, Golden Globes.

RED FLAGS

- Don't point out to anyone in media that the only Emmys that matter are the primetime ones. There's a good chance that since there are so many Emmys you'll inadvertently offend someone you may be trying to sleep with.

- The most brilliant line about television came from Oscar winner and playwright Christopher Hampton (*Dangerous Liaisons*), who wrote in his play *The Philanthropist*, "Masturbation is the thinking man's television." Genius, but again, masturbation may be all you're doing if you use that when you're trying to seduce someone who works in television. Unless they're British. When they'll agree with you and want to sleep with you because you're an admirer of Chris Hampton. And because they know this is true.

THE FASHION

The unifying theme in all of these red carpets events is the fashion. This product placement is a serious business for the fashion houses and also the actresses (and indeed actors now) sporting their wares. For the designers it's all about free advertising; for the thespians it's about personal branding, even leading to lucrative advertising contracts (allude to Charlize Theron, Keira Knightley, Julianne Moore, and Scarlett Johansson). In 2015 there may have been a backlash against the "mani-cam" (a camera that focuses on manicures), with some actresses being proponents of the #AskMeMore movement, but the red carpet pageant has made them rich, so if you find yourself with limited sympathy for them, you are not alone.

The term *stylist* didn't come into vogue until the mid-1990s, basically because the late, great Joan Rivers started making mischief on the red carpet and making fun of all the terrible outfits. Rachel Zoe, who pretty much invented the size 00 (don't get me started), was one of the pioneers of the Power Stylist. Now they are front and center of the assault to get gowns and merchandise on nominees and presenters, with fashion and jewelry houses flying in reps, collections, and seamstresses to Los Angeles for the final push.

TALKING POINTS

- Prada entered the popular lexicon thanks to a lilac gown worn by Uma Thurman to the Oscars in 1995.
- If there's a red carpet, Nicole Kidman, thanks to her musician husband at time of going to press, is normally on it, as between them they always have an excuse to be there. Note that Kidman always pushes the envelope in her sartorial choices and

cite her at the 1997 Oscars in Christian Dior by John Galliano (the dodgy green and gold one that everybody loved), and ten years later in the bright red Balenciaga with a dramatic red bow at the neck. You are also allowed to make a comment about her Botox and filler levels.

- Some trends need to stay on the red carpet, as they just don't translate to ordinary people. Recall when Michelle Williams started the mustard fashion craze in Vera Wang, 2006. She looked great. Nobody normal did.

- Occasionally you'll get an actress remembering her roots as she mixes high fashion with highly stylized main street, most memorably Sharon Stone in Gap and Vera Wang in 1998.

- For Oscar fashion, remember the good: Hilary Swank in Guy Laroche, 2005—the backless dress (she also won the Oscar that year for *Million Dollar Baby*). The leg: Angelina Jolie in Atelier Versace, 2012. And the ugly: the backward suit: Céline Dion in Christian Dior by John Galliano, 1999. And then there's Cher in all those Bob Mackie numbers.

- Lupita Nyong'o's navigation of the 2014 awards season will go down in history as a master class for every starlet out there. Within a few months, she went from an unknown actress in *12 Years a Slave* to Oscar winner (for Best Supporting Actress), a contract with Lancôme, household name, and *People* Magazine's World's Most Beautiful person of the year. Her (and her stylist's) flawless fashion choices on red carpet after red carpet turned her into a superstar.

- Jennifer Lopez wore a belly-button Versace scarf dress to the Grammys in 2000. Completely appropriate for that event (you need to go edgy, fun), but not, obviously, something for the Oscars. That point can be expanded when commenting on every event: "right dress, right event" or "great dress, wrong event" as applicable.

RED FLAG

At the Golden Globes in 2006 Scarlett Johansson got her globes, well, groped by fashion designer Isaac Mizrahi in the middle of an interview. It's that obvious globe joke that we just don't do, remember?

WISE WORDS

To refuse awards is another way of accepting them with more noise than is normal.

—Peter Ustinov

SOCIAL SURVIVAL STRATEGY

Argument: "Celebrities may deny it, but they've all dreamt up acceptance speeches for the Grand Slam—the EGOT. The Emmy, Grammy, Oscar, and Tony. Most are no Richard Rodgers or Whoopi Goldberg, though."

All involved may claim it's about the craft. For some of them this might even be true, but these people are human beings with all their associated vices and they have all dreamed of winning the EGOT—just that most aren't good enough to win anything. This is a solid conversation topic and also may serve to make you feel less inadequate in the admittedly unlikely but possible scenario that someone who is up for a gong was several grades below you in high school.

Crisp Fact: "Since 1950, winners (and family members) can't sell Oscars without first offering them to the Academy for the princely sum of a dollar."

The Academy Awards is all about the money. No more, no less.

Pivot: "Who would you thank in your Oscar acceptance speech? Don't pretend you haven't practiced it in front of the bathroom mirror!"

Ask this, and the answer you receive may assist in deciding whether you want to bed the person you're talking to or not. Everyone has thought about it, and their answers can be quite revealing.

CONCLUSION

School's out. Feeling like a know-it-all yet? Well, perhaps not that, but you surely now have enough to cover cocktail conversation, which is the most important type of discussion most of us have to deal with on a regular basis.

I'm aware that as with when Google Earth was released and the first thing you did was check out the street where you live before venturing to unknown locales, your initial instinct with this book was to head to the Cheat Sheet you were already an expert in, and it will have done nothing for you. However, I hope that you then went on to others that provided a soupçon of enlightenment. Yes, these Cheat Sheets are but an overview, but isn't that the most important type of knowledge to possess? To understand the news today, what we really need to know is how stories fit into their larger themes. Life is a jigsaw puzzle.

In this noisy day and age, with all the "expert" opinions out there, it can be tricky to separate truth from "truthiness," the Orwellian tendency to believe something regardless of the facts. Maybe, just maybe, this book has helped you with this. I hope that it has given you some sane arguments and one or two "crisp facts," which are essential if you're ever to clinch the case you are making for whether Jennifer Lawrence should have worn purple or that the only security guarantee for dictators is nuclear weapons.

If I've done my job, this volume has become a useful security blanket and perhaps even provided you with a moment of superiority where you need it most. And it will be just a moment. A long dispute and both of you are wrong. At the very least, you'll now know how to subtly switch the chat onto a terrain that you are comfortable talking about, something that all good generalists are specialists at.

But most of all, I hope that *The Intelligent Conversationalist* made you smile. What other tome out there even attempts to cover both an actress's sartorial and SCOTUS's decisions, after all?

WISE WORDS

Don't raise your voice, improve your argument.

—Desmond Tutu

ABOUT THE AUTHOR

Caitlin McNaney

Imogen Lloyd Webber is a New York–based British author, broadcaster, PEOPLE Now's Royals correspondent & Broadway.com's senior editor. Educated at Cambridge University and a former MSNBC contributor and Fox News regular, she has made hundreds of appearances on air talking everything from Hillary Clinton to *Hamilton*. Her cheat sheets got her through all but two of them.